Hospitality

AN EAST TEXAS COOKBOOK

HARVEY WOMAN'S CLUB

PALESTINE, TEX.

FOR THE COLLECTION OF

AN EAST TEXAS COOKBOOK

HARVEY
WOMAN'S CLUB

PALESTINE, TEXAS

Additional copies of *HOSPITALITY* may be obtained by sending $11.95 plus $2.00 postage and handling to the following address. (Texas residents please add $.60 for state tax.) Make check payable to *HOSPITALITY.*

HOSPITALITY
Harvey Woman's Club
P.O. Box 1058
Palestine, Texas 75801

First Printing, October 1983, 10,000

Library of Congress Catalog Card Number 83-81013
ISBN 0-9611654-0-5

Printed in the United States by
Hart Graphics, Inc.
8000 Shoal Creek Blvd.
Austin, Texas 78758

Welcome

HOSPITALITY! That is the one word that best describes Palestine, a lovely town set in a profusion of graceful dogwoods, towering pines, and majestic oaks.

Our town is well known for its Victorian homes, outstanding cuisine, and a gracious style of entertaining, a style which has not changed since the days when Southern hospitality gained its reputation. This gracious way of life is symbolized by the pineapple which is our hallmark. It will lead you throughout the book in discovering that world of charming hospitality so evident when you enter one of these homes filled with the aroma of freshly baked bread, the glow of candlelight, and a table laden with a bountiful repast. You can hear the appreciation of family and friends who partake of these delicious offerings.

You'll fine a delightful meld of the various influences in our area which is an extension of the Deep South. There are recipes typical of East Texas, Louisiana Cajun Country, and the various ethnic groups who have contributed so much to our area.

Each recipe included herein has been thoroughly tested during the extensive preparation for this book. Our warmest thanks go to all who worked so diligently on this project, thereby sharing their own hospitality with you, the reader.

Come with us, the Harvey Woman's Club, on a trip to a world where the door is always open, where you are welcomed with a smile and an embrace, and where a stranger is never a stranger for very long.

The Cookbook Committee

Chairman
Mrs. Jack H. Hanks

Co-Chairman
Mrs. Cad E. Williams

Recipes and Testing

Mrs. Leo F. Mizell   Mrs. James C. Boone, Jr.

Special Advisors

Mrs. R. L. Kenderdine   Mrs. G. L. Gaines
Mrs. Robert E. Jordan   Mrs. Stewart Kenderdine
Mrs. John E. Presley

Division Chairmen

Mrs. Gordon B. Broyles   Mrs. Joe P. Bryant
Mrs. J. G. Crook   Mrs. David J. Dial
Mrs. F. H. Eilenberger, Jr.   Mrs. Paul E. Elliott, Jr.
Mrs. Lester Hamilton   Mrs. Ben W. Hearne
Mrs. A. G. Jeanes   Mrs. J. E. Johnston
Mrs. Joe Ed Johnston   Mrs. C. Gerald Joyce, Jr.
Mrs. C. L. Kolstad, III   Mrs. Curtis Mann
Mrs. Robert H. Miller   Mrs. Frank McCreary
Mrs. John B. McDonald   Mrs. John Ballard McDonald
Mrs. Daniel F. Rex   Mrs. Tucker K. Royall
Mrs. Reo Stolzenburg   Mrs. H. E. Sullivan
Mrs. Jeff Walker   Mrs. Dennis E. Ward
Mrs. Howard T. Winkler.

Typists

Mrs. Max G. Alldredge   Mrs. M. D. Chennault
Mrs. K. G. Johnson

Metric Conversions
Daniel F. Rex

Graphics
Crouse & Co., Austin, Texas

Table of Contents

Hospitality and the pineapple . . . the two have been linked since colonial times when captains of sailing ships would return from the South Seas bringing this exotic fruit as a prize for family and friends.

History records that the sea captains on their return to Newport or Nantucket would place a pineapple over the spikes of an iron gate. This was public notice that the captain had returned and was holding open house for all!

The traditional link continued into antebellum days of the Deep South when this beloved fruit was carved above the doors of many southern mansions as a symbol of hospitality. There could be no finer hallmark of Palestine and Harvey Woman's Club than the pineapple, a symbol of their spirit. Palestine is a town in which hospitality and gracious entertaining have been a way of life for generations. Harvey Woman's Club carries on that spirit . . . a symbol of that tradition . . . the pineapple.

To that spirit so beautifully embodied in this treasured fruit and for your enjoyment we offer you . . . *HOSPITALITY.*

APPETIZERS
AND
BEVERAGES

Artichoke

1	large artichoke	1	bay leaf
4	T. vinegar	2	whole peppercorns
Water		½	t. salt
1	T. salad or olive oil		

Slice about 1 inch off the top of artichoke, and cut thorny tips from any remaining leaves. Cut off just enough of bottom so artichoke will stand up. Immerse artichoke in 1 quart of water and 3 tablespoons of vinegar for 10 to 15 minutes. Bring 1 quart of water to a boil. Add 1 tablespoon vinegar, bay leaf, pepper, and salt. Add artichoke and boil about 45 minutes or until stem end pierces readily. Lift from cooking liquid and drain. Remove choke spiney center with a spoon and discard. Then fill with sour cream, cream cheese, or your favorite vegetable dip. Leaves can be plucked off and arranged in sunburst with heart cut in small wedges in center. Fill heart area with dip.

Mrs. F. H. Eilenberger, Jr. (Claire Barnes)

Stuffed Artichokes

1	artichoke	¼	c. oil
½	c. bread crumbs	Salt and pepper to taste	
½	c. grated Romano cheese	Parsley to taste	
4	cloves garlic, finely chopped		

Mix together bread crumbs, Romano cheese, garlic, parsley, salt, and pepper by rubbing in hands. Cut top and bottom from artichoke and turn upside down and mash slightly to open leaves. Fill each leaf from outside in by using the top of each leaf. Then pour oil over stuffed piece. Steam in covered pot in a little water 45 minutes or longer. Done when leaf pulls off easily.

Mrs. Paul E. Elliott (Ann Craft)

Artichoke Dip

3   or 4 slices bacon, cooked   ⅓   c. mayonnaise
    crisp and crumbled   1   T. chopped onion
1   16. oz. can artichoke   Salt, pepper, cayenne to taste
    hearts, drained   Juice of ½ lemon

Fry bacon until crisp. Drain and set aside. Chop artichoke hearts to a pulp. Add all other ingredients, stir well, and season to taste. Chill. Serve with corn chips.
Mrs. Dennis Ward (Jamie Brown)

Italian Artichoke Dip

1   8½ oz. can artichoke   1   pkg. dry Italian Dressing
    hearts   Mix (net wt. 0.6 oz.)
1   c. mayonnaise

Chop artichokes, add other ingredients, and mix well. Serve with crackers, chips, or raw vegetables.
Mrs. Lucylle Mac Naughton

Broccoli Dip

1   10 oz. pkg. cut broccoli,   2   T. horseradish
    frozen in cheese sauce   1   2 oz. jar sliced pimiento,
1   8 oz. pkg. cream cheese,   drained
    softened

Whirl broccoli in blender until creamy smooth. Mix with cheese, horseradish, and pimiento. One 14½ oz. can asparagus, drained, may be used instead of broccoli. Serve with raw vegetables.
Mrs. F. Bailey Summers (Christine Hughes)

Beer Cheese

1	lb. sharp Cheddar cheese	1	t. salt or to taste
1	lb. American cheese	1	t. dry mustard
2	or 3 cloves garlic	Dash Tabasco or cayenne
1	c. beer, more or less	pepper
3	T. Worcestershire sauce		

Grind cheese with garlic. Mix with Worcestershire sauce, salt, mustard, and Tabasco. Place in bowl. Using an electric mixer, beat in beer slowly until mixture is smooth and spreads easily. Store in covered jars and refrigerate.
Cookbook Committee

Fried Brie

½	lb. Brie	½	c. packaged bread crumbs
Flour		2	T. butter
1	egg	1	loaf French bread
1	T. water		

Remove and discard paper and plastic wrap. The cheese should be in one piece. Coat all surfaces with flour. Beat egg in water in a pie plate until foamy. Dip cheese in egg, then in crumbs, coating well. Heat butter in a small skillet until it foams. Put Brie in skillet, cover, and cook over low heat about 5 minutes or until golden brown on 1 side. Turn and cook covered on other side. Remove from heat and make a cut in the cheese so it will run. Serve at once with bread cut into pieces.
You may prepare ahead by dipping and coating the cheese and refrigerate. Cook at serving time.
Cookbook Committee

Stuffed Gouda or Edam Cheese

1 17 oz. Gouda or Edam cheese	1 T. Worcestershire
Mayonnaise	Dash Tabasco
	½ c. chopped walnuts

Hollow out cheese leaving a shell ⅛ inch thick. Grate cheese and mix enough mayonnaise to moisten. Season with Tabasco and Worcestershire and add nuts. Mix well and put back in shell. Chill. Let stand at room temperature for 20 minutes before serving. Serve with thin crackers.

Mrs. J. G. Crook (Maxine Schultz)

Swiss Cheese Dip

12 green onions and tops, chopped	1 lb. Swiss cheese, finely grated
1 bunch parsley, chopped	Salt to taste
1 c. butter	Cayenne to taste
4 T. flour	4 T. sherry
1 pt. light cream	1 lb. shrimp or crabmeat, optional

Saute chopped green onions and parsley in butter. Add flour and cream and stir until smooth. Add cheese and stir until it melts. Add salt, cayenne, and sherry. Add shrimp or crabmeat, if desired. Serve hot in chafing dish with small toast squares or rounds.

Yields approximately 1 quart or 2 quarts if adding seafood.

Mrs. John B. McDonald (Dorothy Crider)

Tamale Dip

2	medium onions, chopped	1½	T. chili sauce
1	28 oz. can tomatoes	1	6 oz. can ripe olives,
1	14 oz. can tomato sauce		drained and chopped
2	28 oz. cans tamales, chopped		Salt, pepper, and chili powder to taste
1	clove garlic, minced		Cheddar cheese
	Dash Tabasco		Corn chips

Mix first 3 ingredients and simmer covered for 3 hours. Add tamales with sauce from can and other ingredients. Serve hot from a chafing dish with corn chips. Sprinkle with grated Cheddar cheese.
Mrs. Joe Ed Johnston (Marilyn Hardgrave)

Party Mold

1	T. unflavored gelatin	1	6¾ oz. can deviled ham
⅓	c. hot water	1	T. prepared mustard
⅔	c. beer	1	T. minced onion
1	c. cottage cheese	½	t. Tabasco
4	or 5 ozs. blue cheese, grated		

Dissolve gelatin in hot water. Add beer and set aside. Blend cottage cheese until smooth; add blue cheese, deviled ham, mustard, onion, and Tabasco. Add beer and gelatin mixture. Pour into a 1 quart ring mold, and refrigerate for at least 4 hours. May be made several days in advance. When ready to serve, unmold on tray and fill center with olives and surround with fancy crackers.
Serves 20 to 25.
Mrs. Erle Dickson (Daphne White)

Tomato Cheese Appetizer

1	10¾ oz. can tomato soup	½	c. finely chopped green
1	3 oz. pkg. lemon gelatin		pepper
1	8 oz. pkg. cream cheese	1	2¼ oz. pkg. sliced
1½	c. finely chopped celery		almonds
½	c. finely chopped onion	1	c. mayonnaise

Place soup, gelatin, and cream cheese in a double boiler. Mix with electric mixer over hot water until smooth. Stir in celery, onion, green pepper, almonds, and mayonnaise. Pour into 4 cup ring mold that has been greased with salad oil. Chill until firmly set.
Mrs. J. G. Crook (Maxine Schultz)

Dill Dip for Raw Vegetables

1	pt. mayonnaise	3	T. grated onion
1	pt. sour cream	3	T. dill weed
3	T. minced fresh parsley or	1½	T. seasoned salt
	1 T. dried parsley		

Blend all ingredients together and chill before serving. May be made several days in advance.
Yields approximately 4½ cups.
Mrs. Ben W. Swinney (Linda Jenkins)

Marinated Mushrooms

1	large thinly sliced onion	1	clove garlic, pressed
1	8 oz. bottle zesty Italian	2	lbs. sliced or whole
	dressing		mushrooms
½	c. white wine		

Simmer all ingredients for 10 minutes. Chill. Serve on crackers or as relish.
Mrs. R. L. Kenderdine (Daphne Dunning)

Pickled Mushrooms

3	medium onions	½	t. mustard seed
¾	c. water	1	T. salt
¾	c. vinegar	Few drops of hot sauce	
½	t. leaf marjoram	½	lb. fresh mushrooms
¼	t. whole cloves	¼	c. olive oil
½	t. celery seed		

Cut onions in ½ inch slices and cook in water, vinegar, and spices for 5 minutes. Add mushrooms and cook 5 minutes longer. Remove mushrooms and add olive oil to remaining liquid and onions. Bring to boil and pour over mushrooms. Let stand for 3 hours or longer, and serve as hors d'oeuvre or salad.
Serves 10 to 12.
Mrs. J. R. Parker (Pat McCrary)

Sherried Mushrooms

1	medium onion, minced	Salt, garlic salt, and pepper to
2	T. butter	taste
½	lb. fresh mushrooms,	¼ c. light cream
	finely chopped	1 T. sherry or to taste
2	T. lemon juice	Toast rounds or wheat thins
1	t. Worcestershire sauce	Parsley
1	T. flour	

Saute onion in butter. Add mushrooms and cook several minutes. Stir in lemon juice, Worcestershire sauce, and flour; remove from heat and cool. Add salt, garlic salt, pepper, and light cream. Stir in sherry to taste. Mold and chill. Garnish with parsley. Serve with favorite crackers.
Serves 6 to 8.
Cookbook Committee

Stuffed Mushrooms

12 large mushrooms	½ c. heavy cream
2 to 3 T. butter	3 T. fresh parsley
Salt and pepper to taste	Salt and pepper to taste
2 T. minced shallots	¼ c. grated Swiss cheese
2 T. butter	1 to 2 T. butter
½ T. flour	

Remove mushroom stems and reserve. Wash and dry the caps, brush with melted butter; arrange hollow side up in baking dish. Season lightly with salt and pepper. Wash and dry the stems and mince. By the handful, twist in the corner of a towel to extract as much juice as possible. Saute with shallots in butter for 4 or 5 minutes until the pieces begin to separate. Lower heat, add flour, and stir for 1 minute. Stir in cream and simmer for a minute or two until thickened. Stir in parsley and seasonings. Fill the mushroom caps with this mixture. Top each with 1 teaspoon of cheese, and add a few drops of melted butter. Set aside until ready to cook. Fifteen minutes before serving, bake in 375° oven until tender. Serve warm.
Serves 4.
Mrs. David G. Bucher (Cynthia Westfahl)

Mediterranean Eggplant Appetizer

1 large egg plant	¼ t. oregano
4 T. olive oil	¼ c. vinegar
¼ c. chopped green peppers	1 c. tomato sauce
½ c. finely chopped onion	1½ t. salt
¼ c. chopped celery	¼ t. pepper
¼ c. chopped parsley	1 T. white wine
2 cloves chopped garlic	

Bake eggplant in 350° oven for 1 hour or until soft. Slit eggplant so steam escapes. Cool. Peel and chop finely. Saute eggplant in 3 tablespoons olive oil. Add other ingredients except wine, simmering for 10 minutes. Stir in wine and chill. Serve on crackers and garnish with parsley.
Mrs. Cad E. Williams (Francis Bailey)

Spinach Spread

1	10 oz. pkg. frozen chopped spinach	3	small green onions, chopped
1½	c. sour cream	1	c. water chestnuts, chopped
1½	c. mayonnaise		
1	pkg. Knorr's vegetable soup mix		

Thaw spinach, squeeze dry, and chop. Add to remaining ingredients. Chill for several hours or overnight. Serve with Hawaiian Bread.

Mrs. Carolyn Hamilton, Austin, Texas

Water Chestnut Hors d'Oeuvres

1	c. soy sauce	2	8 oz. cans water chestnuts, drained
½	c. catsup		Brown sugar
½	c. salad oil		Bacon
1	t. garlic powder		
1	t. pepper		

Mix soy sauce, catsup, salad oil, garlic powder, and pepper. Marinate water chestnuts in sauce for at least 24 hours in the refrigerator. In greased 9 x 12 pan, sprinkle ¼ to ½ inch layer of brown sugar. Wrap each water chestnut in ⅓ slice of bacon, stick with wooden toothpick, and place on bed of brown sugar. Bake 30 to 40 minutes at 350° until bacon is done. Serve hot. Marinade can be reused and keeps in the refrigerator for about 1 month.

Yields approximately 24.

Mrs. Norman E. Bonner (Susan Beyette)

Eggs Elegante

1 doz. hard-cooked eggs,
    halved
1 10 oz. box frozen
    chopped spinach,
    cooked and well
    drained
1 t. salt
Red pepper to taste

1 t. lemon juice
1 T. butter, softened
1 4 oz. pkg. cream cheese,
    softened
Mayonnaise
1 t. Durkee's Dressing
Paprika

Press all liquid from spinach. Add salt, pepper, and lemon juice. Mix butter and cream cheese. Add to spinach mixture and mix well. Mash egg yolks. Add mayonnaise, Durkee's dressing, salt, and pepper to taste. Stuff egg whites with spinach mixture. Top each egg with a dollop of yolk mixture and sprinkle with paprika.
Cookbook Committee

Cheese Ball

3 8 oz. pkgs. cream cheese
1 20 oz. can crushed
    pineapple, well drained
5 T. finely chopped bell
    pepper

5 T. finely chopped celery
3 T. finely chopped onion
½ t. seasoned salt
¼ t. garlic salt
5 drops Tabasco
½ c. chopped pecans

Mix well and form a ball or log. Roll in pecans. Place in foil and refrigerate overnight.
Variation Toasted coconut may be used in place of nuts.
Mrs. R. G. Abernathy (Mildred Porter)

Cheese Ball Appetizers

2   3 oz. pkgs. cream cheese,   ¼   c. finely chopped dried
     softened   beef
1   T. horseradish   ½   c. crushed potato chips
1   t. milk   ½   c. finely chopped parsley

Blend cream cheese and horseradish until smooth. If too stiff, add milk. Add dried beef and potato chips, and blend thoroughly. Chill. Shape into small balls, roll in parsley, and serve on toothpicks.
Yields 24 balls.
Mrs. C. F. Sizer (Mary Cordray)

Cheese Ring

1   lb. sharp Cheddar cheese,   1   medium onion, grated
     grated   1   clove garlic, pressed
1   c. chopped pecans   ½   t. Tabasco
¾   c. mayonnaise   1   c. strawberry preserves

Combine all ingredients except preserves and mix well. Lightly oil an 8 inch ring mold. Put cheese mixture in mold and chill well. Unmold and fill center with strawberry preserves. Serve with melba rounds or crackers.
Mrs. Daniel F. Rex (Emory Hill)

Chutney Cheese

3   8 oz. pkgs. cream cheese,   1   t. curry powder
     softened   ½   c. finely chopped pecans
½   9 oz. jar Major Grey's   Unsweetened shredded
     chutney   coconut

Mix cream cheese, chutney, curry powder, and pecans. Form into ball or log and roll in coconut. This is good even without the coconut.
Mrs. Howard Winkler (Joyce Bell)

Dill Bread Squares

1	loaf thinly sliced white bread	Dill weed
Butter		Paprika

Trim crusts from thin slices of white bread. Brush the slices with melted butter. Sprinkle with dill weed and a little paprika. Cut into squares and triangles. Toast slowly in a 225° oven until crisp.
Freezes.
Mrs. Ben W. Hearne (Esther Johnson)

Deviled Cheese Bites

2	3 oz. pkgs. cream cheese, softened	½ c. chopped pecans
		Onion juice to taste
1	4 oz. pkg. blue cheese, crumbled	½ to 1 c. finely chopped parsley
2	4½ oz. cans deviled ham	Thin pretzel sticks

Combine cream cheese and blue cheese; blend until smooth. Stir in deviled ham, pecans, and onion juice. Chill. Shape into balls the size of small walnuts and roll in parsley. Chill until serving time. To serve, use pretzel sticks to spear cheese balls.
Yields about 40 appetizers.
Mrs. Bruce Barber (Brenda Wilson)

Ham Wafers

½	c. butter
4	4½ oz. cans deviled ham
1	t. fresh lemon juice
¼	t. red pepper
2	T. plus 2 t. Worcestershire sauce
¼	t. sugar
10	drops Tabasco
2	t. curry powder, optional
2	c. unsifted flour

Cream butter. Add ham and continue mixing until well blended. Add seasonings and mix well. Sift in flour and beat and stir thoroughly. Divide into 4 parts. With lightly floured hands, mold into 1½ inch rolls on plastic wrap. Freeze well wrapped rolls. After removing from freezer, let stand at room temperature for 10 minutes; then slice about ⅛ inch thick. Bake on lightly greased cookie sheet at 375° until lightly brown, approximately 10 to 12 minutes. If not used within a few hours, store tightly covered in refrigerator or freezer.

Yields 12 dozen wafers.
Mrs. Lester Hamilton (Frances Edmunds)

Cheese Fingers

3	loaves day-old bread
2	eggs
1½	c. milk

Melted margarine
3   8 oz. cans Parmesan cheese

Remove crusts from bread. Combine eggs and milk in a bowl. In a second bowl, place melted margarine; in a third bowl, place cheese. Dip 1 slice bread in egg mixture, and place between 2 slices dry bread. Cut into 4 fingers. Dip each finger in margarine, then in cheese, leaving bottom side clean. Place clean side down on cookie sheet. Bake at 350° for 10 minutes. Allow at least 3 per person.

Yields about 80.
Cookbook Committee

Cheese-Rice Crisps

2	c. sharp cheese, grated	3	c. crisp rice cereal
2	sticks margarine, softened		Dash of cayenne pepper
2	c. sifted flour		

Mix cheese, margarine, and cayenne pepper. Add flour and mix well. Add rice cereal and mix well. Shape into small balls, and place on ungreased cookie sheet. Flatten each ball with a fork which has been dipped in flour. Bake at 375° about 10 minutes or until lightly brown.
Yields about 90.
Mrs. Wayne Walker (Katherine Cray)

Cheese Straws

1	c. grated cheese	1	egg yolk
½	c. butter or margarine	2	T. milk or water
1	c. flour	1	t. curry powder, optional
½	t. baking powder		Pinch cayenne pepper
1	t. paprika		

Mix all ingredients. Knead well and roll thin. Cut into strips ½ inch wide and bake at 375°.
Yields 48 straws.
Mrs. E. D. Cleveland (Yvonne Teel)

Date-Nut Crisps

½	c. butter	½	t. salt
½	lb. grated sharp cheese	½	t. red pepper
1½	c. flour		Dates and pecans

Soften butter to room temperature. Cream with cheese. Add flour, salt, pepper, and blend. Cut in half. Pinch off small amount of dough and mold in palm of hand around date stuffed with a pecan to fit. Bake at 400° until lightly brown, about 15 minutes. Store in tins. These stay crisp for days.
Yields approximately 75 to 80.
Cookbook Committee

Dressing Bites

2	6 oz. pkgs. white corn bread mix	2	t. salt
8	slices bread, toasted	½	t. pepper
2	c. chopped onion	4	T. sage
3	c. chopped celery	4	eggs, beaten
3	T. margarine	2	c. turkey or chicken broth

Prepare corn bread mix according to directions on package. Toast bread slices in slow oven until crisp. Saute onion and celery in margarine. Crumble cornbread and toast into a large bowl. Add onion, celery, salt, pepper, and sage. Add well beaten eggs. Mix. Add warm broth and mix well. Shape into balls or pieces resembling fried oyster and place on *lightly* greased cookie sheet. Bake in 375° oven for 15 to 20 minutes. May be baked ahead of time and quickly reheated at serving time.
Yields 125 bites and serves 55 to 60.
Mrs. Jack H. Hanks (Jackie Rayburn)

Jalapeno Pie

6	eggs	10	to 12 oz. Cheddar cheese, grated
Chopped jalapeno peppers			

Cover bottom of 1 quart baking dish with chopped jalapeno peppers. Spread cheese evenly over peppers, covering entire dish. Beat eggs and pour over cheese. Bake 25 to 30 minutes at 350°.
Great hors d'oeuvers. Could be served for brunch.

Mushroom Rolls

1	lb. mushrooms	4	T. finely chopped green
½	c. butter		onions
6	T. flour	1	t. lemon juice
1	t. salt	1	loaf sandwich bread
1	c. light cream		

Saute mushrooms in butter for 5 minutes; chop finely, return to pan, add flour, and salt. Stir in cream and cook until thickened. Add green onions and lemon juice. Remove crust from bread and roll each slice thin; spread with mushroom mixture. Roll as for jelly roll and freeze. Cut into slices. Bake at 400° until brown.
Yields 100 slices.
Mrs. Jackson R. Hanks (Helen Reeves)

Olive-Cheese Triangles

1½	c. grated sharp Cheddar cheese	½	c. finely chopped onion
½	c. vegetable oil	¼	t. curry powder
1	c. chopped ripe olives	¼	t. salt
1	c. chopped, stuffed green olives	1	pkg. English muffins

Combine first seven ingredients. Split 1 package English muffins in half. Spread with above mixture. Cut in ¼'s or ⅛'s and bake in 350° oven for 10 minutes. Can be frozen. Add 5 minutes to cooking time.
Yields 40 pieces if cut in ¼'s.
Mrs. Frank C. Hicks (Helen Davenport)

Petite Quiches

Pastry for 1 crust 9 inch pie	1 c. shredded natural Swiss cheese
¾ c. light cream	
2 eggs, slightly beaten	1 T. flour
¼ t. salt	4 slices bacon, crisply cooked
Dash of pepper	

Line miniature muffin pans with pastry. Combine cream, eggs, and seasonings. Mix well. Toss cheese with flour. Add cheese and bacon to egg mixture. Fill muffin pans ⅔ full. Bake at 325° for 30 to 35 minutes or until lightly browned. A variation is to substitute ¾ cup sour cream for light cream and omit flour.
Yields 24. Freezes.
Mrs. Harry Brown (Carol Albright)

Spinach Pies (Spanakopeta)

1½ c. finely chopped green onions	4 T. butter
	¼ c. flour
1 T. oil	½ t. salt
1 T. dill weed	2 eggs, beaten
½ c. minced parsley	½ c. feta cheese, crumbled
1 10 oz. pkg. frozen chopped spinach, thawed	¼ t. baking powder
	1 16 oz. box phyllo (filo)
	1 c. melted butter

Saute onions in oil, add parsley, dill weed, and spinach. Melt 4 tablespoons butter, add flour, salt, eggs, feta cheese, and baking powder. Stir into spinach mixture. Thaw phyllo and keep covered with damp dish towel. Take one sheet of phyllo and brush with melted butter. Cover this with a second sheet of phyllo, and cut into 6 strips. Put about 1 tablespoon spinach mixture on end of each. Roll up like little flags. Freeze on plate. Do not stack unless frozen. Bake 350° for 20 minutes. Run under broiler to brown.
Yields about 48 pies.
Mrs. Jackson R. Hanks (Helen Reeves)

Peanut Butter Sticks

Use 3 day-old bread. Cut off crust. Cut each slice in 4 strips. Toast crusts and strips in 250° oven for an hour or until the bread is very crisp but not brown. Roll crusts into very fine crumbs.

Mix equal parts of smooth peanut butter and salad oil until smooth. Dip each toasted slice of bread in mixture. Then roll in crumbs and drain on brown paper. Store in tin box. These keep well. Also they freeze well. *They are good with drinks as an appetizer or at a morning coffee.*

Mrs. David J. Dial (Margery Hombs)

Bacon and Egg Spread

1	doz. hard-cooked eggs, chopped	½	t. prepared mustard
Salt and pepper to taste		6	slices crisp bacon, crumbled
½	c. mayonnaise	1	c. grated Cheddar cheese
½	t. grated onion		

Mix all ingredients and chill well. Spread on thin sliced bread. *A nice addition to a morning coffee!*

Cookbook Committee

Olive-Nut Sandwich Spread

6	oz. cream cheese	1	c. chopped salad olives
½	c. mayonnaise	2	T. olive juice
½	c. chopped pecans	Dash of white pepper	

Let 6 ounces of cream cheese stand at room temperature until it is soft. Mash with fork and add mayonnaise. Add pecans and olives to cream cheese mixture. Add two tablespoons of olive juice and a dash of pepper. Stir well. This will be mushy and is supposed to be. Put this into a pint jar and refrigerate for at least 24 to 48 hours. It will then become thick. Serve on very thin toast or fresh thinly sliced bread. Will keep a long time. This recipe was used in an Austin Tea Shop years ago and was printed in Heloise's column.

Mrs. Cad E. Williams (Francis Bailey)

Pecan Spread

1	8 oz. pkg. cream cheese, softened	2	T. dehydrated onion flakes
2	T. milk	½	t. garlic salt
1	2½ oz. jar dried beef, finely chopped	½	c. sour cream
¼	c. finely chopped bell pepper	2	T. mayonnaise
		¼	t. pepper
		¼	t. salt
		½	c. chopped pecans

Mix all ingredients except pecans and put in 8" pie plate. Heat and crisp pecans in melted butter and sprinkle on top. Bake at 350° for 20 minutes. It can be frozen before adding pecans. Double recipe fills 9½ inch quiche plate.
John D. Saunders

Clam Cream Fondue

1½	T. minced green onion	2½	T. flour
4	T. butter, divided	1	c. clam juice adding milk to make the cup
1¼	c. canned minced clams, reserving liquid	1	egg yolk
⅓	c. dry white wine or vermouth	¼	c. heavy cream
Salt and pepper		¼	c. grated Swiss cheese or Gruyere
½	t. tarragon		

Cook green onions in 2 tablespoons butter over low heat. Stir in the clams and cook slowly over low heat for 2 or 3 minutes. Add the wine, cover, and simmer for 1 minute. Uncover, raise heat, and boil rapidly until liquid has almost disappeared. Add salt and pepper to taste and the tarragon. Bring clam juice and milk to a boil. In a separate saucepan, cook the remaining butter and flour slowly for a few minutes. Remove from heat and beat in the boiling liquid. Return to a boil and stir for 1 minute. Beat egg yolk and cream in a bowl. Remove sauce from heat and beat into egg-cream mixture. Return to saucepan and boil for 1 minute, stirring constantly. Sauce should be very thick. Fold in the clam mixture, then the cheese. Adjust seasoning. If not used immediately, dot top of sauce with butter to prevent a skin from forming. This may be frozen and then heated in top of double boiler. Serve in chafing dish as a dip for bread rounds or as filling for pastry shells.
Yields approximately 2 cups. Freezes.
Mrs. Jackson R. Hanks (Helen Reeves)

Caviar Surprise

3   pkgs. unflavored gelatin   ¾   c. cold water

Egg Layer
4   hard-cooked eggs,   1   large green onion, minced
    chopped   ¼   t. salt
½   c. homemade mayonnaise   Tabasco to taste
¼   c. minced parsley   Freshly ground white pepper

Avocado Layer
1   medium avocado, pureed   2   T. homemade mayonnaise
1   medium avocado, diced   ½   t. salt
    just before adding   Tabasco to taste
1   large shallot, minced   Freshly ground black pepper
2   T. fresh lemon juice

Sour Cream and Onion Layer
1   c. sour cream   Fresh lemon juice to taste
¼   c. minced onion   Thinly sliced pumpernickel
1   3½ or 4 oz. jar black or   bread
    red caviar

Line bottom of an 8 inch spring form pan with foil extending 4 inches beyond rim of dish on 2 sides. Oil lightly. Soften gelatin in cold water. Liquefy gelatin by setting cup in hot water. This will be divided into 3 parts.
For Egg Layer Combine all ingredients with 1 part of gelatin mixture. Taste and adjust seasoning. Neatly spread egg mixture into prepared dish, smoothing top.
For Avocado Layer Combine all ingredients with 1 part of gelatin mixture. Adjust seasoning. Gently spread mixture evenly over egg layer.
For Sour Cream and Onion Layer Mix sour cream, onion, and remaining gelatin mixture. Spread carefully over avocado layer. Cover dish tightly with plastic wrap and refrigerate overnight.
Just before serving, place caviar in fine sieve and rinse gently under cold running water. Sprinkle with lemon juice. Drain. Transfer mold to a serving dish. Spread caviar over top. Serve with thin slices of dark pumpernickle bread.
Serves 12 to 16.
Mrs. F. H. Eilenberger, Jr. (Claire Barnes)

Crabmeat Dip

6	T. flour	1	t. salt
6	T. butter	¼	t. cayenne pepper
½	onion, finely chopped	2	6½ oz. cans crabmeat
2	c. milk	4	to 6 T. sherry
½	t. dry mustard	Bread crumbs as needed	
½	t. paprika		

Saute onion in butter until tender not brown. Add flour, dry mustard, paprika, salt, and cayenne pepper. Blend thoroughly over low heat. Add milk and after mixture is smooth and thick, add crabmeat. Put saucepan over hot water, and add sherry and bread crumbs for thickening. May be made a day or two ahead, but always reheat over hot water. Add sherry the day it will be served.
Mrs. Everett Hutchinson (Elizabeth Stafford)

Crabmeat Rolls

1	lb. crabmeat	1	t. salt
1	lb. cream cheese	½	t. white pepper
1	egg yolk	Egg roll skins	

Mix well and place 1 teaspoon in center of egg roll skin. Fold skin over filling and seal by moistening with flour and water paste. Fry in deep hot fat until golden brown.

Dipping Sauce

1	c. salad oil	2	T. lemon juice
½	c. catsup	2	T. soy sauce
⅓	c. vinegar	2	T. Worcestershire
⅓	c. honey	Salt	
		Grated onion	

Combine ingredients for sauce and serve with crabmeat rolls.
Mrs. F. H. Eilenberger, Jr. (Claire Barnes)

Crab Swiss Bites

1	pkg. of 1 doz. butterflake rolls	½	c. mayonnaise
1	7½ oz. can crabmeat, drained and flaked	2	T. minced green onion, tops and bottoms
1	6 oz. can water chestnuts, drained and diced	½	T. dill weed
		1	t. lemon juice
1	c. shredded Swiss cheese		Salt and pepper to taste
			MSG

Separate each roll into 3 layers. Place on ungreased baking sheet. Mix all other ingredients and spoon onto top of each roll. Bake at 350° for 15 minutes. May freeze before or after cooking. For smaller hors d'oeuvres, use Tiny Tart Shells recipe on page 246.
Yields 36.
Cookbook Committee

Deviled Oyster Dip

1	qt. oysters		Small piece of bay leaf
3	small onions, minced	2	dashes thyme
2	cloves garlic, minced	½	c. butter
1	T. shortening		Fine bread crumbs

Chop or grind oysters fine, reserving some of liquid. Saute onions and garlic in shortening until brown. Add bay leaf, thyme, and oysters. Cook until oysters stop drawing water. Add juice, butter, and bread crumbs until good dipping consistency.
Mrs. F. H. Eilenberger, Jr. (Claire Barnes)

Nana's Oyster Patties

24	small tart shells	½	c. flour
3	pts. oysters	4	cloves garlic, finely
1	8 oz. can mushrooms		chopped
½	c. finely chopped celery		Tabasco to taste
½	c. finely chopped green	1	T. Worcestershire sauce
	pepper	½	t. chili powder
½	c. finely chopped fresh		Salt and pepper to taste
	green onions	4	T. sherry
2	T. cooking oil	2	T. lemon juice
½	c. margarine		Parsley

Drain oysters and mushrooms. Reserve liquid. Finely chop oysters and mushrooms. Saute celery, green pepper, and green onions in small amount of cooking oil. Melt margarine in heavy Dutch oven. Add flour. Cook on low heat but do not brown. Add garlic and cook a few minutes. Add sauteed celery, pepper, and onions. Add juices a little at a time, stirring frequently. Add Tabasco and Worcestershire sauce, chili powder, salt, pepper, sherry, and lemon juice. Simmer slowly 45 minutes. Fill shells and sprinkle with parsley. Bake about 15 minutes in 350° oven. *Excellent for cocktail party.* Recipe for tart shells is found on page 246.
Yields 24 patties.
Mrs. John B. McDonald (Dorothy Crider))

Salmon Ball

1	16 oz. can salmon	2	t. chopped fresh parsley
1	8 oz. pkg. cream cheese	1	t. prepared horseradish
1	T. fresh lemon juice	½	c. chopped pecans
1	t. chopped onion		

Mix ingredients in order given. Roll in large ball. This can be rolled in additional chopped parsley.
Mrs. F. H. Eilenberger, Jr. (Claire Barnes)

Curried Shrimp Dip

½ lb. shrimp, finely chopped
1 10¾ oz. cream of shrimp soup, undiluted
1 8 oz. pkg. cream cheese, softened
½ t. curry powder

1 4 oz. can chopped ripe olives
2 t. lemon juice
Dash of garlic salt
Salt and white pepper to taste

Combine all the ingredients, and refrigerate several hours before serving. Serve with assorted crackers and/or melba toast.
Serves 10 to 15 generously.
Mrs. Albert Rucker (Lois Brymer)

Hot Cheese Shrimp Dip

1 c. cream of mushroom soup
1 10¾ oz. can cream of shrimp soup
1 6 oz. roll garlic flavored cheese

1 T. grated onion
1 T. lemon juice
1 4 oz. can sliced mushrooms
1 c. grated American cheese
1 c. boiled shrimp

In double boiler combine first 7 ingredients. Heat until melted and well blended. Add shrimp.
Mrs. Joe Ed Johnston (Marilyn Hardgrave)

Shrimp-Cucumber Spread

2 T. mayonnaise
1 3 oz. pkg. cream cheese, softened
2 T. catsup
1 t. dry mustard

Dash of garlic salt
1 t. lemon juice
1 4½ oz. can shrimp, drained
¼ c. minced cucumber
1 t. grated onion

Combine mayonnaise, cream cheese, catsup, mustard, and garlic salt in a medium bowl. Mix until smooth. Add shrimp, lemon juice, cucumber, and onion; stir well. The canned shrimp will break up well. Serve with corn chips, crackers, or party rye.
Mrs. Marion Boyd (Lucile Sutton)

Shrimp Crab Spread

1	10¾ oz. can cream of shrimp soup		Salt and pepper to taste
2	10¾ oz. cans cream of mushroom soup	3	4¼ oz. cans shrimp, rinsed and drained
1	8 oz. pkg. cream cheese	3	6 oz. cans crabmeat
1½	t. Tabasco	2	8 oz. cans sliced water chestnuts
1	t. dry mustard		
2	T. Worcestershire sauce	3	8 oz. cans mushroom stems and pieces, drained

In top of a double boiler, heat soups. Add cheese and stir until melted. Add seasonings and mix well. Fold in shrimp, crabmeat, water chestnuts, and mushrooms. Serve hot in a chafing dish with toast rounds or your choice of crackers.
Serves 70.
Mrs. Jack H. Hanks (Jackie Rayburn)

Shrimp Dip

1	8 oz. pkg. cream cheese, softened	3	t. Tabasco
1	c. Thousand Island Dressing	1	T. seasoned salt
½	c. mayonnaise	1	T. horseradish
2	pimientos, minced	2	lbs. shrimp, cooked, shelled, and finely chopped
1	small onion, grated		
½	c. minced green onions		Dash of lemon juice

Blend together cream cheese, dressing, and mayonnaise. Stir in remaining ingredients. Chill.
Yields 3 pints.
Mrs. Dick Hartt (Dorothy Marshall)

 When using canned shrimp, soak in ice water for a few minutes before proceeding with recipe. This improves flavor.

Tuna Balls with Hot Mustard Sauce

1	12 oz. can tuna	½	c. minced onion
¾	c. dry bread crumbs		Salt and pepper to taste
2	eggs, slightly beaten		

Combine tuna, bread crumbs, eggs, onion, salt, pepper. Mix at medium speed with mixer, scraping the bowl with a rubber spatula. Shape mixture into cocktail size balls and place on lightly buttered cookie sheet. Cover and refrigerate. Bake uncovered at 400° for 12 to 15 minutes or until lightly browned. Serve with Hot Mustard Sauce.

Sauce

¼	c. dry mustard	½	t. salt
¼	c. cider vinegar	1	egg
2	t. sugar	½	c. mayonnaise

Combine all ingredients in a saucepan *except mayonnaise.* Cook over low heat until mixture is just thickened, stirring constantly. Refrigerate until cooled and then stir in mayonnaise.

Mrs. Albert Rucker (Lois Brymer)

Pate

1	lb. liverwurst	½	t. sweet basil
½	small onion, chopped		Salt and pepper to taste

Cream cheese topping

1	8 oz. pkg. cream cheese	½	t. Tabasco
		1	t. mayonnaise

Mash liverwurst with fork. Combine with onion, basil, salt, and pepper. Shape into ball on a plate and chill. Mix cream cheese, Tabasco, and mayonnaise. Spread over pate. Serve with party rye bread.

Mrs. F. H. Eilenberger, Jr. (Claire Barnes)

Kibbie

| 2 | lbs. lean round steak | 1½ | c. fine boulghour |
| 2 | medium onions | | Salt and pepper to taste |

Wash and soak wheat for two hours. Drain. Grind meat, onion, and wheat twice. Mix by hand. Can be served raw, or cooked in clarified butter. Shape as little footballs.
Yields 70 to 80 balls.
Mrs. Curtis C. Mann (Jay Nemer)

Meat Balls

1	lb. ground chuck	4	t. soy sauce
1	lb. lean pork sausage	2	c. seasoned bread cubes
1	8 oz. can water chestnuts,	1	slice extra thin bread
	drained and chopped	1	5.33 oz. can evaporated
1	t. salt		milk
1	t. pepper		

Combine meat mixture and other ingredients. Form into balls and bake at 350° for 20 to 30 minutes.
Yields 100 balls.
Mrs. Lawrence S. McWhorter (Elma Cornelius)

Olive Meat Balls

1	lb. lean ground beef	¼	t. onion salt
⅓	c. bread crumbs	⅛	t. pepper
¼	c. milk	36	stuffed green olives
1	egg, beaten	½	c. French dressing
¼	t. salt		

Mix together with hands everything but olives and French dressing. Shape meat mixture around olives forming balls. Fry in French dressing, turning to brown.
Yields 36 appetizers.
Mrs. Haskell Adcox (Eleanor Tilley)

Tamale Balls

1	lb. lean ground beef	2	t. salt
1	lb. lean ground pork	¾	c. tomato juice
1	T. chili powder	4	medium garlic cloves,
1½	c. corn meal		crushed
½	c. flour		

Mix beef and pork together. Add all other ingredients. Mix well with hands and form into small balls the size of walnuts.

Sauce

6	c. tomato juice	2	T. chili powder
2	t. salt		

Mix above ingredients. Pour sauce into a large shallow roaster. Add balls to sauce and simmer covered for 2 hours. Serve in chafing dish.
Yields 100 balls.
Mrs. Jack H. Hanks (Jackie Rayburn)

Chutney Sausage Bites

1	lb. Little Smokies	8	ozs. sherry
1	8 oz. jar chutney, chopped fine	1	c. sour cream

Cook sausage. Drain fat. Mix chutney, sherry, and sour cream. Cook gently a few minutes and pour over sausage.
Yields 48 to 50.
Cookbook Committee

Sausage Balls

1	lb. hot sausage	1	8 oz. jar Cheese Whiz
2½	to 3 c. Bisquick		

Mix with hands. Shape into small balls. Bake 15 or 20 minutes in 350° oven. These are good made ahead and reheated at serving time. Jalapeno Cheese Whiz may be substituted for the regular.
Yields 6 dozen. Freezes.
Mrs. Andrew Frantzen (Louise Lowe)

Sausage Rolls

Bisquick or any biscuit recipe   **1   lb. hot sausage, room temperature**

Make a dough using recipe on box for biscuits. This is a soft dough so knead in flour to roll out. Divide dough into 2 parts. Roll each half *very thin.* Spread each with sausage. Roll as for a jelly roll. Refrigerate or freeze. Slice as for cookies and bake at 400° for 10 minutes. These slice more easily if half frozen.
Mrs. A. M. Barnes, Athens, Texas

Sausage Stroganoff

1   clove garlic
2   lbs. Little Smokies sausage
3   T. flour
2   c. milk
2   large onions, chopped
2   8 oz. cans mushroom
        stems and pieces,
        drained

4   T. margarine
2   t. soy sauce
2   T. Worcestershire
Salt, pepper, and paprika to
        taste
1   16 oz. carton sour cream

Rub large 12 inch skillet with garlic and heat. Brown sausage, pouring off any grease. Sprinkle flour over sausage, add milk, and simmer until slightly thickened. Set aside. Saute onions, mushrooms, and seasonings in margarine; add sausage. When mixture bubbles, add sour cream. Serve hot in chafing dish with melba toast, biscuits, or small pastry shells. Double the recipe to serve more than 50 people. When doubling, use only 3 onions. May be made in advance and frozen, eliminating sour cream. When preparing to serve, heat, and add sour cream. May be served as an entree over rice for six people.
Cookbook Committee

Swiss Sausage Bits

1	8 oz. can crescent rolls	½	c. light cream
2	lbs. sausage		Salt and pepper to taste
½	c. chopped onion		Basil and oregano to taste
½	c. chopped green pepper	2	c. grated Swiss cheese
4	eggs		

Cook sausage and drain well. Mix sausage, onion, and green pepper; spread over dough. Combine eggs, light cream, salt, pepper, basil, and oregano. Pour over sausage mix. Sprinkle with cheese. Bake at 375° for 30 minutes or until done.
Yields 63 squares.
Mrs. A. J. Rettig, Stuart, Florida

Smoked Turkey Dip

Grind turkey. Add small amount of mayonnaise. Strain picante sauce and add enough tomato mixture for a nippy taste. Serve cold with crackers. This is great for left over smoked turkey.
Mrs. F. H. Eilenberger, Jr. (Claire Barnes)

Wild Game en Chafing Dish

Use a combination of game such as dove, quail, duck, goose, and turkey. Season game with salt and pepper. In heavy skillet, brown in margarine. Remove game to a baking dish. Make sauce in skillet by adding flour, water, and Burgundy wine. Adjust seasonings to taste. Pour sauce over game. Cover and bake in a slow oven until game falls away from bones. Additional wine may be added during baking period. Debone and shred game before serving in sauce in chafing dish. Serve with toast rounds.
This recipe was created to use an abundance of game stored in the freezer for a long while. A very popular recipe, especially with the men! The Wild Game Dip is a variation of this recipe.
Mrs. Cad E. Williams (Francis Bailey)

Wild Game Dip

A combination of game such as duck, quail, goose, and dove. Parboil game with bay leaves, salt, pepper, and garlic. Debone and shred meat. Make a white sauce using light cream. Add enough sauce to game to make it dipping consistency. Heat all thoroughly, and add Burgundy wine to taste. Serve in chafing dish with melba toast rounds or biscuit halves.

Mrs. F. H. Eilenberger, Jr. (Claire Barnes)

Cocktail Pecans

2	c. pecans	15	to 20 chili peppers,
8	t. salt		crushed
		2	c. water

Boil water with salt and crushed peppers. Add pecans for 5 minutes. Drain for 2 hours. Then place in 225° to 250° oven for 2 to 3 hours. Turn several times.

Mrs. John E. Presley (Lucinda Hanks)

Spiced Pecans

1	c. sugar	½	t. cinnamon
⅓	c. evaporated milk	1	t. vanilla
2	T. water	1½	c. pecan halves

Mix sugar, milk, water, and cinnamon in saucepan. Cook, stirring constantly, about 2 minutes. Remove from heat. Add vanilla and pecans. Stir until well coated. Drop on waxed paper.

Mrs. Ben W. Hearne (Esther Johnson)

Christmas Chocolate

1	lb. box Nestle's Quik	1	3 qt. box instant milk
½	lb. box powdered sugar	1	7 oz. jar non-dairy creamer

Mix all together and store in container. When ready to use add ⅔ cup of boiling water to ⅓ cup of mixture.

Mrs. K. G. Johnson (Betty Fister)

Instant Cappuccino

1   part sugar
1   part instant coffee
1   part cocoa

2   parts non-dairy creamer
    or more to taste

Mix all ingredients and store in an air tight container. To serve, dissolve 2 or 3 tablespoons of mix in one cup of hot water.
Mrs. Doug Lowe (Evie Johnston)

Christmas Punch

1   qt. cranberry juice
       cocktail
2   c. apple juice
1   T. lemon juice

1   16 oz. bottle Sprite
Lemon slices

Combine juices and Sprite. Float lemon slices.
Yields 12 cups.
Mrs. A. J. Overton, Jr. (Lila May Morriss)

Fruit Slush

2   c. hot water
1½ c. sugar
2   8½ oz. cans crushed
       pineapple
1   10 oz. box frozen
       strawberries

2   6 oz. cans frozen orange
       juice
6   ripe bananas, chopped
6   cans water

Mix water and sugar and stir until sugar dissolves. Cool. Mix remaining ingredients. Add cooled sugar and water. Freeze in 8 ounce serving cups. Set out two hours to thaw to a slush.
Mrs. H. Green (Bennie Eubanks)

Golden Punch

8	c. water	2	12 oz. cans frozen orange
4	c. sugar		juice
2	qts. pineapple juice,	½	c. lemon juice
	unsweetened	5	large bananas, whipped in blender

Boil water and sugar for 5 minutes; cool. Mix orange juice according to directions on can. Mix all ingredients together and freeze in 3 half gallon containers. Add 2 quarts ginger ale when ready to serve.
Serves 50.
Mrs. A. C. Murray (Acie Graham)

Hot Spiced Punch

9½	c. cranberry cocktail juice	4½	t. whole cloves
9½	c. pineapple juice	4	sticks cinnamon
4½	c. water	¼	t. salt
1	c. brown sugar		

Place spices in basket of 30 cup perculator and juices in bottom. Plug in and allow to heat through. *Delightful during holiday season.*
Mrs. K. G. Johnson (Betty Fister)

Orange Julius

1	6 oz. can frozen orange	¼	c. sugar
	juice	½	t. vanilla
6	oz. milk	8	ice cubes
6	oz. water		

Whirl in blender for 30 seconds.
Yields 4 large servings.
Mrs. H. Green (Bennie Eubanks)

Punch

2	3 oz. pkgs. lemon gelatin			
1	to 1½ c. sugar	1	12 oz. can frozen orange
3	c. boiling water		juice
1	46 oz. can pineapple juice	1	1 oz. bottle almond
1	12 oz. can frozen		extract
	lemonade	1	2 liter bottle Sprite

Combine gelatin, sugar, and boiling water. Stir until gelatin is dissolved. Add remaining ingredients except Sprite. Mix well and freeze. To serve, partially thaw and add Sprite.
Serves 100.
Mrs. A. J. Overton, Jr. (Lila May Morriss)

Milk Punch

3	qts. whole milk	2	or 3 T. vanilla
3	c. bourbon		Nutmeg to sprinkle on each
1	c. sugar		serving
½	c. water		

Mix sugar and water into a simple syrup. Combine ingredients and freeze at least a day ahead in gallon or half gallon milk cartons. Stir while freezing. This will freeze indefinitely. Remove from freezer 30 minutes before serving. Stir as punch thaws.
Make 3 recipes for 50 people.
Serves 16 to 18 while still icy.
Mrs. Cad E. Williams (Francis Bailey)

Papa's Egg Nog

12 eggs, separated	3 T. sugar
1¼ c. bourbon	9 T. sugar
1 qt. heavy cream	Nutmeg to taste

In electric mixer beat egg yolks at medium speed for 20 minutes or until they are light lemon colored and very fluffy. Continue beating and add bourbon a drop at a time, This may be done the night before and placed in covered container in refrigerator. Whip cream until it stands in peaks. Add 3 tablespoons sugar, and fold egg yolks into whipped cream. Beat egg whites until they are dry and have completely lost their gloss. This step is very important. It is the secret of the eggnog's "standing up" quality. Add the 9 tablespoons of sugar to egg whites 1 tablespoon at a time, and continue beating about 10 minutes after all sugar has been added. Fold egg whites into cream and egg yolk mixture. Continue to blend with a folding motion until well mixed and smooth. Very rich.
Serves 12.
May B. Bachtel, M.D. (May Bradley)

Brandy Flips

2 eggs	6 to 8 ice cubes
¾ c. brandy	4½ c. milk
1 t. vanilla	Nutmeg
2 t. sugar	

Place first 6 ingredients in blender and whirl until well mixed. Pour into glasses and sprinkle with nutmeg.
Serves 4 to 6.
Mrs. Jack H. Hanks (Jackie Rayburn)

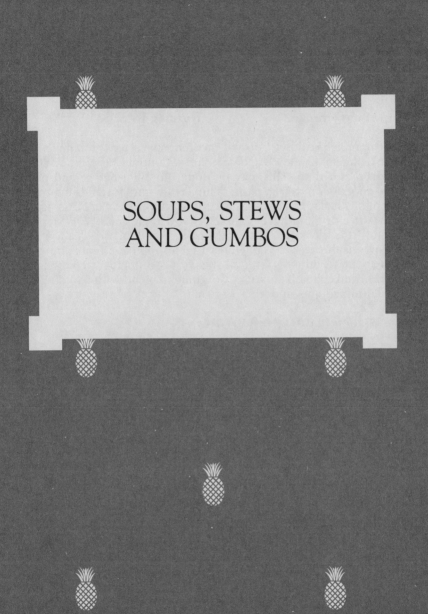

SOUPS, STEWS
AND GUMBOS

Avocado en Gelee Waldershare

2 ripe but firm avocados	Salt and pepper to taste
1½ tins consomme soup	Dry sherry to taste
Juice of 1 lemon	Finely chopped chives

Put consomme soup into a bowl, add plenty of lemon juice, freshly ground pepper, a little salt, chopped chives, and sherry to taste. Stir ingredients well and leave in refrigerator for 3 to 4 hours or longer, stirring occasionally. Just before serving, place the gelee on the serving dish and slice the avocados and arrange around the consomme en gelee. Serve fairly quickly because of the avocado discoloring and, of course, the consomme melting.
The Countess of Guildford, Waldershare Park, near Dover, Kent, England

Avocado Soup

4 avocados	Salt and pepper to taste
1 T. grated onion	Dash of cayenne pepper
2 c. chicken broth	Sour cream and chives to
1 c. light cream	garnish
2 T. finely chopped parsley	

Peel avocados and cut in large pieces. Place all ingredients in blender and process until well blended. Serve cold and garnish with a dollop of sour cream and a bit of minced chives.
Serves 8.
Mrs. Jack Hanks (Jackie Rayburn)

Cold Tomato Soup

2 c. Bloody Mary cocktail	½ t. curry powder
mix	Salt and pepper to taste
2 c. canned chicken broth	Lemon slices
1 t. lemon juice	Sour cream
1 t. sugar	

Bring Bloody Mary mix and chicken broth to a boil. Add lemon juice, sugar, curry powder, salt, and pepper. Simmer 10 minutes. Chill. When serving garnish with lemon slices or a dollop of sour cream.
Serves 6.
Cookbook Committee

Canadian Cheese Soup

¼ c. butter
½ c. finely diced onion
½ c. finely diced carrots
½ c. finely diced celery
¼ c. flour
1½ T. cornstarch
1 qt. chicken stock

1 qt. milk
⅛ t. soda
1 c. grated processed
 Cheddar cheese
Salt and pepper
2 T. finely chopped parsley

Melt butter in large saucepan; add onions, carrots, and celery and saute over low heat until soft. Add flour and cornstarch and cook until bubbly. Add stock and milk and make a smooth sauce. Add soda and the cheese. Season with salt and pepper. Add parsley a few minutes before serving.
Serves 8.
From The Driskill Hotel, Austin, Texas
Mrs. Cad E. Williams (Francis Bailey)

Cheesy Broccoli Soup

½ c. chopped onion
¼ c. chopped green pepper
2 T. margarine
1 10 oz. pkg. frozen
 chopped broccoli,
 cooked (no salt added)

1 10¾ oz. can cream of
 chicken soup
1¼ c. milk
¾ lb. processed American
 cheese, cubed

Saute onions and green pepper in margarine. Cook broccoli and drain well. Add broccoli and remaining ingredients to onions and peppers. Cook on low until cheese is thoroughly melted or cook in microwave for 6 to 8 minutes.
Serves 6.
Mrs. Robert E. Jordan (Margaret Haygood)

Chilled Green Pea Soup

2	10 oz. pkgs. frozen peas	1	10¾ oz. can condensed
¾	c. water		chicken broth
½	c. minced green onion	½	c. heavy cream
½	t. salt		Freshly grated nutmeg
			Chopped chives

Combine peas, water, onion, and salt in medium saucepan and bring to boil. Cover and simmer 15 minutes, stirring occasionally. Cool slightly. Pour into blender or food processor to puree. Add chicken broth. Chill thoroughly. Stir in cream and nutmeg to taste. Refrigerate until ready to serve. Ladle into individual bowls and sprinkle with chopped chives.
Serves 4 to 5.
Mrs. John H. Cumby (Darlen Herrington)

Cream of Carrot Soup

½	c. thinly sliced onion	1	small apple, peeled and
2	c. thinly sliced carrots		diced
1	c. chicken broth	1	t. salt
2	c. milk		Few drops Tabasco
			Nutmeg, optional

Cook onions and carrots in broth until tender. Add milk and apple. Blend in processor or blender. Cool. Season with salt and Tabasco. *May sprinkle with nutmeg when serving. Serve hot or cold.*
Serves 6.
Mrs. Robert Miller (Rosemary Hajenian)

Creamy Chicken Soup

1	10¾ oz. can cream of	1	8 oz. can whole kernel
	chicken soup		corn, drained
1½	c. milk	2	T. finely chopped
1	c. diced cooked chicken		pimiento

In medium saucepan, combine soup and milk; blend until smooth. Add chicken and corn. Heat, stirring occasionally. Season to taste. Garnish with pimiento. *This is a good way to use left over chicken or turkey.*
Serves 5.
Mrs. Jack Graves (Pauline Thompson)

Cream of Onion Soup

2	T. margarine
2	to 3 large onions, sliced thin
2	c. water
Salt to taste	
Pepper to taste	

2	boiled and well mashed potatoes
2	c. boiling milk
Toasted bread	
Minced parsley	

Put margarine into a 2 quart saucepan, and when this is hot, add the sliced onions; stir and cook until they are translucent. Be sure they do not burn. Add water, salt, and pepper to taste. Boil 15 minutes. Add two boiled and well mashed potatoes, stirring in smoothly. Add the boiling milk. Let simmer for a few minutes. Put a piece of toasted bread in bottom of each plate, pour over the soup, and serve hot. Garnish with minced parsley.
Serves 6 to 8.
Mrs. Jim Bob Parker (Pat McCrary)

French Onion Soup

5	c. thinly sliced onions
¼	t. sugar
¼	c. butter
3	10½ oz. cans beef broth
4	c. water
½	t. salt

Freshly ground black pepper to taste	
2	T. brandy
6	slices buttered French bread, toasted
½	c. grated Parmesan cheese

Sprinkle onions with sugar. Saute slowly in butter until a delicate gold. Add beef broth and water. Cover and simmer 45 minutes. Add salt, pepper, and brandy. Place in large tureen or individual bowls. Top with French bread and sprinkle with cheese. Bake a few minutes in 400° oven.
Serves 6.
Mrs. W. G. Darsey, Jr. (Roberta Deerman)

  A peeled potato added to salty soup will absorb some of salt.

Curried Lemon Soup

1	10¾ oz. can cream of chicken soup	⅓	c. lemon juice
2	c. light cream	2	t. curry powder or to taste
			Salt and pepper to taste

Whirl in blender until blended. Serve chilled. Dust with paprika. May be served hot. Heat slowly; do not boil.
Serves 4.
Mrs. Frank C. Hicks (Helen Davenport)

Gazpacho

2	16 oz. cans stewed tomatoes	½	to 1 jalapeno pepper, seeded
1	t. Jane's Crazy Salt		

Place above ingredients in blender and blend well. Serve with garnishes.

Garnish
Croutons
Chopped fresh tomatoes
Chopped cucumber

Chopped celery
Chopped zucchini

Serves 6.
Mrs. Jack Hanks (Jackie Rayburn)

Gazpacho - Summer Soup

1	15 oz. can tomato sauce	3	T. wine vinegar
1	18 oz. can tomato juice	2	T. olive oil
¾	c. chopped celery	1	t. salt
¾	c. chopped cucumber	¼	t. pepper
½	c. chopped onion	½	t. Worcestershire sauce
½	c. chopped avocado	⅛	t. garlic powder
¼	c. chopped green pepper	1	t. hot sauce
1	T. parsley flakes		

Mix all ingredients and add to tomato juice and sauce. Makes 2 quarts. Serve in demitasse cups or small glasses.
Serves 12.
Mrs. Clifford Bassett (Thelma Hamlitt)

Vichyssoise

2	T. butter	2	c. light cream
2	c. green onions, finely chopped		Salt and pepper to taste
			Minced parsely
3	c. diced white potatoes		Chives
2	qts. chicken broth		

Melt butter; add green onions and simmer until tender. Do not brown. Add potatoes and chicken broth to onions. Cook until potatoes are soft. Let mixture cool slightly and then pour into a blender ½ cup at a time. After all is blended, add cream. Heat slowly and add salt and pepper to taste. May be served hot or cold, but it is much better cold. When served cold, sprinkle minced parsley or chives on each portion. This keeps 4 to 5 days in the refrigerator. It tastes better if made a few days before serving.
Serves 6 to 8.
Mrs. P.A. Kolstad, Jr. (Dottie Ondus)

Vichyssoise - The Easy Way

1	10¾ oz. can potato soup	1	to 2 t. chives
1	soup can milk		Pinch of dill weed
1	3 oz. pkg. cream cheese		Seasoned salt
2	t. minced onion		Pepper and Tabasco to taste
1	t. chicken stock base		Paprika

Place potato soup, milk, and cream cheese in blender. Whirl to blend. Add remaining ingredients except paprika and blend well. Adjust seasonings. Chill. When serving, garnish with paprika.
Serves 6.
Cookbook Committee

Potato Soup

2	medium potatoes, cut to bite size	2	T. butter
1	medium onion, cut to bite size	⅓	t. pepper
3	to 4 c. milk		Salt to taste (about 2 t.)
			Chopped green onion

Cover potatoes and onions with water and cook about 20 minutes at a medium boil. Drain. Add remaining ingredients. Bring to a full boil, about 2 minutes. Garnish with chopped green onion.
Serves 4 to 6.
Mrs. Vernon Fritze, Jr. (Kathy Duderstadt)

Green Pea and Potato Soup

4	to 6 medium new potatoes, peeled and diced	2	T. margarine
1	t. salt	1½	c. milk
1½	c. water	⅛	t. pepper
1	slice bacon	1	hard-cooked egg, grated
1	10 oz. pkg. frozen green peas		

Put salt, water, and bacon in pan and bring to boil. Add potatoes and cook almost done. To potatoes add peas and cook until peas are done. Add margarine, milk, pepper, and bring to boil. Garnish with grated egg. Serve with cornbread and green salad.
Serves 6.
Mrs. Lucylle Pope MacNaughton

Split Pea Soup

4	T. butter		
1	11 oz. pkg. dried split peas	1	bay leaf
2½	qts. water, divided	½	t. paprika
1	2½ oz. can deviled ham	1	T. lemon juice
⅔	c. finely chopped carrots	½	t. lemon pepper
⅔	c. finely chopped onions	2	t. salt or to taste after
⅔	c. finely chopped celery		soup has cooked

Melt butter in a heavy 3 quart saucepan. Pour in split peas and stir to coat thoroughly with butter. Add 2 quarts water, stir in deviled ham, mixing well. Cover and simmer for 2 hours. Use remaining water for desired consistency. Add carrots, onions, celery, bay leaf, paprika, lemon juice, and lemon pepper. Simmer for 45 minutes to 1 hour. Add salt to taste. *This is a delicious thick soup for a cold winter night. Best made a day ahead.*
Serves 6 to 8.
Mrs. John H. Cumby (Darlen Herrington)

Tortilla Soup

1	onion, chopped	1	t. each ground cumin, chili powder, salt, and sugar
1	large jalapeno pepper, seeded and chopped		
2	or 3 cloves garlic, mashed	½	t. lemon pepper
1	T. oil, or more, if needed	2	t. Worcestershire
1	16 oz. can stewed tomatoes	1½	t. Tabasco
		4	corn tortillas
4	to 6 c. chicken or beef broth	2	c. grated sharp cheese
		2	avocados, peeled and chopped
1	10½ oz. can tomato soup	1	8 oz. carton sour cream

Saute onion, pepper, and garlic in oil until limp. Add stewed tomatoes, chicken broth, and tomato soup. Mix well and add seasonings, Worcestershire sauce, and Tabasco. Simmer uncovered for 1 to 1½ hours. Cut tortillas in thin strips like noodles. Add tortillas to soup the last 10 minutes of cooking. To serve, put a bit of grated cheese in the bottom of each bowl. Ladle hot soup over cheese. Top with chopped avocado and a dollop of sour cream.
Mrs. Everett Hutchinson (Elizabeth Stafford)

Yellow Squash Soup

3 to 4 yellow squash, straightneck or crookneck	1 c. light cream
	Curry powder to taste
	Salt and white pepper to taste
1 fresh leek or onion	Chopped parsley for garnish
2 to 2½ c. chicken stock	

Wash and trim squash, slice thickly, and parbroil several minutes in a small amount of water in a saucepan. Follow the same method for the leek. Drain the squash well and puree through a food mill or in a food processor and set aside in a bowl. If you prefer a smoother puree, pass it through a fine sieve to remove any bits of seed that may still be firm. Repeat with the leek. Place half the squash puree, 1 tablespoon leek puree, 1 cup chicken stock, and ½ cup cream in a blender, and process until smooth. Remove to a bowl and repeat with the second half of ingredients. If the mixture seems too thick, blend in a little chicken stock. Combine the two batches, stir in curry powder, salt, and pepper to taste, and chill until ready to serve. Sprinkle with parsley just before serving.

For **Broccoli Soup** substitute 1 bunch fresh broccoli which has been washed, trimmed, pared, and cooked in a small amount of water. Continue with recipe omitting curry powder. This soup is great heated.
Serves 4 to 6.
Mrs. John H. Cumby (Darlen Herrington)

Corn Chowder

½ c. cut up bacon	Pepper to taste
½ c. chopped onion	½ bay leaf
½ c. chopped celery	3 T. flour
1 c. diced raw potatoes	½ c. cold milk
2 c. water	1½ c. hot milk
1 t. salt	2 to 3 c. whole kernel corn, drained
¼ t. paprika	Chopped parsley

Brown bacon. Add onion and celery and saute until golden brown. Stir in potatoes, water, salt, paprika, pepper, and bay leaf. Cook on medium 30 to 45 minutes or until potatoes are tender. Mix flour and ½ cup cold milk together until smooth. Add to potato mixture. Stir in 1½ cups hot milk and corn. Heat, but do not boil. Serve with chopped parsley.
Serves 5 to 6.
Mrs. Sam Martin (Tommie Bell)

Fresh Corn Chowder

6	to 8 ears of corn	2	c. cubed potatoes
6	slices bacon, diced	2	t. salt
1	c. chopped onions	⅛	t. white pepper
¼	c. flour		Dash of Tabasco
2	c. chicken broth	2	c. milk
1	c. water	2	T. butter or margarine

Remove the husks and silk from corn; rinse and drain. Remove kernels from the cob by cutting with a sharp knife. Measure kernels to equal 4 cups. In a 3 quart saucepan, cook bacon until crisp. Remove bacon with slotted spoon; drain on paper towel. Discard all but 1 tablespoon bacon drippings. Add onions and saute until tender, about 5 minutes. Gradually stir in flour. Pour in chicken broth and water, stirring constantly until blended. Add corn, bacon, potatoes, and seasonings. Heat to boiling. Reduce heat to low and simmer covered, for 15 to 20 minutes, stirring occasionally. Add milk and continue cooking until well heated. Top with butter or margarine. Serve immediately. You may reserve chopped bacon and use as a garnish.
Serves 8.
Mrs. Alexander Nemer II (Vicki Burke)

Manhattan Clam Chowder

¼	c. finely cut bacon	1	c. water
¼	c. minced onion	⅓	c. diced celery
1	pt. shucked fresh clams with liquor or two 7 oz. cans minced clams, drained	1	16 oz. can tomatoes
		1	t. salt
		⅛	t. pepper
		2	t. minced parsley
2	c. finely diced raw potatoes	¼	t. thyme

Saute bacon and onion in large kettle. Drain and grind clams and set aside. (If using canned clams, drain and set aside.) Add clam liquor, potatoes, water, and celery to bacon and onions. Cook until potatoes are tender. Add clams, tomatoes, and seasonings. Simmer for flavor. Do not overcook, as tomatoes tend to toughen clams.
Serves 4.
Mrs. Frank C. Hicks (Helen Davenport)

Boeuf Bourguignon

1	6 oz. chunk salt pork or thick sliced bacon, cut into 1 inch strips	2	c. beef bouillon
		1	T. tomato paste
Olive oil or cooking oil		2	or 3 cloves garlic, pressed
3	lbs. lean boneless beef, cut into 2 inch chunks	½	t. thyme
		1	bay leaf
3	c. red Burgundy wine	Salt to taste	

Brown the pork lightly in a large skillet, adding a small amount of oil if necessary, to render out the fat; this will be used for browning the beef. Remove the browned pork to a plate, add oil to film skillet, and turn heat to moderate high. When skillet is almost smoking, brown the beef a few pieces at a time, turning often to brown on all sides. As the beef chunks brown, place in a 4 quart baking dish.

Pour browning fat out of skillet, pour in the red wine, scraping up all the brown bits, and then pour over the beef. Add the browned pork to the dish and enough of the bouillon to cover the meat. Stir in the rest of the ingredients and bring to a simmer. Cover the dish, place in a 325° oven, and simmer slowly for 2½ to 3 hours or until beef is fork tender.

Mushrooms and Onions

1	lb. fresh mushrooms, washed and sliced	24	small white onions
2	T. butter	1	T. butter
Salt		½	t. salt
		Water	

Brown mushrooms in heated butter over high heat for 3 to 4 minutes. Set aside and sprinkle with salt.

Peel onions carefully; to prevent onions from bursting while cooking, cut an ''X'' ¼ inch deep in the root ends. Making 1 layer, place onions in a heavy saucepan, adding butter and salt and enough water to partially cover onions. Cover and simmer slowly 20 to 30 minutes or until tender. Set aside, reserving onion liquid.

Sauce

3	T. softened butter	3	T. flour

When beef is done, drain the cooking liquid into a saucepan. This should equal about 2½ cups; if liquid has boiled down too much, add some beef bouillon. Skim off fat, bring to a simmer, and adjust seasonings. Cream the butter and flour in a small container to make a smooth paste. Add a little of the beef liquid and whisk to blend. Then blend into the beef liquid. Pour in reserved onion juices and bring to a simmer. Stir until sauce thickens.

Add the mushrooms and onions to the beef, pour on the sauce, cover, and simmer 5 minutes to meld. Swirl the dish to baste the meat and vegetables with the sauce. Serve with rice.
Serves 6.
Mrs. Cad E. Williams (Francis Bailey)

Chili

2	lbs. lean ground beef	2	c. tomato juice
2	cloves garlic, crushed	6	c. water
4	T. flour	1	t. cumin seed
5	T. chili powder	2	15 oz. cans Ranch Style
2	t. salt		beans, undrained

Brown meat and garlic. Drain fat. Mix flour, chili powder, and salt. Mix well with meat mixture. Add tomato juice, water, and cumin seed. Bring to a boil. Reduce heat and simmer for about 2 hours. Stir from bottom and scrape sides of pan as mixture cooks. Skim any fat that might surface. When proper consistency is reached, add Ranch Style beans. Adjust seasonings.
Serves 5 or 6.
Mrs. Jack Hanks (Jackie Rayburn)

Five Hour Stew

2	lbs. beef stew cubes	1	10½ oz. can beef
1	8½ oz. can English peas,		consomme
	drained	½	c. water
1	c. cubed carrots	½	c. red wine
2	medium onions, quartered	1	large potato, cubed
1	t. salt	¼	t. oregano
1	t. pepper	½	bay leaf, optional

Put all ingredients in large covered pan or dish. Bake covered in 275° oven for 5 hours. Can also be cooked in slow cooker, omitting ½ cup water.
Serves 6.
Mrs. Harry Clark (Nancy Hable)

Lamb Stew with Dumplings

1	large onion	Salt and pepper to taste
4	lbs. lamb shoulder, cut	6 medium carrots, sliced
	into 1 inch squares	1 10 oz. pkg. frozen English
	Flour for dredging	peas

Dumplings
1	c. flour	Dash of salt
½	t. cream of tartar	1 t. margarine
½	t. baking soda	½ c. milk

Cut one large onion into small pieces and saute in oil until slightly brown-ed. Dredge trimmed meat squares in flour, salt and pepper to taste, add to onions, and brown. Onions will be well cooked, but don't worry as this is where you get the flavor. Cook carrots in salted water until tender. Cook peas according to package directions. Add the water from these vegetables to the meat, cover, and simmer until meat is tender. Have liquid enough to just come to the top of meat. When meat is tender, add vegetables, and stir to mix well. Drop dumplings by spoon, cover, and simmer another 15 minutes. Do not lift lid. *Very unusual flavor and very good.*

Dumplings Sift dry ingredients once. Cut in margarine and add enough milk to give a very thick consistency so that when dropped from spoon, dump-lings keep their shape.
Serves 4.
Jack W. Meeker

Play Golf Stew

2	lbs. beef stew meat, cubed	1 t. salt, dash of pepper
1	c. sliced carrots	1 10½ oz. can tomato soup
1	or 2 chopped onions	½ can water
1	c. sliced celery	2 large raw potatoes, sliced

Place stew meat in a 3 quart casserole which has a tight fitting lid. Add car-rots, onions, celery, salt, and pepper. Mix soup and water and add to casserole. Add potatoes. Place lid on top and put casserole in 275° oven. It will cook happily by itself and be done in 4½ to 5 hours.
You may use cream of celery or mushroom soup instead of tomato.
Serves 6.
Mrs. Frank C. Hicks (Helen Davenport)

Texas Cabbage Patch Stew

1 ½ lbs. ground meat	1 15 oz. can Ranch Style
1 ½ c. shredded cabbage	beans, undrained
½ c. chopped celery	½ t. oregano
1 large onion, thinly sliced	½ t. sweet basil
1 garlic clove, minced	Salt and pepper to taste
1 16 oz. can tomatoes	

Brown ground meat and add cabbage, celery, onions, and garlic and cook
10 minutes. Add salt, pepper, spices, tomatoes, and beans. Let simmer 30
minutes.
Meal in one.
Serves 8 to 10.
Mrs. K. G. Johnson (Betty Fister)

Ham Jambalaya

1 c. raw rice	1 14 oz. can tomato sauce
3 T. oil	2 c. boiling water
1 medium bell pepper,	Salt and pepper to taste
minced	Worcestershire to taste
1 medium onion, minced	Dash of Tabasco
2 cloves garlic, minced	2 c. chopped ham

In a heavy saucepan lightly brown the rice in oil. Add pepper, onion, and
garlic; saute. Add tomato sauce, boiling water, and seasonings. Bring to a
boil. Stir in ham. Reduce heat and simmer about 15 minutes or until rice
is tender.
Serves 6.
Miss Theresa Pessoney

Sausage Jambalaya

1 lb. beef sausage, sliced into bite size pieces	1 c. boiling water
1 green pepper, chopped	1 beef bouillon cube
1 medium onion, coarsely chopped	1 c. instant rice, uncooked
4 celery stalks, chopped	Salt and pepper to taste
4 to 6 green onions with tops, chopped	Dash Worcestershire
1 16 oz. can whole tomatoes, drained	Dash garlic powder
	½ lb. shrimp, cooked and deveined

Brown sausage in deep skillet. Drain all fat, reserving 1 tablespoon. Add green pepper, onion, celery, and green onions to drippings and stir until wilted. Add bouillon cube to water and stir until dissolved. Add to wilted vegetable mixture. Stir in rice, salt, pepper, Worcestershire, and garlic powder. Stir, cover, and cook until rice is done. One-half pound shrimp may be added with rice and water.
Serves 4 to 6.
Mrs. John R. Elliott (Helen Laws)

Easy Shrimp Gumbo

4 T. bacon drippings, melted	2 T. flour
2 large onions, chopped	2 c. water
1 large bell pepper, chopped	1 16 oz. can tomatoes
1 or 2 cloves garlic, optional	1 8 oz. can tomato sauce
1 10 oz. pkg. frozen cut okra, thawed	Salt and pepper to taste
	1 bay leaf, optional
	1 to 1½ lbs. shrimp, cooked
	1 6 oz. can crabmeat
	Tabasco to taste

Saute onions, bell pepper, and garlic in bacon drippings. Add okra. Add flour; blend well. Add water, tomatoes, tomato sauce, bay leaf, salt, and pepper. Cook covered until well blended, about 1 hour. Add shrimp and crabmeat. Adjust seasonings, adding several dashes Tabasco or to taste. Serve over rice.
Serves 6.
Mrs. Jeff Walker (Kathy Kolstad)

Basic Gumbo

1	medium onion	1	small stalk celery
4	cloves garlic	¾	c. vegetable oil
1	medium bell pepper	½	c. flour

Chop onion, garlic, celery, and bell pepper. In a 4 quart Dutch oven make a roux with the oil and flour. This is done by heating the oil on medium low and adding the flour to brown. The color of the roux should be the color of chocolate. To keep the browning even, stir constantly. When roux has browned, add chopped vegetables and saute. It may be necessary to remove from heat, but the seasonings generally reduce the heat sufficiently. Add 2 quarts *cold* water.

A variety of things may be used in gumbo. Cut up broiler or fryer, wild duck, dove or shrimp and oysters. When using poultry or duck or dove, brown the pieces and add to the liquid and cook over medium low heat until meat is tender. Serve over cooked rice in soup bowls. When using seafood, gumbo should be cooked about 45 minutes before adding the seafood. Seafood gives off liquid as it cooks so let the liquid reduce enough to allow for this. Shrimp takes about 20 minutes to cook and oysters about 7 minutes. A combination of shrimp and oyster is delicious, and oysters are delicious added to fowl or wild game. Serve this over rice in soup bowls also. Garnish with gumbo file.

Serves 6 to 8.

Mrs. J. E. Johnston (Marie Orgeron)

Shrimp and Chicken Gumbo

1   2 to 3 lb. chicken, cooked,
     reserving stock (about 3
     quarts)

Roux
5   T. oil or bacon drippings   4   T. flour
                                    1   T. Kitchen Bouquet

Stirring constantly, cook oil and flour until dark golden. Add Kitchen Bouquet to make it darker.

6   small green onions with   ½   to ¾ t. garlic powder or 2
     tops, chopped   cloves garlic, pressed
1   medium onion, chopped   Dash of pepper
1   small green pepper,   Dash of Tabasco
     chopped   4   or 5 dashes of
4   stalks celery, chopped   Worcestershire
5   c. cut okra, fresh or   2   lbs. shrimp, cooked and
     frozen   deveined
2   T. salt, more or less   ½   lb. crabmeat, optional
                                  File to taste

Add vegetables to roux and stir and cook until wilted. Add this to chicken stock, bring to a boil, and add chicken which has been boned and cut into pieces. Add okra and season with salt, garlic, pepper, Tabasco, and Worcestershire. Simmer for a few minutes. Add shrimp. Serve over rice and add file to taste.
Sausage may be used instead of seafood.
Serves 10 to 12.
Mrs. John R. Elliott (Helen Laws)

SALADS
AND
DRESSINGS

Chicken Mousse

1	3 oz. pkg. lemon gelatin	2	T. vinegar
2	c. chicken broth	1	t. salt
2	c. diced chicken	½	pt. heavy cream
2	c. finely chopped celery		Dash of cayenne
1	7 oz. jar chopped pimientos		

Dissolve gelatin in hot broth; chill. When cold and slightly thickened, beat until consistency of whipped cream. Mix chicken, celery, pimientos, vinegar, salt, and cayenne. Add to gelatin and fold in whipped cream. Turn into a 3 quart mold to set.
Serves 10 to 12.
Mrs. W. A. Schmidt (Dora Campbell)

Ham Vegetable Mousse

1	or 2 bunches spinach	2	lbs. assorted vegetables such as green beans, artichoke hearts, asparagus, squash, or broccoli flowerets
4	c. finely ground lean ham		
4	egg whites		

Clean and remove stems from spinach leaves. Blanch in boiling water for 30 seconds or until leaves are pliable. Remove and carefully pat dry. Mix egg whites (unbeaten) and ham and blend until mixture makes a fine paste. Wash vegetables and cut into thin julienne strips. Cook vegetables briefly in boiling water just until tender crisp. Drain well and pat dry with paper towels. In a greased 9 x 5 loaf pan, carefully overlap spinach leaves around sides and bottom of pan. Press ⅓ of the ham mixture (layer will be thin) into the bottom of pan, making sure corners are filled. Arrange ½ of the vegetables in lengthwise rows over the ham layer. Repeat layering, ending with ham. Press loaf lightly to be sure there are no air pockets. Cover pan tightly with foil and place in a larger pan containing 1 inch of hot water. Bake at 350° for 1 hour or until mixture is firmly set. Cool, then refrigerate overnight. To unmold, place pan briefly in hot water and shake gently to loosen. Run knife along sides, then turn out onto a platter. Serve with Cucumber Dressing found on page 78.
Serves 10 to 12.
Hugo Neuhaus, Houston, Texas

Congealed Chicken Salad

2	c. diced cooked chicken	1	c. chopped celery
1½	c. chicken stock	½	c. chopped pimiento or ½
1½	T. plain gelatin		c. sliced olives
1	8 oz. pkg. cream cheese	¾	c. chopped nuts
½	c. mayonnaise		

Dissolve gelatin in hot chicken stock. Mix in cream cheese and mayonnaise. Then add chicken and remaining ingredients. Put into 1½ quart mold and refrigerate for three hours. Serve on lettuce or on tomato slices.
Serves 6.
Mrs. Harry Clark (Nancy Hable)

Hot Chicken Salad

4	c. diced cooked chicken		Salt to taste
4	hard-cooked eggs, sliced	3	T. grated onion
1	10¾ oz. can cream of	2	T. lemon juice
	chicken soup	¼	t. pepper
2	c. chopped celery	1	c. grated cheese
1	c. mayonnaise	1	3 oz. can fried onion rings
1	c. sour cream	½	c. slivered almonds
1	c. sliced water chestnuts		

Spread soup in bottom of a 2 quart casserole. Slice eggs and spread over soup in rows. Salt and pepper lightly. Mix celery, mayonnaise, sour cream, water chestnuts, onion, lemon juice, and pepper. Then add chicken and pour over eggs. Top with cheese. Bake at 350° for 30 minutes. Add onion rings last 5 minutes. Does not freeze well.
Serves 8 to 10.
Mrs. John B. McDonald (Dorothy Crider)

 A 3½ pound chicken will yield about 3 cups diced chicken. Two whole chicken breasts will yield 1½ to 2 cups cooked chicken.

Turkey Salad

4	c. chopped turkey breast	1	T. curry powder
1	8 oz. can water chestnuts, drained and sliced	2	T. soy sauce
2	c. thinly sliced celery	2	T. lemon juice
2	c. toasted, slivered almonds	1	20 oz. can pineapple chunks
3	c. mayonnaise	1	lb. seedless green grapes

Combine chopped turkey, water chestnuts, pineapple, celery, and almonds in large bowl. Mix mayonnaise, curry powder, soy sauce, and lemon juice in a separate bowl and then combine with other ingredients. Add grapes and mix gently.
Serves 12.
Mrs. Harold L. Kennedy (Helen Hancock)

Crab Louis

1	c. mayonnaise	1	large head lettuce
¼	c. heavy cream, whipped	2	6½ oz. cans crabmeat, chilled or 3 c. fresh crabmeat
¼	c. chili sauce		
¼	c. chopped green peppers		
¼	c. chopped green onions and tops	2	large tomatoes, cut in wedges
1	t. lemon juice	2	hard-cooked eggs, cut in wedges
Salt to taste			

Mix mayonnaise, whipped cream, chili sauce, green peppers, green onions, and lemon juice; salt to taste. Chill. Makes 2 cups dressing.
Remove bits of shell from crabmeat and arrange on lettuce leaf. Circle with wedges of tomato and eggs; sprinkle with salt and pour desired amount of dressing over each salad. Sprinkle with paprika and serve with your favorite crisp crackers or toast points dusted with Parmesan cheese.
Serves 4.
Mrs. Thomas B. Bailey (Sue Simmons)

Tomato-Shrimp Mold

1½ T. gelatin	2 T. chopped green peppers
½ c. cold water	1 t. grated onion
1 10¾ oz. can tomato soup	½ c. broken nuts
1 8 oz. pkg. cream cheese	1 lb. cooked and cleaned
1 c. mayonnaise	shrimp or
1 c. chopped celery	Two 4½ oz. cans shrimp

Soften gelatin in cold water. In a double boiler heat tomato soup, add cheese and whisk until smooth. Add softened gelatin. Cool. Add remaining ingredients and refrigerate in a 1½ quart rectangular mold which has been rubbed with mayonnaise. May substitute tuna for shrimp or omit both. The nuts may also be omitted.
Serves 8 to 10.
Mrs. Robert B. Bristow (Jimmie Reta Inmon)

Molded Tuna Salad

2 6½ oz. cans tuna	1 c. mayonnaise
2 hard-cooked eggs,	1 c. sour cream
chopped	1 T. minced onion
½ c. sliced stuffed olives	1 t. salt
½ c. chopped celery	¼ c. lemon juice
1 T. gelatin	2 T. chopped parsley
¼ c. cold water	

Drain tuna and flake. Combine with eggs, olives, and celery in a large mixing bowl. Soften gelatin in cold water for at least 5 minutes. Dissolve over hot water. Stir into mayonnaise. Add sour cream, onions, salt, lemon juice, and parsley. Combine with tuna. Pour into small molds. Refrigerate. These need to be made one day in advance.
Serves 8.
Mrs. Jack Grigsby (Edith Fetters)

Artichoke Salad

1	8 oz. box chicken flavored Rice-A-Roni	4	to 6 chopped green onions, tops included
2	6 oz. jars marinated artichoke hearts, reserving liquid from one jar	20	pimiento stuffed olives, sliced
⅓	c. mayonnaise	½	c. chopped green pepper
½	t. curry powder	½	c. toasted slivered almonds
			Paprika and parsley to garnish

Prepare rice according to directions, omitting butter. Slice artichokes. Mix reserved liquid with mayonnaise. Combine all ingredients and blend well. Refrigerate until served. This recipe is better prepared a day ahead.
Serves 6.
Mrs. Frank Hicks (Helen Davenport)

Cabbage-Potato Salad

3	c. diced cooked potatoes	2	T. diced pimiento
2	T. salad oil	2	T. diced bell pepper
1	T. wine vinegar	3	T. grated onion
Salt and pepper to taste		1½	c. shredded cabbage
½	c. sliced ripe olives	¾	c. mayonnaise
¼	c. diced dill pickle	1	t. prepared mustard
1	c. shredded carrots		

Place potatoes in mixing bowl and toss with oil and vinegar. Salt and pepper to taste. Add the next seven ingredients. Combine mayonnaise with mustard and pour over salad. Mix well and refrigerate. *Better if prepared day before serving.*
Serves 4 to 6.
Mrs. M. D. Chennault (Anne Johnston)

Cool Bean Salad

2	16 oz. cans French style green beans, drained	½	onion, thinly sliced into rings
12	pitted ripe olives, sliced	¼	t. pepper
½	c. sliced water chestnuts	¼	t. garlic powder
1	6 oz. can sliced mushrooms, drained	2	T. grated Parmesan cheese
			Commercial Italian salad dressing

Combine all ingredients except salad dressing; toss until well mixed. Add enough salad dressing to almost cover vegetables. Cover and refrigerate at least 2 hours. Drain off excess dressing before serving.
Serves 6.
Mrs. J. G. Crook (Maxine Schultz)

Cole Slaw

1	medium head cabbage, shredded	¼	c. light cream
4	carrots, grated	¼	onion, minced
1	c. mayonnaise		Salt and pepper to taste

Mix together mayonnaise, cream, and onion. Let stand at least 30 minutes. Pour over vegetables. Season to taste. Refrigerate immediately. The colder the better.
Serves 8.
Mrs. Curtis C. Mann (Jay Nemer)

Danish Cucumbers

4	medium cucumbers	1	c. sugar
½	c. salt		Cider vinegar
	Ice water		

Wash and thinly slice cucumbers. Salt in layers in bowl. Cover with ice water. Let stand at least 2 hours covered with a lid. Drain. Add sugar and enough cider vinegar to cover cucumbers. Let marinate for several hours. Keeps indefinitely in refrigerator.
Serves 6 to 8.
Mrs. Carmon L. Greenwood (Frances Samuell)

Dilled-Rice Salad

1	10 oz. pkg. frozen green peas, cooked	⅓	c. chopped dill pickles
1	c. rice, cooked	3	T. chopped green onion
¼	c. vegetable oil	½	t. salad herbs
⅓	c. dill pickle liquid		Salt and pepper to taste

Cool peas and rice. Combine in bowl with remaining ingredients. Toss and chill. Makes approximately 5 cups. Pretty served in a crystal bowl.
Serves 8.
Mrs. Jeff Walker (Kathy Kolstad)

Hot Caesar Salad

½	c. salad oil	3	to 6 anchovy fillets, minced (optional)
1	clove garlic, cut in half	1	T. lemon juice
¼	t. salt	1	egg, beaten
	Dash of black pepper	1	c. croutons
1	t. Worcestershire sauce	½	c. grated Parmesan cheese
1	large head romaine lettuce, washed, dried, and torn into bite-sized pieces		

In large skillet heat oil and garlic. Remove garlic and add salt, pepper, and Worcestershire sauce, stirring occasionally. Tossing gently add romaine, anchovies, and lemon juice. Add beaten egg and toss again. Add croutons and cheese; toss. Serve immediately.
Serves 4.
Mrs. James N. Parsons, III (Karen Hawkins)

Marinated Carrots

2	lbs. carrots, peeled and sliced or 2 16 oz. cans sliced carrots, drained	1	10¾ oz. can tomato soup, undiluted
1	small onion, sliced into rings	¾	c. sugar
		¼	c. salad oil
1	bell pepper, sliced into rings	¾	c. apple cider vinegar
		1	T. dry mustard
1	c. chopped celery	1	t. Worcestershire sauce
		1	t. salt
			Dash Tabasco

Cook sliced carrots in salted water until tender crisp. Drain and cool. Then add onion, bell pepper, and celery. Heat soup, sugar, oil, vinegar, and seasonings. Pour over vegetable mixture. Cover and refrigerate 24 hours.
Serves 8.
Cookbook Committee

Marinated Vegetable Salad

1	9 oz. pkg. frozen artichoke hearts	1	15 oz. can white asparagus, drained
1	8 oz. bottle low calorie Italian style dressing	1	12 oz. can julienne carrots, drained
1	16 oz. can whole green beans, drained	1	T. finely chopped onion
		½	t. dried basil leaves
1	16 oz. can small whole beets, drained	1	large tomato
		1	T. chopped parsley
1	15 oz. can green asparagus, drained		

Cook artichoke hearts as package directs, drain. Turn into bowl and toss with 3 tablespoons dressing. Cover and refrigerate 4 hours. Meanwhile in large, shallow baking dish, arrange drained green beans, beets, asparagus, and carrots in separate mounds. Sprinkle vegetables with onion and basil. Spoon remaining dressing over vegetables to coat well. Cover, refrigerate 4 hours. To serve, slice tomato. Arrange slices attractively with other vegetables, on large platter. Spoon over them any dressing remaining in baking dish. Sprinkle white asparagus with chopped parsley.
Makes 8 servings.
Mrs. Harry Brown (Carol Albright)

Sauerkraut Salad

½   c. sugar
½   c. vinegar
1   16 oz. can sauerkraut,
     drained
1   c. minced celery

1   large onion, minced
1   green pepper, minced
1   2 oz. jar pimiento,
     chopped

Place sugar and vinegar in saucepan and bring to a boil. Cook until sugar is dissolved. Cool. Mix with next 5 ingredients and refrigerate. Keeps indefinitely. You may add chopped apple if desired.
Serves 6 to 8.
Mrs. Curtis C. Mann (Jay Nemer)

Shoe Peg Salad

1   12 oz. can shoe peg corn,
     drained
1   2 oz. jar diced pimiento,
     drained
1   c. chopped celery
1   small bell pepper,
     chopped

1   small onion, chopped
½   c. salad oil
1   t. salt
1   t. pepper
1   T. mustard
1   t. sugar
2½ T. vinegar

Combine salad oil, vinegar, and seasonings and pour over first 5 ingredients.
Serves 8.
Mrs. Chester Hendrick (Olive Hinson)

Tabouli Salad

1 c. ground wheat	1 dill pickle, chopped, optional
1 bunch fresh parsley, finely chopped	2 medium tomatoes, diced
1 bunch green onions, finely chopped	1 jalapeno pepper, finely chopped, optional
1 c. finely chopped fresh mint	¼ to ½ c. lemon juice
2 cucumbers, finely chopped	¼ c. salad oil
	Salt and pepper to taste

Wash wheat several times. Cover with water to soak and refrigerate. Thirty minutes before serving, drain all water from wheat, and squeeze dry until just moist and fluffy. Add remaining ingredients and mix well. To serve, spoon onto a bed of romaine or other lettuce.
Serves 8.
Mrs. Jesse George (Agnes Totah)

Fresh Spinach Salad

Dressing

¾ c. salad oil	¾ t. salt
¼ c. fresh lemon juice	1 T. sugar
2 T. Parmesan cheese	1 clove garlic, minced
	Pepper and paprika

Salad

1 lb. fresh spinach	2 avocados, sliced
1 8 oz. pkg. fresh mushrooms, sliced	1 c. seasoned croutons
6 green onions, sliced	Morton's Natures Seasoning

Combine first 8 ingredients. Mix well and chill. Wash spinach and tear into bite-sized pieces. Add mushrooms, onions, avocados, and croutons to spinach. Pour dressing over salad and sprinkle with Morton's Natures Seasoning.
Serves 6.
Mrs. Pete Eckert (Judy Jordan)

Spinach and Mandarin Orange Salad

1½	lbs. fresh spinach, washed and torn	12	bacon strips, fried and crumbled
1	11 oz. can mandarin oranges, drained	2	avocados, peeled and sliced

Sesame Seed Dressing

1	c. sugar	1	T. grated onion
1	t. paprika	2	c. salad oil
½	t. dry mustard	1	c. cider vinegar
1	t. salt	½	c. toasted sesame seeds
1	t. Worcestershire sauce		

Place sugar, seasonings, and onion in a bowl and beat until combined. Add oil gradually, then vinegar, a little at a time. Add toasted sesame seeds. Keep in covered jar in refrigerator. Makes approximately 1½ pints. Combine salad ingredients and toss with dressing. A choice of artichoke hearts, hearts of palm, and pineapple chunks may be added.
Serves 6 to 8.
Mrs. Joe Ed Johnston (Marilyn Hardgrave)

Spinach Salad

1	lb. spinach, washed and drained	5	slices bacon, fried and crumbled
1	8 oz. can sliced water chestnuts, drained	15	fresh mushrooms, sliced
2	hard-cooked eggs, chopped	10	radishes, sliced

Dressing

1	c. salad oil	2	T. Worcestershire sauce
⅓	c. catsup	½	c. sugar
¼	c. vinegar	1	small onion, grated

Mix thoroughly. Pour over salad ingredients. Dressing may be prepared days ahead.
Serves 8 to 10.
Mrs. Lucylle Pope MacNaughton

Tex-Mex Salad

1½	heads lettuce, torn into small pieces	1	12 oz. pkg. corn chips, crushed
3	large tomatoes, chopped	1	15 oz. can pinto beans, well drained
3	large avocados, chopped		
½	c. chopped onion	2	8 oz. bottles Catalina dressing
1	10 oz. pkg. Monterey Jack cheese, grated		

Combine all ingredients in large salad bowl and toss well. If prepared ahead of time do not add corn chips or dressing until serving time. One pound browned and drained ground beef may be added.
Serves 8 to 10.
Mrs. Jeff Walker (Kathy Kolstad)

Tomatoes Vinaigrette

8	thick tomato slices, peeled	2	garlic cloves pressed or 2 t. garlic salt
1	c. salad oil		
½	c. red wine vinegar	½	t. pepper
2	t. ground oregano	½	t. dry mustard
1	t. salt		Parsley

Arrange tomatoes in flat dish. Mix remaining ingredients except parsley and pour over tomatoes. Cover; refrigerate 2 or 3 hours (overnight is better). At serving time sprinkle with parsley. Keeps several days in the refrigerator.
Serves 3 or 4.
Mrs. Dennis E. Ward (Jamie Brown)

 To improve flavor of winter tomatoes, peel; cut into desired size; and toss with fresh lemon juice. Chill several hours before serving.

Tossed Romaine Salad

1   large bunch romaine   3   hard-cooked eggs,
    lettuce, torn   chopped
                                 Salt and pepper to taste

Dressing
½   lb. Romano cheese   2   c. salad oil
Juice of 3 cloves garlic   4   T. lemon juice

Place dressing ingredients in a 1 quart jar and shake well. Pour over salad.
Serves 4.
Mrs. Joe Ed Johnston (Marilyn Hardgrave)

Asparagus Soup Salad

1   10¾ oz. can cream of   ¾   c. chopped celery
    asparagus soup   ½   c. chopped green pepper
1   3 oz. pkg. lime gelatin   ½   c. chopped pecans
1   8 oz. pkg. cream cheese,   1   T. grated onion
    softened   ½   t. lemon juice
½   c. cold water   Pinch of salt
½   c. mayonnaise

Heat soup to barely boiling. Add gelatin and whisk until dissolved. Add cold
water, cream cheese, and whisk until blended. Mix in remaining ingredients.
Chill in a 1½ quart mold until firm. Plain gelatin may be substituted for lime
gelatin.
Serves 10 to 12.
Mrs. Stewart Kenderdine (Jane Kukar)

Avocado Mold

1   T. plain gelatin   ½   c. sour cream
½   c. cold water   1   c. mashed avocado pulp
1   c. boiling water   Salt, pepper, and cayenne to
1   t. sugar   taste
1   T. unstrained lemon juice

Mix gelatin. Chill until it begins to thicken. Add avocado sieved. Season
highly with salt, pepper, and cayenne.
Serves 6.
Mrs. N. C. Woolverton (Jettie Seagler)

Guacamole Mold

1½	T. unflavored gelatin	1	t. grated onion
½	c. cold water	2	dashes Tabasco sauce
¾	c. boiling water	2½	c. mashed ripe avocado
2	T. lemon juice	1	c. sour cream
1¼	t. salt	1	c. mayonnaise

Soften gelatin in cold water; dissolve in boiling water. Add lemon juice, salt, onion, and Tabasco. Cool to room temperature; stir in avocado, sour cream, and mayonnaise. Turn into 1½ quart mold and chill 6 hours or overnight.
Serves 8.
Mrs. Paul E. Elliott, Jr. (Ann Craft)

Beet Salad

1	3 oz. pkg. lemon gelatin	1	t. grated onion
1	16 oz. can beets, diced	3	T. horseradish
1	c. beet juice	1	c. chopped celery
½	c. water	½	c. diced cucumber,
3	T. tarragon vinegar		optional
½	t. celery salt		

Drain beets, reserving liquid. Dissolve gelatin in boiling beet juice. Add water and seasonings. Chill until they are about set. Fold in celery and beets. Pour into 1½ quart mold and chill until firm. Serve with blue cheese dressing.

Blue Cheese Dressing

1	c. sour cream	3	oz. blue cheese

Combine sour cream with blue cheese, chill, and serve with salad.
Serves 8 to 10.
Mrs. Jack H. Hanks (Jackie Rayburn)

 Inserting a toothpick at the stem of an avocado is a test for ripeness. If it flows in and out freely, it's ready to eat. If it's not ripe, place the fruit in a paper bag at room temperature; this will hasten the ripening process.

Congealed Vegetable Salad

1	3 oz. pkg. lemon or lime gelatin	1	c. raw or cooked carrots
⅓	c. English pea juice	1	c. finely chopped celery
⅔	c. water	1	8½ oz. can English peas
1	T. minced onion	1	c. mayonnaise
¼	T. vinegar	1	T. chopped green bell pepper
1	t. prepared mustard		

Heat English pea juice and water; add gelatin. Stir until dissolved. Cool and add remaining ingredients. Pour into an oiled 1½ quart dish or individual molds and refrigerate. Makes an excellent luncheon salad to serve with cold meat.
Serves 8.
Mrs. H. Green (Bennie Eubanks)

Spinach Mold

8	10 oz. pkgs. frozen chopped spinach	2	T. lemon juice
2	8 oz. pkgs. cream cheese	2	t. salt
2	T. minced onion	1	t. pepper
4	T. chopped cucumber	3	T. unflavored gelatin
		1	14½ oz. can chicken broth

Cook spinach in unsalted water and drain thoroughly, pressing out water in a colander. Add softened cheese to hot spinach. Add onion, cucumber, lemon juice, salt, and pepper. In ¾ cup chicken broth soften the gelatin. Heat remaining chicken broth and add softened gelatin, stirring until completely dissolved. Add to spinach mixture. Pour into oiled mold and refrigerate. Serve with cucumber dressing.

Dressing

1½	c. mayonnaise	4	T. grated cucumber
1	T. lemon juice	1½	T. grated onion

Combine ingredients, chill, and serve.
Serves 26.
Mrs. John B. McDonald (Dorothy Crider)

Tomato Aspic

3	c. tomato juice	2	T. plain gelatin
1	bay leaf	½	c. cold water
2	small stalks celery	2	T. white vinegar
Dash of salt and red pepper		2	T. onion juice

Mix tomato juice, dashes of salt and red pepper, celery, and bay leaf into a saucepan and boil ten minutes. Soften the gelatin in the cold water and add to the hot mixture. Stir until dissolved. Add the vinegar and onion juice. Remove the celery and bay leaf and turn into lightly greased 4 cup ring mold. Chill until set. Unmold and garnish as desired. Mayonnaise, sour cream, or sour cream with chopped cucumbers may be used as a complement to the aspic as it is sliced and served.
Serves 8 to 10.
Mrs. Billy Gragg (Jackie Lockey)

Mustard Ring

4	eggs, beaten	2	T. dry mustard
1	c. water	½	t. tumeric
½	c. vinegar	1	t. salt
½	c. sugar	½	pt. whipping cream,
1½	T. gelatin		whipped

Blend together eggs, water, and vinegar. Mix in sugar, gelatin, dry mustard, tumeric, and salt. Cook in double boiler, stirring constantly until it starts to thicken; cool. Add whipping cream and place in 2 quart ring mold. Especially good with ham.
Serves 12.
Mrs. R. L. Kenderdine (Daphne Dunning)

Apricot Salad

1 12 oz. bottle 7-Up	1 c. sour cream
1 3 oz. pkg. apricot gelatin	1 3 oz. pkg. cream cheese
1 8 oz. can crushed	
pineapple, undrained	

Heat 7-Up, add gelatin and dissolve. Cool. Mix cream cheese, pineapple, and sour cream. Combine with gelatin mixture and pour into 9 x 5 mold and chill.
Serves 8 to 10.
Mrs. Weldon Bynum (Opha Gilbreath)

Schmierkaesesalat
(Cottage Cheese Salad)

1 6 oz. pkg. orange gelatin	1 8 oz. can crushed
2 c. heated pineapple juice	pineapple, drained
2 c. cottage cheese	1 c. whipped cream

Heat pineapple juice to dissolve gelatin. Cool until thickened. Blend thoroughly the remaining ingredients and combine with gelatin mixture. Refrigerate in a 2 quart mold 4 to 6 hours. Maraschino cherries may be used for garnish.
Serves 8 to 10.
Mrs. Vernon V. Fritze, Jr. (Kathy Sue Duderstadt)

Cranberry Mold

1 3 oz. pkg. cherry gelatin	1 c. ground raw cranberries
½ c. hot water	1 orange and rind, ground
¾ c. sugar	1 c. crushed pineapple,
1 T. lemon juice	drained
1 T. plain gelatin	1 c. chopped celery
1 c. pineapple juice	½ c. chopped pecans

Dissolve gelatin in hot water. Add sugar, lemon juice, and pineapple juice to gelatin mixture and stir until blended. Add cranberries, orange, pineapple, celery, and pecans. Pour into 10 inch ring mold.
Serves 10.
Mrs. F. Bailey Summers (Christine Hughes)

Creamy Orange Salad

1	3 oz. pkg. orange gelatin	1	T. frozen lemonade concentrate, undiluted
1½	c. boiling water		
2	3 oz. pkgs. cream cheese, softened	1	11 oz. can mandarin orange sections, drained
⅓	c. frozen orange juice concentrate, undiluted		

Dissolve gelatin in boiling water. Whip cream cheese until smooth; add hot gelatin mixture and beat until well blended. Add orange juice and lemonade concentrates; blend thoroughly. Chill gelatin mixture approximately 1 hour or until slightly thickened; fold in mandarin orange sections. Spoon into an oiled 4 cup mold and chill until firm. Keeps well.
Serves 4 to 6.
Mrs. E. Wayne Craddock (Alpha Boyett)

Frozen Pineapple Salad

1	8 oz. can crushed pineapple and juice	½	c. chopped pecans
3	T. chopped maraschino cherries	2	c. sour cream
		¾	c. sugar
		2	T. lemon juice

Mix the pineapple, pineapple juice, cherries, and pecans. In a separate bowl mix the sour cream, sugar, and lemon juice until the sugar dissolves. Fold the two mixtures together. Add 2 or 3 drops or enough food coloring to make salad a pretty pink color. Put 2½ inch paper baking cups in muffin tins and pour the salad into these. Freeze. When frozen the salads may be removed from the muffin tins and stored in the freezer in plastic bags. Let stand about 10 minutes to soften before serving. To serve peel off the paper baking cup and serve on lettuce.
Serves 12.
Mrs. Joe G. Laumen (Nancy Simpson)

 If you place an orange or grapefruit into a hot oven before peeling, no white fiber will be left on the orange or grapefruit.

Grapefruit Salad

2   pink grapefruit   2   3 oz. pkg. lemon gelatin
2   c. mashed apricots

Cut grapefruit in half. Cut out sections removing membranes. Measure to
make 2 cups with juice. Save shells. Heat mashed apricots and add gelatin,
stirring thoroughly to dissolve. Add grapefruit sections and refrigerate until partly jelled. Clean inside of rind. Fill shells with mixture and complete
jelling. When ready to serve, cut shells in half. Serve on lettuce. Top with
sour cream and chives.
Serves 8.
Mrs. Gordon B. Broyles (Frances Dilley)

Layered Strawberry Salad

2   3 oz. pkgs. strawberry   2   bananas, mashed
      gelatin   1   15¼ oz. can pineapple
2   c. boiling water   bits
2   10 oz. pkgs. frozen sliced   1   3 oz. pkg. cream cheese
      strawberries   1   c. sour cream

Melt strawberry gelatin in water. Add strawberries, pineapple, and bananas.
Place half of gelatin mixture in 9 x 15 dish and chill until set. Mix cream
cheese with sour cream and spread over congealed mixture. Layer with re-
maining gelatin mixture and chill.
Serves 12 to 15.
Mrs. Joe N. Davis (Marguerite Dellis)

Summer Salad

1   3 oz. pkg. lime gelatin   2   c. cottage cheese
½   c. water   ½   c. mayonnaise
½   pt. cream, whipped   1   T. onion juice

Dissolve gelatin in ½ cup boiling water. Cool to room temperature but not
set. Mix cottage cheese, mayonnaise, and onion. Add to gelatin mixture.
Fold in whipped cream quickly so it will be light. Pour in lightly greased
ring mold. Serve with poppy seed dressing. Garnish ring mold with an assort-
ment of fruits and melon balls.
Serves 8.
Mrs. Gordon B. Broyles (Frances Dilley)

Pineapple Cheese Salad

1	3 oz. pkg. lemon gelatin	1	4 oz. carton whipped
1	T. plain gelatin		topping
1	c. boiling water	1	c. grated Cheddar cheese
1	8¼ oz. can crushed	½	c. chopped pecans
	pineapple, undrained		

Dissolve lemon gelatin and plain gelatin in boiling water. Add pineapple. Place in refrigerator and allow to cool. Fold in whipped topping, Cheddar cheese, and pecans. Pour into 1½ quart casserole and chill until firm. Can be put in the freezer for a short period of time to speed up chilling process. Serves 8.
Mrs. C. L. Kolstad, III (Jill McPherson)

Pineapple Cottage Cheese Mold

1	3 oz. pkg. lemon gelatin	½	c. mayonnaise
1	3 oz. pkg. raspberry	1	c. cottage cheese
	gelatin	1	20 oz. can crushed
1	c. boiling water		pineapple, undrained
1	13 oz. can evaporated		
	milk		

Dissolve gelatins in boiling water; cool; add milk, mayonnaise, and cottage cheese. Add pineapple with juice and mix well. Lightly coat a 13 x 9 mold with mayonnaise and fill with pineapple mixture. Cover and refrigerate. Serves 8 to 10.
Mrs. Wayne Walker (Katherine Cray)

Yogurt Fruit Salad

2   to 3 bananas, sliced
2   to 3 apples, cored and cut
    into ½ inch cubes
1   15 oz. can pineapple
    chunks, drained

1   8 oz. carton mandarin
    orange-flavored yogurt
Lettuce, optional

Combine fruit and yogurt and mix well. Chill thoroughly. Serve on lettuce
if desired. This dish may be served for breakfast, salad, or dessert.
Serves 6 to 8.
Mrs. A. Hugh Summers (Ahnise Varnell)

Williamsburg Inn Salad

2   T. unflavored gelatin
½   c. cold water
1   c. boiling water
½   c. cold water
½   c. vinegar
½   t. salt
2   c. sugar

Few drops green food coloring
1   c. slivered almonds,
    blanched
1   c. sliced sweet pickles
1   c. crushed pineapple,
    drained
1   c. sliced stuffed olives

Soften gelatin in ½ cup cold water. Add to boiling water and stir until
dissolved. Add ½ cup cold water, vinegar, salt, sugar, and a few drops of
green food coloring. Chill until mixture thickens. Fold in other ingredients
and pour into a lightly greased 1½ quart mold. Chill until ready to serve.
Nice Christmas salad!
Serves 6.
Mrs. Howard T. Winkler (Joyce Bell)

Pistachio Salad

1	8 oz. carton whipped topping	1	16 oz. can crushed pineapple
1	3 oz. pkg. pistachio instant pudding	1	c. chopped pecans

Mix pudding in whipped topping; whip. Add pineapple with juice and whip until fluffy. Add pecans. Pour into 1½ quart mold and chill. May also be served as a dessert.
Serves 8.
Mrs. Frank McCreary (Irma Holland)

Cold Vegetable Dressing

4	medium tomatoes	1	medium green pepper, sliced in rings
1	medium onion, sliced in rings		Parsley chopped for garnish

Dressing

1	T. sugar	½	c. salad oil
3	T. catsup	1	whole garlic clove
1	T. Worcestershire sauce		Salt and pepper to taste
⅓	c. cider vinegar		

Combine dressing ingredients and chill. Remove garlic clove before serving. Slice cold tomatoes in ¼ inch thick slices. Add onion and green pepper rings. Garnish with chopped parsley. Serve with well refrigerated salad dressing.
Mrs. Robert G. Cox (Louise Spreen)

 To keep garlic, place peeled garlic cloves in a jar of vegetable oil in refrigerator Use garlic as needed and oil to flavor a dish.

Creamy Garlic Salad Dressing

6	T. salad oil	1	egg
5	T. light cream	⅛	t. dry mustard
2	T. vinegar		Salt and freshly ground pepper
1	to 3 cloves of garlic,		to taste
	pressed (according to		
	taste)		

Place ingredients in a blender and blend for 2 to 3 minutes. Keeps well in refrigerator for a week.
Yields approximately ¾ cup.
Mrs. C. G. Joyce, Jr. (Jeanne Dunn)

French Dressing

1	c. sugar	⅔	c. catsup
2	t. celery seed	2	c. salad oil
2	t. dry mustard	2	onions, finely chopped
2	t. paprika	4	T. lemon juice
2	t. salt	1	clove garlic, optional
½	c. vinegar		

Mix all ingredients in deep bowl and beat 7 minutes. Refrigerate. Shake before using.
Yields 1 quart.
Mrs. Pete Eckert (Judy Jordan)

French Horn Salad Dressing

⅓	c. cider vinegar	⅓	c. sugar
⅔	c. salad oil	4	T. water
1	t. salt	¼	t. Tabasco
1	t. dry mustard	¼	c. sesame seeds, toasted

Combine ingredients and serve over romaine and Boston red leaf lettuce. This is a beautiful, tasty green salad. Green onions add a nice touch.
Yields 1 cup.
Mrs. Pete Eckert (Judy Jordan)

Mayonnaise

1	egg	¼	t. paprika
½	t. dry mustard	2	T. lemon juice
½	t. salt	1	c. salad oil

Put egg, seasonings, lemon juice, and ¼ cup oil in blender. Cover and process at medium speed. Remove cap and add remaining oil slowly.
Yields approximately 1 cup.
Mrs. Walter E. Johnston (Lottie Mae Griffith)

Old South Salad Dressing

2	eggs	1	medium onion, chopped
1	pt. salad oil	¾	of a 5 oz. jar Roka blue cheese
1	t. sugar		
1	t. salt	2	T. vinegar
1	t. prepared mustard	2	T. lemon juice
3	small sweet pickles, chopped	Garlic to taste	
½	c. chopped stuffed green olives		

Beat eggs until fluffy. Add oil a few drops at a time, beating thoroughly to avoid separation in dressing later on. Fold in remaining ingredients. Good dip for raw vegetables.
Yields approximately 1 quart.
Mrs. Stewart Kenderdine (Jane Kukar)

Honeyed Mayonnaise

½	c. mayonnaise	Dash onion powder
½	c. honey	Poppy seeds to taste

Mix all ingredients and chill ½ hour before using. Will store indefinitely in refrigerator. Delicious time saver.
Yields 1 cup.
Mrs. W. D. Smith (Marye Jo Green)

Poppy Seed Dressing

¾ c. sugar
⅔ t. salt
⅔ t. dry mustard
1 ½ c. salad oil
⅔ c. vinegar

2 t. onion juice (1 small onion grated)
3 T. poppy seed
1 clove garlic

Mix sugar, salt, and mustard. Add oil and vinegar, beating constantly. Add onion juice, and poppy seed. Pour into a quart jar and add a clove of garlic. Keeps indefinitely in refrigerator.
Yields 2 ½ cups.
Mrs. Curtis C. Mann (Jay Nemer)

Sea Breeze Dressing

1 ⅓ c. salad oil
1 6 oz. can frozen lemonade concentrate

4 T. honey
2 T. chopped parsley
2 T. poppy seed

Mix all ingredients well. Store in refrigerator. Serve with fruits.
Yields approximately 1 quart.
Mrs. Lawrence S. McWhorter (Elma Cornelius)

Thousand Island Dressing

1 c. mayonnaise
½ c. chili sauce

¼ c. pickle relish

Combine and chill two hours before serving.
Yields approximately 1 pint.
Mrs. J. E. Johnston (Marie Orgeron)

BREADS

Bread Tips

Flour:
Wheat flour generally is used for bread making because it contains a protein called gluten. Gluten stretches to form an elastic framework capable of holding the bubbles of gas produced by yeast. Stirring and kneading help to develop the gluten. The various methods of milling and varieties of wheat influence the flour and the amount and kind of gluten which in turn affect the volume and texture of the bread. This is why bread recipes usually say approximate amounts of flour to use and do not indicate an exact number of minutes for the kneading. Today's flour usually does not need to be sifted.

Liquid:
Milk, water, and potato water are the most used in making yeast breads. Water gives a wheaty flavor and crisp crust. Milk makes a velvety grain and creamy white crumbs. Breads made with milk keep better and toast more evenly. Evaporated milk need not be scalded but can be diluted with an even amount of water. When using dry milk solids, mix them to the dry ingredients and use water as the liquid.

Bread Faults and Their Causes

Poorly Shaped Loaf
> Inexperienced in handling.
> Dough too stiff or not stiff enough.
> Dough too light (too much rising) before baking.
> Oven not hot enough or heat uneven.

Coarse Grain or Texture
> Oven temperature too low.
> Not enough kneading.
> Too much rising before baking.

Streaks
> Dough allowed to dry on top during rising.
> Uneven mixing or kneading.
> Dry flour folded into loaves during shaping.
> Dough too heavily greased on top during rising.
> Dough allowed to rise in too warm place; allowing bottom of pan to become too hot.

Crust Splitting on Top or Sides
> Oven too hot at first or uneven heat in oven.
> Size of loaf too large for pan.

Soggy or Heavy
> Insufficient rising or baking.
> Poor yeast or poor flour.

Sour Dough Starter

Step I: 1 yeast cake or 1 pkg. dry yeast in ½ cup lukewarm water. Let stand until dissolved, about 10 minutes. Stir.

Step II:
2   c. lukewarm water
1   T. sugar
1   t. salt
2   c. sifted all-purpose flour

Step III: Add above ingredients to first mixture and mix well. Cover and let stand 3 days in about 78°. Stir mixture daily.

To Use and Continue Starter
Add the following to the above mixture each time you use any portion of it:
1   c. milk
1   c. flour
½   c. sugar
Do not let starter get to less than 1 cup. Try to use some starter at least once a month. Keep covered and refrigerated.

Sour Dough Bread

Mix and let stand 5 to 10 minutes:
2   **pkgs. dry yeast**   1   T. sugar
½   **c. lukewarm water**

In large mixing bowl, place:
1   **c. starter**   ⅓   **c. sugar**
2½   **t. salt**   2   **eggs**
½   **c. oil**

Stir well and add yeast mixture. Beat well. Add 4 cups flour, 1 cup at a time; no need to sift. Add 1 cup warm water with the third and fourth cups of the flour. Add 2 more cups flour and mix well. Turn out on a floured board. Knead for about 10 minutes. Add flour as you require it. You might add 1 cup more extra flour while kneading. When dough is ready, it is no longer sticky.

Grease a large bowl and drop batch of dough in it and turn dough until dough is greased on the top side. Cover and let rise until double. You may put dough in an electric oven at lowest setting, 150°. In about 45 minutes to 1 hour, it is ready. Remove it from the oven, punch it down, and divide

into thirds. Place into three glass loaf pans which have been greased. Cover and return to low setting oven to rise again. Should be about 30 to 45 minutes. Slash tops of loaves and rub with butter. Bake approximately 20 minutes at 400°. Turn out on a rack to cool. Freezes. Also is good for cinnamon rolls. Prepare after first rising of dough.
Mrs. Joe P. Bryant (Gay Lawrence)

Asphodel Bread from St. Francisville, Louisiana

5	c. biscuit mix (Pioneer or Bisquick)	2	c. warm milk
4	T. sugar	2	envelopes dry yeast
¼	t. cream of tartar	4	eggs
		½	t. salt

Combine biscuit mix, sugar, and salt in a large bowl. Add yeast which has been dissolved in warm milk. Beat eggs with cream of tartar and add to mixture. Stir well. Cover and let rise until double in bulk. Stir down and pour into 2 greased 7½ x 3½ x 2½ loaf pans. Cover; let rise again until double. Bake 40 minutes at 350°.
Mrs. John R. Elliott (Helen Laws)

Batter Buns

1⅓	c. warm water	½	c. shortening
2	pkgs. yeast	2	eggs
4	T. sugar	3⅓	c. sifted flour
1	t. salt		

Mix yeast and water. Add sugar, salt, shortening, eggs, and 2 cups flour. Use mixer on low speed and beat until blended. Add remaining flour and beat with scraper until smooth. Fill 24 greased muffin cups ½ full. Let rise 30 to 40 minutes. Bake in 375° oven for 15 to 20 minutes or until lightly browned.
Yields 20 to 24.
Mrs. Clay D. Lockett (Jeanne Adcox)

Pop Up Bread

3	c. flour	½	c. vegetable oil
1	pkg. dry yeast	¼	c. sugar
½	c. milk	1	t. salt
½	c. water	2	eggs

In a large mixing bowl, stir yeast into 1½ cups flour. Beat milk, water, oil, sugar, and salt over low heat until just warm. Stir into flour and yeast mixture. Beat by hand until well blended. Beat in eggs. Add remaining 1½ cups flour. Mix well. Pour into 2 well greased 1 pound coffee cans. Cover with lids. Let rise in warm place about 1 hour until batter is about ½ inch from lids. Remove lids and bake about 35 minutes at 375°.

Mrs. Charles H. Ham (Jane Herrington)

Dilly Casserole Bread

1	pkg. active dry yeast	1	T. butter, melted
¼	c. warm water	2	t. dill seed
1	c. creamed cottage cheese, heated to lukewarm	1	t. salt
		¼	t. soda
2	T. sugar	1	egg, unbeaten
1	T. instant minced onion	2¼	to 2½ c. flour

Soften yeast in warm water. Combine in a mixing bowl cottage cheese, sugar, onion, butter, dill seed, salt, soda, egg, and softened yeast. Add flour to form a stiff dough, beating well after each addition. For first addition of flour, use mixer on low speed, then mix by hand. Cover and let rise in warm place, 85° to 90° F., until light and doubled in size, for 50 to 60 minutes. Stir down dough. Turn dough into well greased 8 inch casserole or two 8½ x 4½ x 2⅝ inch loaf pans or four 5 x 3½ inch baby loaf pans. Let rise in warm place for 30 to 40 minutes or until double. Bake at 350° for 40 to 50 minutes until golden brown. Baking time may be reduced if smaller pans are used. Brush with butter and sprinkle with salt. May be frozen. Serve hot or cold spread with butter. Delicious.

Mrs. John Ballard McDonald (Linda Cole)

Hot Rolls

1	yeast cake or dry yeast	1	c. warm milk
⅓	c. warm water	½	t. salt
2	t. sugar	3	c. flour
2	t. shortening		

Dissolve yeast in warm water and set aside. In mixing bowl combine sugar, shortening, milk, salt, and yeast. Beat in 1½ cups of flour. Knead remaining flour into the mixture. Cover bowl and set in a warm place for 1 hour. Place dough on bread board. Roll out and cut into rolls. Place in a well oiled pan. Let rise for 1½ hours. Bake in a 350° oven until brown, about 15 minutes.
Yields 4 dozen.
Mrs. O. L. Gragg (Inez Hardin)

Refrigerator Rolls

2	pkgs. dry yeast	6½	to 7 c. sifted flour
2	c. warm water	1	egg
½	c. granulated sugar	¼	c. soft shortening
2	t. salt		

Dissolve yeast in water and add sugar, salt, and half of the flour, 1 cup at a time, beating after each addition. Beat thoroughly 2 minutes. Add egg and shortening and beat in remaining flour gradually. Mix with hands until smooth. Place in a bowl and grease top of dough with shortening. Cover with a cool damp cloth and refrigerate. Punch down occasionally. Remove amount needed two hours before baking. Shape into rolls and place on greased baking pan. Let rise about 2 hours before baking. Drizzle with melted butter or margarine and bake at 400° for 12 to 15 minutes.
Mrs. Alexander Nemer, II (Vicki Burke)

Kolache

2	cakes fresh or 2 pkgs. granular yeast	⅔	c. melted shortening
1	t. sugar	¾	c. sugar
1	c. lukewarm water	4	t. salt
2	c. milk, scalded	2	eggs, beaten
		10	to 11 c. flour

Soften yeast and dissolve sugar in water. Cool milk to lukewarm. Add lukewarm milk, shortening, sugar, and salt to yeast mixture. Add eggs and beat well. Add flour to make a soft dough; let stand 10 minutes. Knead on lightly floured surface until smooth and elastic. Place in greased bowl and let rise until doubled. Shape dough into balls, ovals, or squares. Place on greased baking sheet. Depress centers and fill with prepared filling of choice. Let rise again. Brush with egg yolk glaze if desired or brush with mixture of milk and butter after removing from oven. Sprinkle with sugar. Bake in 400° oven about 12 to 15 minutes or until brown. Serve warm.
Yields 3 dozen.

Cinnamon-Apple Filling

4	small apples, peeled and cut up	3	t. cinnamon candies
		⅓	c. water

Cook in saucepan until soft. Drain and press pulp through sieve.

Poppy Seed Fruit Filling

24	cooked prunes or apricots, mashed	¼	c. sugar
½	t. cinnamon	2	T. poppy seeds

Mix above ingredients.

May use strawberry jam or preserves for filling. Press hole with thumb and place filling in hole. Fold over after placing filling in center and pinch edges together. For a 3 inch square, place filling in center. Fold corners to center and pinch together.
Mrs. Leland McReynolds (Annita Verzal)

 To scald milk without scorching, rinse pan in hot water before using.

Pao Doce

(Portuguese Sweet Bread)

2	envelopes active dry yeast	3	eggs, lightly beaten
¼	c. lukewarm water	1	t. salt
Pinch of sugar		5	c. flour
1	c. sugar	½	c. flour for kneading
1	c. milk, scalded	Milk for brushing tops of
½	c. butter, softened		loaves

Dissolve yeast in lukewarm water with a pinch of sugar. In a large bowl combine sugar, scalded milk, and butter which is well softened and cut into pieces. Stir the mixture until the butter is melted. Let it cool to lukewarm. Add the yeast mixture, eggs, salt, and beat in flour, adding 1 cup at a time. Turn dough out onto a floured surface (use about ½ cup flour) and knead it for 10 minutes, or until it is smooth and elastic. Form the dough into a ball, put it in a buttered bowl, and brush the top lightly with melted butter. Let the dough rise, covered, in a warm place for 2 hours or until it is double in bulk. Punch down the dough, divide it in half, and form each half into a round loaf about 8 inches in diameter. Put the loaves in buttered 9 inch pie tins and let them rise, covered, in a warm place for 1 hour and 30 minutes, or until they are double in bulk. Brush the loaves with milk and with a sharp knife cut a cross about ¼ inch deep in the top of each loaf. Bake the loaves in a preheated 350° oven for 45 minutes, or until they are well browned and the bottoms sound hollow when tapped. Remove the loaves from the tins and let them cool on racks.

This bread is slightly sweet. Makes delicious toast, also good for turkey, chicken, or home baked ham sandwiches.
Yields 2 loaves. Freezes.
Mrs. Eugene Fish (Elizabeth Link)

Beer Bread

4	c. Bisquick	1	can beer, room
4	T. sugar		temperature

Mix well and bake in greased 9 x 5 x 2 loaf pan at 350° for 45 to 50 minutes.
Lynda Seat Jenkins

Bacon Muffins

6	to 8 slices bacon	1	c. flour
1	T. bacon drippings	¼	t. salt
1	egg, beaten	4	t. baking powder
1	T. sugar	1	c. white corn meal
1	c. milk	1	T. minced onion, optional

Fry bacon until crisp and set aside. Reserve 1 tablespoon bacon drippings. Crumble cooled bacon and set aside. Mix sugar and milk into beaten egg. Sift flour with salt and baking powder, then mix in corn meal. Stir egg mixture into flour mixture just until moistened. Stir in bacon drippings, onion, and crumbled crisp bacon pieces. Fill greased muffin pan ⅔ full. Bake in a 400° oven for 20 to 25 minutes.
Yields 1 dozen.
Cookbook Committee

Corn Bread for Two

½	c. sifted flour	1	t. salt
¾	c. yellow cornmeal	2	T. bacon drippings
1	to 2 T. sugar	1	egg, beaten
½	t. soda	1	c. buttermilk
½	t. baking powder		

Combine dry ingredients with egg and bacon drippings. Batter will be lumpy. Add buttermilk and stir until smooth. Put a big dab of bacon drippings in an 8 inch skillet and heat in oven until piping hot. Pour batter into hot grease. Return to oven immediately. Bake at 425° for 25 to 30 minutes. Quick and delicious.
Serves 2 or a small family.
Mrs. Joe P. Bryant (Gay Lawrence)

Hush Puppies

2	c. yellow corn meal	¼	c. finely chopped onion
1	T. flour	1¼	c. buttermilk
1	T. sugar	1	egg, well beaten
1	t. baking powder	Shortening	
¾	t. baking soda		

Mix dry ingredients together. Stir buttermilk into beaten egg and add to dry ingredients. Form cakes to desired shape and size. Deep fry only as many cakes as will float uncrowded one layer deep. Fry 3 to 4 minutes or until well browned.

According to East Texas folklore, these morsels were made at hunting time to feed the hungry howling hounds to quiet them, hence "Hush Puppies".

Yields about 1½ doz.

Mrs. Charles C. Davis (Martha Saxton)

Hot Water Corn Bread

1	c. white corn meal	¾	to 1 c. boiling water
1	t. salt	Bacon drippings	

Combine corn meal and salt in a bowl. Stir in enough boiling water to allow the mixture to reach the proper consistency. With wet hands, shape the corn mixture by the tablespoon into flat pones or into fat little rolls. Fry the corn pones on both sides until crisp and brown, turning several times.

Yields 8 to 10 pones.

Mrs. Jack H. Hanks (Jackie Rayburn)

Corn Fritters

1	c. flour	2	eggs, well beaten
¼	c. sugar	1	8¾ oz. can cream style
1	t. baking powder		corn
⅛	t. salt		

Combine dry ingredients. Stir in eggs and corn, mixing well. Carefully drop batter by tablespoons into deep heated oil. Fry until golden brown. Serve with butter and honey.
Yields about 2 dozen. Freezes.
Mrs. C. L. Kolstad, III (Jill McPherson)

Spoon Bread

3	c. milk	2	eggs
1	c. cornmeal	1	T. sugar
1	t. salt	2	t. baking powder
2	T. shortening		

Scald 2 cups of milk, add slowly the cornmeal and salt, stirring constantly. Cook until thick. Cool slightly. Add shortening. Beat in eggs, one at a time. Add remaining milk, sugar, and baking powder. Pour into a heated 1 quart baking dish that has been greased. Bake at 350° for 30 or 40 minutes. Serve hot with a spoon from the baking dish.
Serves 6 to 8.
Mrs. David Dial (Margery Hombs)

Angel Gingerbread

2	c. sifted flour	1	c. sugar
2	level t. soda	2	eggs
1	heaping t. ginger	1	c. vegetable oil
½	t. cinnamon	½	c. ribbon cane syrup (must
½	t. cloves		be ribbon cane)
½	t. nutmeg	1	c. boiling water
¼	t. salt		

Mix dry ingredients and sift three times. This is a must. Add eggs, oil, and syrup. Mix well. Add 1 cup boiling water. Mix and pour into a greased 9 x 13 inch pan. Bake at 350° about 30 minutes or until cake springs back at touch.
Yields 10 to 12 generous servings.
Mrs. Robert F. Herrington (Oma Pinkerton)

Gingerbread

1	c. sugar	1	c. syrup
1	c. vegetable oil	2	t. ginger
3	eggs	2	t. other spices (your
2	c. flour		choice)
1	t. soda	1	c. boiling water
½	t. salt		

Mix sugar and oil. Add eggs. Add remaining dry ingredients. Mix together and add boiling water. Pour batter into a greased and floured 9 x 12 pan and bake at 350° for 25 to 30 minutes. May be topped with Orange Glaze.
Mrs. Jack Graves (Pauline Thompson)

Orange Glaze
1   c. sugar
Juice and grated rind of 1
    orange

Stir over low heat until sugar is dissolved.
Mrs. J.M. Hunt (Doris Leathers)

Moist Gingerbread

1	1 lb. box light brown sugar	1	t. nutmeg
2	c. sifted flour	2	t. cinnamon
1½	sticks margarine	2	eggs, beaten
½	c. chopped nuts	1	t. soda and 1 c. buttermilk, mixed together before adding
½	t. ginger		

Place sugar, flour, and margarine in a bowl and cut together until well blended. Do not use mixer. After blending, remove 1 cup for topping and add chopped nuts. Set aside. To the remainder of the crumbly mixture add remaining ingredients. Mix by hand and pour into a 9 x 13 inch greased and floured pan. Spread the topping evenly over this mixture. Bake 45 minutes to 1 hour at 350°. Cool about 15 minutes and cut into squares. Top with lemon sauce.
Serves 10 to 12.

Lemon Sauce

3	eggs	1	c. sugar
4	T. lemon juice	½	c. butter
Grated rind of 2 lemons			

Using the top of a double boiler, beat eggs with lemon juice and sugar. Add rind and butter. Cook over hot water, stirring constantly, until mixture thickens.
Yields 2 cups.
Mrs. J. W. Sims (Lena Mae Roquemore)

Apricot Nut Bread

1	c. sugar	3	c. flour, unsifted
2	T. shortening	3½	t. baking powder
1	egg, lightly beaten	1	t. salt
¾	c. milk	¾	c. chopped walnuts
¾	c. fresh orange juice	6	oz. dried apricots,
4	t. freshly grated orange rind		plumped in ½ c. boiling water

Preheat oven to 350°. Thoroughly blend sugar, shortening, and egg. Stir in milk, orange juice, and orange rind. Sift dry ingredients and stir in nuts. Add to liquid mixture. Drain and coarsely chop apricots. Blend into batter and pour into 2 small 7 inch loaf pans. Let stand 20 minutes. Bake for 1 hour and 10 minutes or until toothpick inserted in center comes out clean. Cool in pans for 10 minutes on a rack, remove from pans, and cool completely. Wrap in foil and let stand in refrigerator for 2 days to allow flavors to blend.
Yields 2 small loaves.
Cookbook Committee

Cottage Cheese Hot Cakes

3	eggs, separated	¼	t. salt
½	c. milk		Pinch white pepper
1	scant c. flour	2	T. cooking oil
1	t. baking powder	1	c. cottage cheese, small or
2	T. sugar		large curd

Beat egg yolks with milk. Combine dry ingredients, add to milk mixture, and beat well. Add oil while beating. Add cottage cheese and mix well. Beat egg whites until stiff and fold into batter. Pour ¼ cup batter for each hot cake onto a heated and well greased skillet and cook on both sides until golden brown.
Yields 16 hot cakes.
Jack W. Meeker

Easy Sticky Buns

½	c. butter or margarine	¼	t. cinnamon
½	c. brown sugar, firmly packed	⅔	c. milk
2	c. Bisquick	1	egg
2½	T. sugar	6	T. chopped pecans or 36 pecan halves
1	t. nutmeg		

Heat oven to 400°. Spray muffin cups with vegetable cooking spray. In each of 12 medium muffin cups, place 2 teaspoons each butter and brown sugar. Place in oven to melt. Mix all else except pecans. Batter will be slightly lumpy. Do not over mix batter. Remove muffin tins from oven; place 1 teaspoon chopped pecans or 3 pecan halves in each cup. Fill muffin cups ½ full. Bake about 15 minutes. Immediately invert pan to remove muffins. **Yields 18.**
Mrs. C. L. Kolstad, III (Jill McPherson)

Breakfast Muffins

1	egg	¾	c. sugar
½	c. milk	2	t. baking powder
¼	c. salad oil	½	t. salt
1½	c. flour		

Heat oven to 400°. Spray muffin tins with vegetable oil. Beat egg and stir in milk and oil. Mix in remaining ingredients just until flour is moistened. Batter should be lumpy. Fill muffin tins ⅔ full. Bake 20 to 25 minutes or until golden brown. Remove from pan immediately.
Variations:
Blueberry — fold in 1 cup fresh or ¾ cup well drained frozen, thawed blueberries.
Cranberry Orange — fold in 1 tablespoon grated orange rind and 1 cup cranberries, chopped.
Jelly Filled — fill muffin cups ½ full. Drop in 1 teaspoon preserves in center of each and add batter to fill to ⅔ full.
Yields 12 medium or 36 miniature muffins.
Mrs. C. L. Kolstad, III (Jill McPherson)

Banana Muffins

½	c. shortening	1	t. nutmeg
1	c. sugar	1	t. soda dissolved in 2 T.
1	egg		hot water
1½	c. flour	1	t. vanilla
1	c. mashed bananas		

Grease and flour muffin tins. Cream shortening and sugar. Add egg, flour, and banana alternately. Then add nutmeg, vanilla, and soda. Bake in 350° oven for 20 to 25 minutes or until brown.
Yields 24 muffins.
Mrs. E. D. Cleveland (Yvonne Teel)

Banana Nut Muffins

½	c. honey	½	c. raw wheat germ
2	eggs, beaten	½	t. salt
½	c. vegetable oil	1	t. soda
½	t. vanilla	3	bananas, mashed
¼	t. almond extract	½	c. pecan pieces
1½	c. whole wheat flour		

Combine honey, eggs, oil, vanilla, and almond extract. Beat well. Mix flour, raw wheat germ, salt, and soda. Add to honey mixture. Add bananas and pecans and mix well. Grease muffin tins with margarine and fill them ⅔ full. Bake in 325° oven for 25 minutes.
Yields 20 medium muffins or 50 minature muffins.
Jack W. Meeker

Fruit Bread

2½	c. sugar	3	eggs, well beaten
1½	c. ripe bananas, mashed	¾	c. vegetable oil
1	8 oz. can crushed pineapple	2½	c. flour
		¼	t. salt
1	8 oz. jar maraschino cherries, drained and cut up (optional)	¾	t. soda
		1	t. vanilla
		1	c. chopped pecans

Mix sugar, bananas, pineapple, cherries, and eggs. Combine with oil. Combine flour, salt, and soda. Stir into the first mixture. Add nuts and vanilla. Grease and flour tube pan or loaf pan. Bake 1 hour and 30 minutes at 300°. You may make miniature muffins. Bake in 300° oven for 35 minutes. **Yields 8 dozen.**

Lemon Tea Bread

½	c. butter or margarine	1½	c. all-purpose flour
1	c. sugar	1	t. baking powder
2	eggs, beaten		Juice and grated rind of 1 lemon
½	t. salt		

Combine butter and sugar. Add eggs, salt, flour, and baking powder. Stir in lemon juice and rind and mix well. Spoon batter into a greased 9 x 5 x 2 inch loaf pan. Bake at 350° for 1 hour. Spread glaze over warm loaf.

Glaze
¼   c. sugar
Juice and grated rind of 1
   lemon

Slowly beat lemon juice and sugar until sugar dissolves. Add grated rind. **Yields 1 loaf or 36 miniature muffins.**
Mrs. J. B. Bellican (Lucile Beasley)

Orange Nut Bread

2	T. butter or margarine	½	c. orange juice (about 1 orange)
½	c. boiling water		
2	c. sifted flour	2	T. grated orange rind
1	t. soda	1	c. sugar
1	t. baking powder	2	t. vanilla
½	t. salt	1	egg, slightly beaten
		½	c. chopped nuts

Melt butter or margarine in boiling water in medium sized bowl. Sift flour, soda, baking powder, and salt together. Add orange juice, grated orange rind, sugar, and vanilla to the butter and water. Add egg. Sift dry ingredients over orange mixture, add nuts and stir until flour is all dampened. Batter will be lumpy. Pour into a greased and floured loaf pan and bake at 350° for 1 hour or until toothpick inserted in center comes out clean. Remove from pan and cool on wire rack. Wrap in wax paper and store. It slices better the next day. Use cream cheese as filling for sandwiches.
Yields 1 large loaf or two small.

Pumpkin Bread

⅔	c. shortening	1½	t. salt
2⅔	c. sugar	½	t. baking powder
4	eggs	1	t. cinnamon
1	16 oz. can pumpkin	1	t. cloves
⅔	c. water	⅔	c. coarsely chopped nuts
3½	c. flour	⅔	c. raisins
2	t. soda		

Heat oven to 350°. Grease 2 loaf pans 9 x 5 x 3 inch or 6 small loaf pans. Soak raisins in small amount of water or sherry to plump. Cream shortening and sugar thoroughly. Add eggs, pumpkin, and water. Blend in dry ingredients except nuts and raisins. Stir in nuts and raisins. Bake in prepared pans 65 to 75 minutes or until wooden pick inserted in center comes out clean.
Yields 2 loaves.
Mrs. Dale Holloway (Delia Pearce)

Bran Refrigerator Muffins

2	c. boiling water	1	qt. buttermilk
2	c. 100% bran cereal	5	c. flour
1	c. shortening or corn oil	5	t. soda
3	c. sugar	1	t. salt
4	eggs	4	c. All-Bran cereal

Pour boiling water over the 100% bran cereal. Set aside to cool. In a large bowl cream together the shortening and sugar. Add eggs, one at a time, beating well after each addition. Add buttermilk. Mix flour, soda, and salt. Add to liquid mixture. Add the cooled bran mixture and fold in the All Bran cereal only until moistened. Pour into 4 one quart glass jars and refrigerate. Will keep more than two weeks. Bake as many as desired, using greased muffin cups, in a 400° oven for 15 to 20 minutes.
Mrs. Robert B. Bristow (Jimmie Reta Inmon)

Graham Muffins

½	c. sifted flour	1	c. whole wheat flour, stirred
¼	c. sugar		
1	t. salt	1	egg, well beaten
4	t. baking powder	1	c. milk
		3	T. butter, melted

Sift flour, sugar, salt, and baking powder; stir in whole wheat flour. Combine eggs, milk, and butter. Make a well in center of dry ingredients and add liquid all at once. Stir just until flour is moistened. Fill greased muffin cups ⅔ full. Bake in 425° oven for 15 to 18 minutes.
Yields 10 large or 35 small muffins.
Mrs. Bruce Barber (Brenda Wilson)

Whole Wheat Nut Bread

1	c. sifted flour	¾	c. sugar
2	t. baking powder	2	eggs
¼	t. salt	⅔	c. milk
½	t. cinnamon	½	t. vanilla
¼	t. nutmeg	½	c. chopped walnuts or
¼	t. allspice		pecans
½	c. whole wheat flour	½	c. raisins, optional
¼	c. butter		

Sift together first 6 ingredients; stir in whole wheat flour. Cream butter, sugar, and eggs. Add dry ingredients alternately with milk and vanilla to creamed mixture. Beat smooth after each addition. Stir in nuts and raisins. Pour batter into an 8½ x 4½ x 2½ inch lightly greased loaf pan and bake at 350° for 55 minutes. Cool 10 minutes in pan.
Mrs. Bruce Barber (Brenda Wilson)

Sour Cream Coffee Cake

1	c. margarine	2	c. flour
2	c. sugar	1	t. baking powder
2	eggs		Pinch of salt
1	T. vanilla	1	c. sour cream

Topping mix

1	c. chopped nuts	2	t. cinnamon
4	T. sugar		

Sift flour, baking powder, and salt. Cream margarine, sugar, eggs, and vanilla using mixer on low speed. Add flour mixture and sour cream alternately to creamed mixture. Pour in a 9 x 12 greased and floured pan. Add half of batter and sprinkle with ½ of topping mix; then add the rest of batter and sprinkle with remaining topping mix. Bake in a 325° oven for 1 hour or until toothpick inserted into center comes out clean. This makes a very moist cake and needs to be covered tightly when cake is cooled.
Mrs. John Ballard McDonald (Linda Cole)

Monkey Bread Coffee Cake

2	8 oz. cans biscuits	½	c. chopped nuts
½	c. sugar	½	c. butter
½	t. cinnamon	½	c. brown sugar

Cut biscuits in quarters. Mix cinnamon, sugar, and nuts together. Roll biscuits in mixture. Drop in greased 9 x 9 inch pan or bundt pan. Sprinkle remaining sugar mixture on top. Melt butter and brown sugar in small pan. Boil and stir about ½ minute or until brown sugar and butter are well mixed, and pour over biscuits. Bake at 350° for 20 to 30 minutes. Remove from oven and let set about 5 minutes before inverting pan onto platter.
Mrs. Norman E. Bonner (Susan Beyette)

Praline Toast

6	T. butter or margarine	10	slices of white bread
¼	c. evaporated milk	⅔	c. chopped pecans
1	c. light brown sugar		

Melt butter or margarine on low heat. Stir in milk, sugar, and pecans. Cut each slice of bread into four strips and toast on one side. Spread untoasted side with pecan mixture. Broil for 1 to 2 minutes, or until mixture bubbles. This mixture may be made in quantity and stored in an air tight container in the refrigerator. Delicious with coffee.
Yields 40 pieces.
Mrs. Wayne Walker (Katherine Cray)

Orange Bread

1	egg	1	c. milk	
6	T. vegetable oil	1½	T. candied orange peel	
1	c. sugar	½	t. orange flavoring	
3	c. flour	½	t. lemon flavoring	
½	t. salt	1	t. vanilla	
3	t. baking powder			

Beat together the egg, oil, and sugar. Mix the flour, salt, and baking powder. Add alternately with the milk to sugar mixture. Add peel and flavorings. Mix well. Pour batter into a greased and floured 8½ x 4½ x 2½ loaf pan. Bake at 275° for 1½ hours or until wire test comes out clean.
Jack W. Meeker

Orange Toast

2	T. butter	1	t. grated orange rind
½	c. sugar	6	slices bread
¼	c. orange juice		

Melt butter. Mix with sugar, juice, and rind. Toast bread on one side. Spread the other side with the orange mixture. Place on cookie sheet and broil or bake in a hot oven until golden brown.
Serves 3 to 6.

Basic Crepe

1¼   c. flour   1½   c. milk
Pinch of salt   2   T. butter, melted
3   eggs, beaten

Place all ingredients in blender or mixer and beat well. Let batter stand 1 hour for more perfect crepes. Stir batter before using. Chicken or beef bouillon can be substituted for all or part of milk. The addition of onion, garlic, or celery salt can also create a tasty crepe.
Serves 8 to 10. Freezes.
Mrs. Jim Bob Parker (Pat McCrary)

Variations:
Parmesan crepes - add ¼ c. grated Parmesan cheese to batter.
Vanilla crepes - add 1 or 2 t. vanilla extract and 1 T. sugar to batter.
Dessert crepes - add 1 or 2 T. of sugar to batter. Then add one of the following:
2 t. grated lemon rind plus 2 more T. sugar,
2 t. grated orange rind or
1 T. brandy or favorite liqueur plus 1 more T. sugar.

Quick Drop Biscuits

1½   c. flour   ⅜   t. salt
2   t. baking powder   1   c. heavy cream

Sift dry ingredients together. Add cream and stir until soft dough is formed. Drop by spoonfuls on ungreased baking sheet. Bake at 450° for 12 to 15 minutes.
Yields 12.

CHEESE, EGGS
AND
RICE

Cheese Souffle

1 c. hot milk	2 t. butter
1 c. coarsely broken soft bread crumbs	3 eggs, separated
	Pinch of salt
¼ c. grated cheese	

Combine milk, bread crumbs, cheese, and butter. Beat yolks until thick and lemon colored; add to milk mixture. Stiffly beat egg whites adding a pinch of salt. Fold in egg whites. Pour into 1 ½ quart casserole. Bake immediately in 350° oven for about 30 minutes.
Serves 2.
Mrs. David Dial (Margery Hombs)

Crab Quiche

1 9 inch deep dish pie shell	¾ c. sour cream
1 4 oz. can sliced mushrooms	¼ c. mayonnaise
	½ t. salt
1 c. canned crab	1 t. flour
1⅓ c. or ⅓ lb. finely diced Gruyere or Swiss cheese	3 eggs, slightly beaten
	Light cream
	½ t. Tabasco
1 t. butter	

Bake pastry in 450° oven for 10 minutes. Drain mushrooms, reserving liquid. Saute mushrooms in butter 2 minutes. Scatter in partially baked pie shell. Remove any membrane from crab and scatter crab and cheese over mushrooms. Mix sour cream and mayonnaise with reserved mushroom liquid, salt, and flour. Add enough light cream to mixture to make 2 cups. Blend in eggs and Tabasco and pour into shell. Bake in 350° oven 55 minutes or until set. Let stand 15 minutes before cutting.
Serves 6.
Mrs. Jack H. Hanks (Jackie Rayburn)

 Freeze very soft cheese 15 minutes to make shredding easier.

Spinach Quiche

1	9 inch deep dish pie shell, partially baked	½	t. salt
1	10 oz. pkg. frozen chopped spinach	⅛	t. pepper or to taste
		Pinch	nutmeg
2	T. chopped onion	3	eggs
2	T. butter	1½	c. heavy cream
		1½	c. grated Swiss cheese

Cook and drain spinach. Saute onions in 2 tablespoons butter until tender. Stir in salt, pepper, and nutmeg. Combine eggs and cream. Add spinach and cheese. Add additional salt and pepper if necessary. Pour mixture into pie shell. Bake in preheated 375° oven 30 to 40 minutes.
Serves 6.
Cookbook Committee

Quiche Lorraine

1   10 inch deep dish pie
    shell

Filling

¼	lb. Swiss cheese, grated	3	large eggs, beaten well
1	T. flour	2	c. milk or cream
½	lb. bacon, fried and crumbled or 1 c. chopped ham	⅛	t. nutmeg
		¾	t. salt
		¼	t. pepper
¼	lb. mushrooms, sliced	¼	t. garlic powder

Combine cheese, flour, bacon or ham, and mushrooms and place in bottom of pie shell. Blend remaining ingredients well. Pour egg mixture over the cheese mixture. Place pie shell in preheated 425° oven. Lower oven to 375°; bake 20 to 30 minutes. Done when knife tip inserted in center comes out clean. Cool on wire rack 10 minutes.
Serves 6 to 8.
Mrs. V. A. Gordon (Gwendolyn Stark)

 To keep quiche crust from getting soggy, try brushing the crust with Dijon mustard before filling. You may also toss the cheese with a small amount of flour and spread over the crust before filling with the custard mixture.

Eggs Benedict

4   rounds of bread or 4
     English muffin halves
Ham, Canadian bacon, or fried
   bacon
	Broiled tomatoes, optional
	Poached eggs
	Simple hollandaise sauce

Toast bread or English muffin halves. Cover with slices of ham, Canadian bacon or bacon strips, tomatoes, and poached eggs. Serve with hollandaise sauce.

Simple Hollandaise Sauce

1	T. flour	2	T. lemon juice
2	T. butter	2	egg yolks
½	c. boiling water		Salt and cayenne to taste

In a double boiler, blend flour and butter well. Add boiling water. When thick, add lemon juice. Remove from heat and pour over well beaten egg yolks. Season with salt and cayenne. May be returned to double boiler to keep warm. If a thinner sauce is desired, more boiling water may be used.
Serves 4.
Mrs. Tucker K. Royall (Ann Boyd)

Egg Casserole

1½	c. croutons	2	c. milk
1	c. shredded Cheddar cheese	1	T. prepared mustard Salt, pepper, and onion salt to
4	eggs		taste

Spread croutons in a buttered 10 x 6 dish. Sprinkle with cheese. Mix remaining ingredients and pour over cheese. Set aside for 5 minutes. Bake at 325° for 50 minutes.
Serves 6.
Mrs. Tucker K. Royall (Ann Boyd)

Breakfast Casserole

1	lb. sausage	1	t. dry mustard
3	slices white bread, trimmed and cubed	1	4 oz. can sliced mushrooms, drained
6	eggs, beaten		Salt to taste
2	c. light cream	1	c. grated cheese

Brown sausage and drain. In 9 x 13 casserole layer sausage and bread. Combine eggs, light cream, mustard, mushrooms, and salt to taste. Pour over sausage; top with cheese. Cover and refrigerate overnight. Bake at 350° for 45 minutes.
Serves 12.
Mrs. Tate McCain (Peggy Moore)

Make-Ahead Egg Casserole

½	c. chopped onion	1	10¾ oz. can cream of chicken soup
½	c. chopped green pepper		
1	4 oz. can mushrooms, drained	1	10¾ oz. can golden mushroom soup
⅓	c. butter	1	c. grated processed cheese
2	doz. large eggs	1	t. salt
½	c. milk	½	t. pepper
			Tabasco to taste

Saute onion, green pepper, and mushrooms in butter. Beat eggs, add milk, combine with onion, pepper, mushroom mixture, and soft scramble. Stir in soups, cheese, and seasonings. Pour into buttered 9 x 13 inch casserole. Bake at 225° uncovered for 45 minutes.
May be prepared a day in advance. Reheat before serving.
Serves 12 to 14.
Mrs. R. L. Kenderdine (Daphne Dunning)

Hot Eggs with Horseradish Sauce

6	hard-cooked eggs	¾	t. salt
⅛	t. black pepper	2	T. cream

Sauce

1	T. butter	½	t. salt
2	T. flour	1	t. sugar
¼	c. prepared horseradish	1	c. milk
⅛	t. pepper		Parsley

Mash yolks well with seasonings and cream. Fill whites with yolk mixture and place in greased 9 inch baking dish.

Sauce Blend melted butter and flour, add seasonings, and horseradish. Add milk and stir constantly until thick. Pour over eggs and bake at 325° about 10 minutes. Garnish with parsley.

Serves 4 to 6.

Mrs. George E. Glober (Catherine Crain), Austin, Texas

Ridglea Eggs

2	doz. hard-cooked eggs, halved	1	c. plain yogurt
1	c. mayonnaise	1	2 oz. bottle capers
1	c. sour cream		Salt and pepper to taste

Place eggs in 2 quart container. Mix other ingredients and pour over eggs. Refrigerate. Keeps several days.

Serves 12.

Cookbook Committee

 Make a tiny pin hole in the large end of an egg before dropping into boiling water; this will keep egg from breaking while cooking.

Woodstock

6	T. butter	1	6 oz. can mushrooms,	
½	c. flour		drained	
2	c. milk	2	T. sliced pimiento	
½	t. salt	¼	c. thinly sliced green	
Pepper to taste			pepper	
½	lb. sharp Cheddar cheese,	6	hard-cooked eggs	
	cubed	English muffin bread or toast		

Melt butter in saucepan. Stir in flour and mix well. Gradually add milk and stir with wire whisk constantly until sauce thickens. Add salt, pepper, and cheese. Stir until cheese is melted. Add mushrooms, pimiento, and green pepper. Slice eggs into a 1 quart casserole. Pour sauce over eggs and serve immediately over English muffins or toast.
Serves 6.
Mrs. R. L. Kenderdine (Daphne Dunning)

Oven Rice

1	c. margarine	2	8 oz. cans mushrooms,
2	c. raw rice		drained
2	10¾ oz. cans onion soup	2	8 oz. cans sliced water
2	14½ oz. cans chicken		chestnuts, drained or
	broth		halved almonds or both

Place in 2 quart casserole. Bake covered in 350° oven 1 hour. Good with any kind of meat. May be prepared ahead and baked later. *To speed cooking time heat margarine and soups before combining.*
Serves 8 to 10.
Mrs. Ed Montgomery (Dorothy Meador)

 To make rice white and fluffier, add 1 teaspoon lemon juice to each quart of cooking water.

Armenian Rice

½ c. butter	1 10¾ oz. can beef
1 medium bell pepper, slivered	consomme
1 medium yellow onion, slivered	1 chicken bouillon cube dissolved in 1 c. boiling water
1 c. raw rice	½ c. sliced almonds
1 8 oz. can sliced mushrooms and liquid	

Saute pepper and onion in butter. Combine with remaining ingredients in 2½ quart casserole. Cover and bake at 325° for 45 minutes. You may wish to stir the mixture once approximately halfway through baking.
Serves 10. Freezes.
Mrs. Helmut Loth (Marigrace Stutts)

Baked Rice

½ c. butter	1 10¾ oz. can onion soup
1 c. raw rice	1 10¾ oz. can beef broth
1 10¾ oz. can mushroom soup	

Saute rice in butter until golden. Add soups and mix well. Spoon into a 1 quart casserole. Cover and bake at 350° for 1 hour.
Serves 6 to 8.
Mrs. J. B. Bellican (Lucile Beasley)

Cumin Rice

¼ c. chopped onion	1 T. Worcestershire sauce
1 c. raw rice	¼ t. cumin seed
2 T. bacon drippings	¼ t. salt
2 10¾ oz. cans beef consomme	

Brown onion and rice in bacon drippings in large skillet. Add remaining ingredients. Cover tightly, bring to boil, lower heat, and simmer 20 minutes.
Serves 4 to 6.
Mrs. Stewart Kenderdine (Jane Kukar)

Rice Dressing

2	c. long grain rice	2	t. salt or to taste
2	lbs. ground beef	1	t. black pepper
2	T. butter	½	t. allspice
2	large onions, chopped		Hot water to cover

Wash rice in cold water. Brown meat and drain fat. Add butter and chopped onions. Cook until onions brown lightly. Add seasonings, drained rice, and cover with hot water. Simmer, covered, until rice is done. You may stuff turkey with this mixture, or serve as side dish. May be served with baked chicken or cornish hen.

For a change brown ½ cup pinenuts or almonds in butter and garnish on top or add to rice and meat mixture after it is done.

You may cook rice separately, and then add to meat mixture.

Serves 12.

Mrs. Jesse George (Agnes Totah)

Green Rice

1	c. long grain rice	2	eggs
2	c. water	1	clove garlic, minced
1	t. salt	1	medium onion, chopped
1	c. chopped fresh parsley	½	lb. Cheddar cheese, grated
2	c. milk, divided	½	c. vegetable oil

In 3 quart saucepan bring 2 cups water and 1 teaspoon salt to boil. Add rice, cover, and simmer for 25 minutes. Mix parsley, 1 cup milk, garlic, onion, and eggs in blender. Pour into large mixing bowl. Then blend in blender remaining 1 cup milk and vegetable oil. Add to parsley mixture with rice and grated cheese. Pour into 2½ quart casserole. Bake at 350° for 1 hour.

Serves 12.

Mrs. Robert E. Jordan (Margaret Haygood)

Jalapeno Rice Casserole

1	c. raw rice	1	4 oz. can chopped green chilies
1	c. sour cream		
1	4 oz. can jalapeno peppers, chopped,seeded, and drained, or	1	c. grated Monterey Jack cheese
		1	10¾ oz. can mushroom soup

Cook rice. Combine with remaining ingredients. Pour into a greased 2 quart casserole and bake at 350° for 20 to 30 minutes.
Serves 8. Freezes.
Mrs. Jeff D. Walker (Katherine Kolstad)

Orange Rice

3	T. slivered almonds	1	c. buttermilk
1	c. chopped onion	¼	t. oregano
¼	c. chopped green pepper	½	t. salt
2	T. butter	2	oranges, peeled and cut into small pieces
1	c. long grain rice		
1	c. orange juice		Paprika

In 350° oven bake almonds for 5 to 10 minutes. Cook onion and green pepper in butter until tender but not browned. Add the rice and brown lightly, stirring constantly for about 3 to 5 minutes. Add orange juice, buttermilk, oregano, and salt. Stir once and bring to a boil over high heat. Cover and reduce heat. Simmer for 25 minutes or until liquid is absorbed. Do not raise lid. Stir the orange pieces and almonds into the cooked rice. Garnish with paprika.
Mrs. R. L. Kenderdine (Daphne Dunning)

Orange Rice with Fresh Parsley

¼	c. butter or margarine	2	c. chicken broth
1	c. raw rice	½	c. dry white wine
½	t. salt		Juice and rind of 1 orange
	Dash white pepper		Chopped parsley

Combine first 6 ingredients. Cover. Bake at 350° for 45 minutes. Add orange juice and rind. Return to oven for 10 mintues uncovered. Taste for seasoning. Toss with a fork. Sprinkle with chopped parsley.
Serves 4.
Mrs. Willard W. Johnson, Jr. (Nancy Earle)

Wild Rice Casserole

1	c. raw wild rice, washed	½	c. white wine, optional
1	onion, chopped	2	T. butter
3	stalks celery, chopped	1	qt. chicken broth
1	t. seasoned salt		Salt and pepper to taste

Combine ingredients. Place in buttered 2 quart casserole. Bake covered at 325° for 2 hours. May be prepared in advance.
Serves 6 to 8. Freezes.
Mrs. W. H. Shuller (Mary Plemons)

Boulghour (Cracked Wheat)

10 T. butter or margarine   6   c. chicken broth or
1   small to medium onion,   consomme
    finely chopped   Salt and pepper to taste
3   c. boulghour (medium
    cracked wheat)

Saute onion in 2 tablespoons of butter until golden brown. Set aside. Melt 8 tablespoons of butter in a 12 inch iron skillet. Add boulghour and braise, stirring constantly, until butter begins to bubble. At this point you may pour ingredients into a 3 quart casserole or continue using the skillet. Add onions, broth, and seasoning. Stir well. Cover and place in a 350° oven for approximately 45 minutes. Remove from oven, stir, and check. If too dry, add a little water. If too moist, leave cover off. Return to oven for about 15 minutes more.
If serving with lamb, use chicken broth. If serving with beef, use consomme.
Serves 12.
Mrs. Daniel F. Rex (Emory Hill)

Rice Ring

2   c. raw rice   ¾   c. grated Cheddar cheese
4   c. water   Tabasco to taste
2   t. salt

Bring water, salt, and rice to a boil. Cover, reduce heat, and simmer for 15 minutes. When done lift lid and allow to steam dry. Stir in cheese, Tabasco, and pack into a greased 8 inch ring mold. Cover ring and let stand in hot water until serving time. To serve loosen ring edges with knife and unmold on hot platter. Center may be filled with vegetables or meat.
Serves 8 to 10.

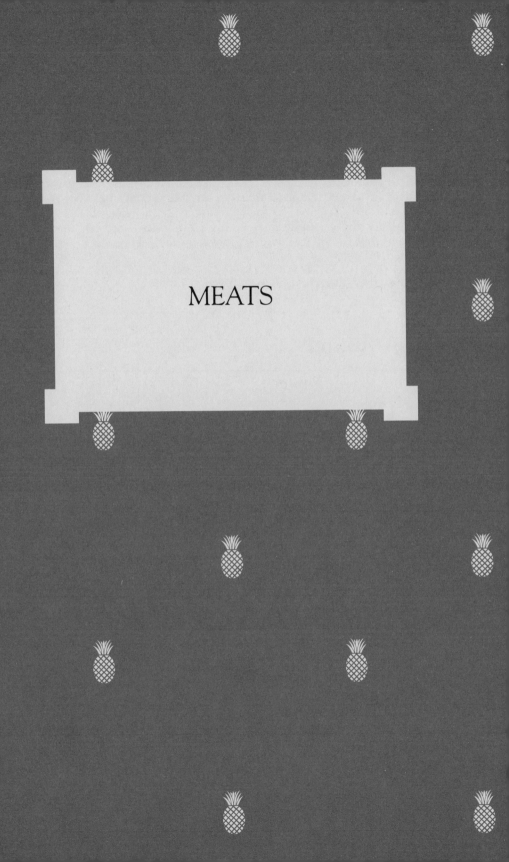

MEATS

Beef Tenderloin

1   2 to 3 lb. tenderloin   Lemon pepper

Preheat oven to 450°. Rub tenderloin with seasoning. Place in shallow roasting pan and roast at 450° for 10 minutes. Reduce heat to 350°, cover pan with foil, and continue to roast for 10 minutes longer. If tenderloin is large, you may want to increase cooking time 5 minutes.
For those who enjoy rare meat!
Serves 6 to 8.
Mrs. Jack H. Hanks (Jackie Rayburn)

Eye of Round

1   4 lb. eye of round roast   Coarse black pepper or choice
                                        of seasoning

Have an eye of round roast at room temperature. Sprinkle with coarse black pepper or your choice of seasoning. Place in roasting pan and bake in a preheated 500° oven 5 minutes per pound. Turn off heat and do not open oven door for 2 hours. Roast will be pink and juicy. Best served in very thin slices. Two roasts may be cooked at same time. To arrive at baking time, multiply total weight by 5.
Mrs. Clyde Hanks (Howard Kolstad), Houston, Texas.

Rare Roast Beef for Two

2   ribs of prime beef
Salt and pepper to taste or
    seasoning of your choice

Place meat on a rack in a roasting pan and bake in 300° oven for 2¼ hours. For smaller servings, bake 1 rib for 1¾ hours.
Serves 2 generously.
Mrs. Daniel F. Rex (Emory Hill)

Roast Beef au Jus

4½ to 5 lb. standing prime rib   Salt and pepper to taste
     roast

Let roast stand at room temperature for at least 1 hour before cooking. Preheat oven to 375°. Rub meat with salt and pepper. Place fat side up in shallow pan. Roast for 1 hour and 10 minutes. Turn off heat and do not open oven door. Leave in closed oven for at least 1½ hours or longer if desired. Thirty to 40 minutes before serving, reheat in oven at 375°. Roast will be brown and crisp on the outside and rare in the middle.
Serves 6 to 8.
A 6 pound boneless rib eye may be substituted and will serve 10.
Mrs. Jack Selden (Gloria McCracken)

Flank Steak

1   2 lb. flank steak, 1 inch
     thick

Preliminary marinade

3   T. finely chopped green   2   T. olive oil
     onions and tops   ½   t. thyme
1½   T. soy sauce   2   to 3 dashes Tabasco
                                     2   T. lemon juice

Combine marinade ingredients in bowl. Score the steak diagonally across the grain on each side and lay flat in a shallow glass dish. Spread on half the marinade; turn and spread with rest of marinade. Cover with waxed paper and set aside for at least 20 minutes or refrigerate overnight or longer. Remove to broiling pan and broil steak 4 inches from heat for 3 to 4 minutes on first side and 2 to 3 minutes on other side. Steak should be rosy rare. Marinade should be increased if steak is larger.
Serves 4.
Mrs. Cad E. Williams (Francis Bailey)

 Never cook a roast cold. Let stand 1 hour at room temperature. Brush with oil before and during cooking. The oil will seal in juices.

Steak Baked with Thyme

3	lbs. boneless steak 2 inches thick, trimmed well	½	T. salt
		½	t. thyme
		3	cloves garlic, unpeeled
Cooking oil		½	c. beef bouillon or wine
1	T. margarine	1	T. margarine

Pat steak dry with paper towels. Rub lightly with oil. Coat a flameproof baking dish with oil, heat, and brown steak a minute or two on each side. Pour out cooking oil. Spread a tablespoon of margarine over the steak and sprinkle with salt and thyme. Place the garlic around the steak. Bake steak in 375° oven for 15 to 20 minutes. If steak is frozen, bake about 30 minutes. Remove steak to a warm platter. Skim excess grease, add bouillon or wine, and heat. Cook with or without garlic until liquid is desired consistency. Stir in butter until absorbed and pour over steak.
Easy method for steak more than 1½ inches thick and for frozen steaks more than an inch thick. Frozen steak should be thawed at room temperature for about an hour or until the outside has become slightly soft.
Serves 6.
Mrs. Cad E. Williams (Francis Bailey)

Brisket

1	8 to 10 lb. brisket	2	oz. liquid smoke
2	T. salt	1	16 oz. bottle barbecue
1	T. pepper		sauce
1	T. garlic salt	3	T. Worcestershire sauce
1	T. celery salt		

Prepare meat for cooking. Season with salt, celery salt, garlic salt, and black pepper. Wrap in foil and pour in liquid smoke and Worcestershie sauce. Place in refrigerator and marinate 12 to 24 hours. Cook covered in 200° oven about 10 hours. Drain off part of liquid and pour in barbecue sauce. Return to 200° oven, and cook 4 to 6 hours.
The amount of seasonings used may vary according to taste and size of brisket.
Serves 18 to 20. Freezes.
Mrs. Joe M. Reed (Potsie Eubanks)

Steak Sauteed with Crushed Peppercorns

4 boneless steaks, cut ¾ inch thick and well trimmed	1 T. oil for rubbing steaks
4 t. peppercorns or 1 T. cracked pepper	1 T. oil plus 2 T. butter for sauteing

Pat steaks dry with paper towels; rub with oil. Crush the peppercorns and press about ½ teaspoon on each side of steaks. Let steaks stand about 2 hours to allow pepper to season the meat. Saute steaks on each side in oil and butter to a medium rare. Remove to a heated serving platter.

Sauce

2 T. finely chopped green onions	1 t. cornstarch blended with ¼ c. beef bouillon
½ c. dry white wine	2 T. butter

Spoon out excess grease from skillet. Add all ingredients for sauce except the butter, and simmer until sauce thickens, scraping bottom of skillet. Stir butter into sauce and pour over steaks.
Serves 4.
Mrs. Cad E. Williams (Francis Bailey)

Deviled Round Steak

1½ lbs. round steak	Dash cayenne
Flour	1 t. prepared mustard
1 onion, minced	1 t. vinegar
1 garlic clove, minced	1 t. horseradish
3 T. shortening	½ c. tomato sauce
2 t. salt	1½ c. hot water
¼ t. pepper	

Cut steak into strips across the grain and roll in flour. Brown meat, onions, and garlic in shortening. Stir in 2 tablespoons flour and seasonings. Add remaining ingredients. Cover and simmer about 1 hour. Good with rice, noodles, or mashed potatoes.
Serves 4.
Mrs. Charles Stanton (Lisa Guarnieri)

Flaming Beef

2	lbs. boneless sirloin cut into 1¼ inch cubes	2	T. vinegar
2	onions, chopped	½	c. salad oil
1	clove garlic, crushed	2	t. salt
1	c. claret or Burgundy wine	½	t. pepper
		Dash cayenne pepper
		¼	t. oregano

Place beef cubes in large bowl and cover with marinade made of remaining ingredients and refrigerate several hours or overnight. Drain meat well, reserving marinade, and thread on skewers alternately with the following:

Onion pieces
Bite sized squares of green
 pepper

Red cherry tomatoes
Pineapple chunks
Fresh mushrooms

Grill on hot charcoal slowly and brush with marinade.
Serves 4.
Mrs. Gordon B. Broyles (Frances Dilley)

Beef Tips in Wine Sauce

1	lb. beef tips	1	T. flour
1	T. oil	2	T. whiskey or Cognac
1	T. butter	6	T. red wine

In a 10 inch skillet brown beef tips in oil and butter. Sprinkle in flour and lightly brown. Pour the whiskey over beef tips and flame. A WORD OF CAUTION: If pot is too hot, there will be a lot of flame. Add the wine and simmer covered until tender. This is also good with white wine and cream substituted for the red wine.
Serves 4.
Mrs. J. E. Johnston (Marie Orgeron)

 To slice meat into thin strips, as for stroganoff, partially freeze and it will slice easily.

Beef Stroganoff

2	lbs. beef sirloin, cubed	2	T. catsup
4	T. butter	¼	t. instant minced garlic
½	lb. mushrooms, sliced	1	t. salt
1	medium onion, finely chopped	½	c. water
		2	T. flour
1	c. water	1	c. sour cream
2	beef bouillon cubes		

In 12 inch skillet brown meat, mushrooms, and onion in butter. Stir in water, bouillon cubes, catsup, garlic, and salt. Reduce heat, cover, and simmer for 15 minutes. Mix ½ cup of water with flour. Stir into meat mixture. Bring to a boil and stir for 1 minute. Add sour cream and heat through. If preparing ahead, sour cream should be added when reheating. Serve over rice or noodles.
Serves 6.
Mrs. C. L. Kolstad, III (Jill McPherson)

Chinese Skillet Dinner

2	lbs. beef sirloin or round steak	1	large bell pepper, cut into strips
Lemon pepper to taste		1	c. sliced mushrooms
MSG to taste		1	14 oz. can Chinese vegetables, drained
Garlic salt to taste			
¼	c. salad oil	¼	c. soy sauce
1	large onion, sliced	2	T. honey

Cut meat into 1 to 2 inch strips, season, and brown in oil on high heat. Add the fresh vegetables and stir cook 2 to 3 minutes. Add the Chinese vegetables, soy sauce, and honey. Stir and cook about 1 minute to heat through. Serve over rice.
Serves 6.
Mrs. Jeff D. Walker (Katherine Kolstad)

Grillades (Gree-yahds)

3	lbs. veal or beef round steak, ½ inch thick	½	t. thyme
4	to 6 T. oil or bacon drippings	2	t. salt
		2	t. pepper
3	T. flour	2	oz. tomato sauce
2	large onions, chopped	1	beef bouillon cube
3	T. minced garlic	2	dashes Worcestershire
1	small green pepper, chopped		Tabasco to taste
			Cayenne to taste
1	stalk celery, chopped	3	c. hot water
1	large tomato, chopped, or one 14½ oz. can tomatoes, chopped and drained	½	c. chopped parsley

Trim fat and cut meat into 2 inch pieces. In a large heavy pot, brown meat in 1 to 2 tablespoons oil. Remove meat and set aside. Add more oil, 2 to 4 tablespoons, and about 3 tablespoons flour. Stir over medium heat to make a dark roux, about 10 minutes. *Be careful not to scorch.* If roux becomes too thick, add a little more oil. Add onions, garlic, green pepper, celery, and tomatoes. Saute until soft. Add thyme, salt, pepper, tomato sauce, bouillon, Worcestershire, Tabasco, cayenne pepper, and 3 cups hot water. Mix well, add browned meat, cover, and simmer about 2 hours. If sauce is too thick, add water; if too thin, remove lid the last 30 minutes of cooking. Meat should be tender enough to cut with a fork and gravy rather thick. Sprinkle with parsley. Serve over hot buttered grits.

If made a day or two ahead and refrigerated, the flavors of the Grillades will meld and improve.

Serves 6 to 8.

Mrs. Paul E. Elliott, Jr. (Ann Craft)

 Bruised greens can be used to keep rare meat rare during reheating. Line a baking pan with greens, layer leftover meat slices on top, then blanket with additional leaves. Warm about 10 minutes in a very slow oven.

Continental Steak Rolls with Sour Cream Sauce

1	lb. sirloin steak, thinly sliced	3	T. finely chopped mushrooms
¼	c. flour	3	T. finely chopped onion
¼	t. salt	1	8 oz. can refrigerated quick cresent dinner rolls
⅛	t. pepper		
2	T. shortening		

Sour Cream Sauce

1	c. sour cream	½	t. parsley flakes
1	T. butter	¼	t. salt

Cut steak into 4 rectangular pieces. Coat with mixture of flour, salt, and pepper; and lightly brown in shortening. Drain on absorbent paper. Saute mushrooms and onions. Place 1½ tablespoons of mixture on one end of browned meat; fold over the other end, covering mushroom mixture well. Unroll dough leaving 2 triangles joined to form a rectangle. Press at perforation to seal. Place meat in center of dough. Fold up sides and ends of dough, sealing edges tightly. Place seam side down on cookie sheet. Bake at 400° for 10 to 12 minutes or until golden brown.

Sour Cream Sauce Combine ingredients for sauce; heat thoroughly, but do not boil. Serve in separate dish along with the steak rolls.

Serves 4.

Mrs. John Ballard McDonald (Linda Cole)

Beef and Beans Across the Border

1	lb. pinto beans, cooked	2	dashes cayenne, optional
¼	c. shortening		Black pepper to taste
3	onions, chopped		Cinnamon or cumin to taste
2	lbs. ground beef	4	c. canned tomatoes
2	T. salt	3	green peppers, chopped
2	T. chili powder		

In a Dutch oven brown meat with seasonings and vegetables. Combine with beans and simmer approximately 30 minutes. May top each serving with shredded lettuce, grated cheese, guacamole, and chips.

Best made day ahead!

Serves 8 to 10.

Mrs. J. T. Davis, Jr. (Ann Weatherly)

Bavarian Beef Balls

⅓	c. water	⅓	t. salt
1	t. caraway seeds	⅛	t. pepper
2	lb. ground beef	½	t. dehydrated onion
1	c. well-drained finely	3	T. flour
	chopped sauerkraut	2	T. oil or shortening
1	egg		

Pour water over caraway seeds and let stand 5 minutes; combine ground beef, sauerkraut, egg, salt, pepper, onion, caraway seeds, and water. Mix well. Shape into 24 balls, allowing about 2 rounded tablespoons of mixture each. Roll balls in flour and brown in fat. Cover and let cook slowly for 30 minutes. Pour the following sauce over the cooked balls when ready to serve.

Sauce

⅔	c. sour cream	½	t. caraway seeds
2	T. milk	¼	t. salt

Combine all ingredients.
Yields 24 balls.
Mrs. Hugh Rives (Frances Corbett)

Beef and Eggplant Casserole

1	lb. lean ground meat	1	14 oz. can whole
1	large onion, chopped		tomatoes, chopped;
2	T. vegetable oil		reserve liquid
Salt and pepper to taste		1	6 oz. can tomato paste
2	medium eggplants	¼	c. water

Cook meat and onion in oil until meat is brown and onion tender. Season with salt and pepper. Set aside. Peel, quarter, and deep fry eggplants until golden brown. Remove from skillet and drain well. Place eggplant quarters in 3 quart casserole. Slit each quarter, widen the opening with a teaspoon, and fill with meat mixture until overflowing. Mix tomato paste with water to make a sauce; add tomatoes and reserved liquid. Pour sauce over the eggplants and bake uncovered at 350° approximately 30 minutes. Serve with rice.
Serves 8. Freezes.
Place covered casserole in cold oven; bake at 350° for 1 hour.
Mrs. William George, Jr. (June Haddad)

Beef and Zucchini Italian Supper

1 8 oz. pkg. noodles, firmly cooked and drained	1 16 oz. can stewed tomatoes
1¼ lb. ground beef	1 8 oz. can tomato sauce
1 c. chopped onion or 2 T. dried onion	1 t. salt
	½ t. seasoned salt
1 c. chopped celery and/or 1 c. chopped green pepper	¼ t. oregano
	¼ t. cayenne pepper
	½ c. water
1 clove garlic, minced	1 c. grated Cheddar cheese
1¼ lb. zucchini, sliced	

In a large skillet or Dutch oven, brown ground beef over medium heat until crumbly. Add onion, celery and /or green pepper, and garlic. Cook about 10 minutes or until meat is well browned. Add zucchini, tomatoes, tomato sauce, seasonings, and water. Cover and simmer until zucchini is tender but firm. Stir in noodles and cover to heat through. Top with cheese and continue to heat until cheese melts.
This one-dish meal needs only a salad, bread, and a sweet bite to complete it.
Serves 6 to 8.
Mrs. Lester Hamilton (Frances Edmunds)

Burgundy Spaghetti Casserole

1 lb. ground meat	¼ t. pepper
1 large onion, chopped	1 4 oz. can mushrooms, drained
1 28 oz. can tomatoes, chopped	¾ c. Burgundy wine
¼ t. thyme	½ lb. thin spaghetti, cooked
1 t. salt	¾ c. grated cheese
2 T. chili powder	

Brown meat in a large heavy pan. Add onion and cook until tender. Add tomatoes and juice, seasonings, mushrooms, and wine. Simmer for 10 minutes, add spaghetti, mix well, and pour into a 2 quart casserole. Top with cheese. Bake covered at 325° for 45 minutes. Uncover and bake 30 minutes more or until cheese is melted.
Serves 8 to 10. Freezes. If freezing casserole, omit cheese until baking time. To bake frozen casserole, pour one jigger of wine over ingredients before topping with cheese.
Mrs. Harvey Bell (Virginia Kimball)

Bohemian Cabbage Rolls

8	or more large cabbage leaves		Salt and pepper to taste
1	lb. ground beef	1	16 oz. can sauerkraut
¾	c. raw rice	1	8 oz. can tomato sauce
2	T. Worcestershire sauce	1	16 oz. can tomatoes
		1	T. caraway seeds

Place cabbage leaves in hot water until limp. Drain and remove heavy center part of each leaf. Mix ground beef, rice, onions, Worcestershire, and salt and pepper. Place enough meat mixture on each leaf to make a nice roll. Roll and tuck the leaf as you go along. Spread ½ can of sauerkraut in large heavy pot and place the cabbage rolls with seam sides down on top of the kraut. Fit the cabbage rolls snugly against each other so they won't come apart. If you make smaller rolls or increase the recipe, you may make a second layer. Place the remaining sauerkraut, tomatoes, tomato sauce, and caraway seeds on top of rolls. *Do not stir.* Bring to boil, reduce heat, cover, and simmer for 1½ to 2 hours. *Tastes better the second day.*
Serves 6 to 8. Freezes.
Mrs. Leland McReynolds (Annita Verzal)

Cabbage Rolls

1	large head cabbage or 2 small heads		Salt and pepper to taste
1½	lbs. coarse ground meat	6	T. lemon juice
1	c. long grain raw rice	3	garlic cloves, chopped
½	c. clarified butter		Dried or fresh mint

Core cabbage; place in boiling water and let leaves wilt. Separate. Cut the middle vein so cabbage will roll evenly. Mix meat, raw rice, butter, and salt and pepper. Put mixture on each cabbage leaf and roll. Stack in pot and pour boiling water over leaves. Add lemon juice and garlic. Sprinkle mint on top. Simmer covered for 1 hour.
Serves 6.
Mrs. Curtis Mann (Jay Nemer)

Cowboy Casserole

2	strips of bacon, chopped	1	16 oz. can pork and beans
1	medium onion, chopped		or Ranch Style beans
2	T. chopped bell pepper	½	t. mustard
1	lb. ground meat	1	t. salt
½	c. catsup	¼	t. pepper
½	c. dark corn syrup	1	T. Worcestershire sauce

In a large skillet saute bacon, onion, and bell pepper. Add ground beef and brown. Stir remaining ingredients into meat mixture and heat to bubbling. *Children love it!*
Serves 4.
Mrs. Dennis E. Ward (Jamie Brown)

Greek Macaroni Casserole

1	12 oz. pkg. elbow macaroni	1	8 oz. can tomato sauce
2	lbs. lean ground beef	2	tomato sauce cans of water
¼	c. margarine	1	recipe cheese sauce (follows)
1	large onion, diced		

Cook macaroni according to package directions. Grease a 9 x 13 casserole. Brown beef and onion in margarine; add salt and pepper and cook over heat until softened. Add tomato sauce and two cans of water. Cook until dry. Layer half the macaroni in the casserole, add meat mixture, remaining macaroni, and cover with cheese sauce. Bake uncovered at 350° until cheese lightly browns.

Cheese Sauce

4	c. milk		Salt and pepper to taste
3	T. corn starch	1	lb. processed cheese

Scald milk. Add small amount of hot milk to corn starch to make a paste. Add this paste to the milk, stirring constantly, and season with salt and pepper. Add cheese and stir over low heat until cheese melts.
Serves 8 to 10.
Mrs. W. T. Condos (Hazel Kojack)

Beef Rice Supreme

1½	lbs. ground chuck	½	c. water
1	onion, chopped	½	t. garlic salt
1	6 oz. box long grain and wild rice	½	t. celery salt
		¼	t. pepper
1	10¾ oz. can cream of mushroom soup	½	t. salt
			Grated cheese, optional
1	10¾ oz. can cream of chicken soup		

Brown meat and onion. Drain excess fat. Add rice, cooked according to directions, and remaining ingredients. Pour into a lightly greased 3 quart casserole. Cover and bake at 350° for 30 minutes. Uncover and continue to cook for an additional 15 minutes. May be topped with grated cheese during final baking time.
Serves 6 to 8. Freezes.
Mrs. Guy Keeling (Lucile DuPuy)

Mexican Casserole

3	lbs. lean ground beef	8	corn tortillas, quartered
1	large onion, chopped	2	c. small curd cottage cheese
1	clove garlic, minced		
¼	c. chili powder	1	egg
2	c. tomato sauce	1	lb. thinly sliced Monterey Jack cheese
1	10 oz. can Rotel tomatoes		
½	t. sugar	1	c. grated Cheddar cheese
1	t. salt	½	c. chopped green onions
1	c. sliced black olives	1	c. sour cream
1	4 oz. can diced green chilies, drained		Guacamole

Brown meat, onion, and garlic in a Dutch oven. Drain excess fat. Sprinkle chili powder over meat and mix well. Add tomato sauce, Rotel tomatoes, sugar, salt, olives, and green chilies. Simmer 15 minutes. Beat cottage cheese and egg together and set aside. Preheat oven to 350°. Spread ⅓ of meat mixture in bottom of a deep 3 quart casserole. Cover with ½ of the Monterey Jack cheese, ½ of cottage cheese mixture, and ½ of tortillas. Repeat, finishing with final layer of meat. Top with Cheddar cheese. Bake uncovered for about 30 minutes or until bubbly. Serve with chopped green onions, sour cream, and guacamole. Casserole can be prepared a day ahead and refrigerated.
Serves 8 to 10.
Mrs. C. L. Kolstad, III (Jill McPherson)

Mexican Cornbread with Ground Beef

1	lb. ground beef, browned	1	16 oz. can cream-style
1	c. yellow corn meal		yellow corn
1	c. milk	1	lb. Longhorn cheese,
2	eggs, beaten		grated
¾	t. salt	1	large onion, chopped
½	t. soda	4	jalapenos, seeded and
½	c. bacon drippings		chopped

Prepare cornbread batter by mixing together corn meal, milk, eggs, salt, soda, and bacon drippings. To this batter add corn and set mixture aside. Grease a 9 or 10 inch cast iron skillet, heat, sprinkle with meal, and allow to brown slightly. Pour half of corn meal batter in skillet. Sprinkle grated cheese evenly on batter and spread cooked meat on top of cheese. Add onion and pepper and top with remaining batter. Bake at 350° for 45 to 50 minutes. Serve hot. *Delicious served with pinto beans on cold winter evening!*
Serves 6.
Mrs. Max Alldredge (Martha Tettleton)

Skillet Spanish Rice with Beef

1	lb. ground beef	1	c. rice, well washed
1	c. chopped celery	1	8 oz. can tomato sauce
1	c. chopped green pepper	1¼	c. water
1	c. chopped onion		Salt to taste

In a Dutch oven brown meat. Drain excess fat. Spread celery evenly over meat. Season with a *little* salt. Layer green pepper over celery and again season with a little salt. Spread onion over green pepper, seasoning with salt. Spread rice over onions and lightly salt. Pour tomato sauce over rice and add water. Cover container and cook at low temperature for 45 minutes to 1 hour. *Do not peep!* At end of cooking time, carefully mix.
Serves 6.
Mrs. Werner K. Kuhne (Mary Jane McMahan)

South of the Border

1	large onion, chopped	2	t. chili powder
2	cloves garlic, minced	2	t. oregano
3	lbs. ground meat	2	t. ground cumin
1	16 oz. can tomato sauce	2	t. salt
2¼	c. water	2	t. MSG

Saute onions, garlic, and ground meat until browned. Add remaining ingredients. Simmer at least an hour.

Garnishes

2	onions, chopped	1	8 oz. jar chopped jalapeno peppers
2	avocados, chopped		
2	tomatoes, chopped	2	4 oz. cans taco sauce or one 8 oz. jar picante sauce
½	to 1 head lettuce, shredded		
		1	bell pepper, chopped
1	lb. sharp Cheddar cheese, grated	2	12 oz. bags regular Fritos
		1	16 oz. carton sour cream
2	c. chopped stuffed olives or ripe olives		

To serve, put Fritos on plate. Ladle meat sauce on Fritos to cover generously. Select garnishes. Top with sour cream.
Serves 8 or more.
Mrs. Gordon B. Broyles (Frances Dilley)

Tamale Pie

¼	c. vegetable oil	1	17 oz. can yellow cream-style corn
2	medium onions, diced		
1	clove garlic, diced	2	T. chili powder
1	lb. ground meat	3	eggs, beaten
1	28 oz. can tomatoes, undrained	1½	c. yellow corn meal
		2	t. salt

Brown onions, garlic, and meat in a 4 quart saucepan. Add tomatoes, corn, and chili powder. Cook for 15 minutes. Add eggs, corn meal, and salt. Simmer 15 minutes. Pour into a 2½ quart greased casserole, and bake at 375° for 40 minutes.
Serves 8.
Mrs. Ben L. Slack (Alice Jeffrey)

Winter Casserole

1½	lbs. ground meat	2	t. chili powder
½	lb. sausage	1	T. Worcestershire sauce
1	medium onion, chopped	1	6 oz. can pitted ripe
1	green pepper, chopped		olives
1	4 oz. can sliced	1	10 oz. pkg. egg noodles,
	mushrooms, drained		cooked
3	8 oz. cans tomato sauce	1	c. grated cheese
1	c. water		

Brown ground meat and sausage. Drain fat. Add next 8 ingredients. Mix well and simmer for 2 hours. Combine noodles and meat sauce. Pour into a 2 quart casserole, top with grated cheese, and bake at 350° for 20 to 30 minutes. Freezes but omit cheese until ready to bake.
Serves 12. Freezes.
Mrs. Dick Hartt (Dorothy Marshall)

Beef Pot Pie

3	T. butter	2	T. chopped parsley
1	large onion, chopped		Pinch of thyme
1½	c. cooked cubed meat	1	t. Worcestershire sauce
1	T. flour	2	T. sherry
1	c. rich meat stock		Salt and pepper to taste
1	c. cooked diced potatoes		Pastry topping
½	c. cooked peas and carrots		

Melt butter, saute onions, add meat, and cook until brown. Sprinkle with flour and gradually add stock (bouillon cube may be substituted). Stir constantly until thickened. Add remaining ingredients and blend. Place in lightly greased 10 inch deep dish pie plate. Top with frozen pie crust or favorite pastry topping. Bake at 350° about 30 minutes.
Great for leftover meat!
Serves 4.
Mrs. Joe Ed Johnston (Marilyn Hardgrave)

Beef and Okra

1 lb. okra, washed and cut	1 6 oz. can tomato paste
Butter	Salt and pepper to taste
2 lbs. stew meat	1 14 oz. can whole tomatoes
2 large onions, sliced	

Saute okra in butter until golden brown. Set aside to drain. Brown meat and onions. Add tomato paste and enough water to make a sauce. Season with salt and pepper. Add tomatoes, bring to a boil, lower heat, and simmer until meat is tender. Add okra and continue simmering for ten minutes. Serve over rice.
Serves 6 to 8.
Mrs. William George, Jr. (June Haddad)

No Peek Casserole

2 lbs. stew meat	
1 10¾ oz. can cream of	½ c. red wine
mushroom soup	1 pkg. onion soup mix
1 4 oz. can mushrooms,	Rice or noodles
drained	

Mix ingredients and pour into a casserole. Cover with a tight fitting lid. Bake 3 hours at 300°. *Do not peek!* Serve over cooked rice or noodles. One 14½ oz. can clear beef broth can be substituted for the wine.
Serves 6. Freezes.
Mrs. Jeff D. Walker (Katherine Kolstad)

Sauteed Liver

1	lb. calf liver	3	T. margarine
Buttermilk		½	c. sliced onion
Corn meal		1	T. water

Slice calf liver in one-third inch strips. Wipe with a damp cloth. Soak in buttermilk for 30 minutes. Remove skin and veins. Dip in corn meal and set aside. Heat margarine in skillet. Saute onions until golden. Remove onions, add liver, and saute 2 minutes on each side or until brown. Place liver on warm platter. Return onions to skillet, and add 1 tablespoon of water. When it bubbles up, pour over liver.
Serves 4.
Mrs. Edwin W. Link (Ann Seymour)

Borju Porkolt (Veal Paprika)

2	lbs. veal cutlets, sliced thin	1	T. sweet paprika
		1	c. water
2	T. butter	1	c. heavy cream
1	garlic clove, minced	½	t. salt

Pound veal well. Pat dry with absorbent paper. Melt butter; brown veal quickly with garlic and paprika. Add water, cover, and simmer for 1 hour. Add cream and salt; heat thoroughly and serve.
Serves 4 to 6.
Mrs. Charles Stanton (Lisa Guarnieri)

Veal Scaloppine in Wine

2   lbs. veal steak   2   bouillon cubes dissolved
Salt and pepper to taste   in 1 c. hot water
Flour   ½   c. dry white wine
6   T. vegetable oil   Fresh parsley sprigs
6   T. butter

Pound the steak until it is thin and cut into 8 scallops. Salt and pepper these lightly and dredge in flour. Use 2 skillets of similar size with 3 tablespoons each of oil and butter in each skillet. Cook the veal quickly on medium heat, turning frequently. Add bouillon and half of the wine in equal parts to each skillet. Cover and simmer for 10 minutes. Transfer to a meat platter. To the liquid left in one skillet, add the remaining wine. Stir and pour over the meat. Garnish with fresh parsley.

This may be prepared for later use by postponing simmering and reserving ¼ cup wine. Store in the refrigerator until just before serving time, then simmer, and add remaining wine.

The beauty of this recipe is that round steak may be substituted for the veal. If round steak is used, trim off fat and pound a great deal until steak is very thin. The steak may be covered by an old tea towel during the pounding to avoid a great deal of spattering. Cook exactly as you do the veal except continue to simmer the meat covered until tender. When served, it is difficult to tell the round steak is not veal!
Serves 4.
Mrs. John E. Presley (Lucinda Hanks)

Char Sui

1   3 to 4 lb. boneless pork   6   T. honey
    loin   1   t. dry mustard
1   c. soy sauce   1   clove garlic
½   to 1 c. bourbon

Place boneless pork loin in heavy duty baggie. Combine remaining ingredients for marinade and pour over loin. Tie securely. Place in refrigerator and turn baggie frequently for several hours or overnight. Bake at 300° for 2 hours or until done. If marinating period has been short, baste loin frequently during cooking time. Basting is not necessary during cooking time if marinated overnight. Slice thin for sandwiches. The marinade keeps indefinitely if refrigerated.
Mrs. Clyde Hanks (Howard Kolstad), Houston, Texas

Casserole of Lamb

1	c. rice	2	c. water
2	c. salted hot water	4	T. margarine
2	lbs. lean beef or lamb, cubed	1	large head cauliflower
1	large onion, chopped	Salt and pepper to taste	

Soak rice in water. In 12 inch skillet brown meat and onion in margarine. Add water and cook until meat is done. Add more water if necessary. In separate skillet break up cauliflower and saute in margarine; remove from skillet and drain well. Add cauliflower to the meat. Layer drained rice over cauliflower and add enough water to cover. Salt and pepper to taste. Bring to boil and simmer covered for approximately 20 minutes.
This could be served as a one dish meal.
Serves 4 to 6.
Mrs. W. T. Condos (Hazel Kojack)

Marinade of Pork Ribs

4	lbs. pork ribs	3	T. brown sugar
⅓	c. lemon juice	2	t. Worcestershire sauce
¼	c. soy sauce	½	t. ground ginger
¼	c. vinegar	½	t. garlic powder
¼	c. honey		

Cut pork ribs into serving pieces. Pour marinade over ribs and refrigerate overnight, turning over once. Two hours before serving, bake ribs uncovered in sauce in a 325° oven for 1 hour. Remove ribs from sauce, place on rack, and continue baking for 1 hour. During the last 30 minutes of baking, brush with favorite barbecue sauce. Ribs are done when meat begins to pull away from bone.
Serves 4.
Mrs. Leo F. Mizell (Muriel Murphy)

Sweet and Sour Pork

1 lb. pork shoulder, cut into ¾ inch cubes	Oil for deep frying

Batter

2 eggs	1 t. salt
1 c. flour	½ c. water

Sauce

1 c. pineapple chunks	¾ c. water
1 green pepper, cut into squares	¼ c. firmly packed brown sugar
½ c. vinegar	1 T. molasses

Thickening

2 T. cornstarch	¼ c. water

Prepare batter. Heat oil in 10 inch frying pan. Dip pork cubes into batter and drop into hot oil. When pork browns, remove and drain. Mix ingredients for sauce and bring slowly to a boil, stirring constantly. Pour thickening into sauce. When thick and smooth, add meat and mix well. Serve hot with rice.
Serves 4.
Mrs. Charles Stanton (Lisa Guarnieri)

Deviled Pork Chops

4 1 inch thick butterfly pork chops	2 T. salad oil
2 T. prepared mustard	1 10¾ oz. can cream of chicken soup
Flour	

Spread both sides of each pork chop with mustard. Dip in flour to coat. Brown in hot oil in skillet. Transfer to ovenproof baking dish. Top with undiluted soup. Cover tightly. Bake at 350° for 1 hour.
Serves 4.
Mrs. S. M. Kenderdine (Jane Kukar)

Hawaiian Pork Chops

4	pork chops	1	8 oz. can crushed
3	T. brown sugar		pineapple
2	T. corn starch	1	T. soy sauce
½	c. catsup	Pinch salt	
1	T. vinegar		

Place pork chops in an 8 inch square pan. Combine other ingredients in a saucepan. Bring to a boil and pour over pork chops. Cover and bake in a 350° oven for 1 hour and 15 minutes.
Serves 4.
Mrs. Leo F. Mizell (Muriel Murphy)

Orange Pork Chops

4	thinly cut pork chops	¼	t. pepper
½	c. orange juice	½	t. dry mustard
1	t. salt	¼	c. brown sugar

Place pork chops in baking pan. Mix all other ingredients. Pour over pork chops. Bake at 350° for 1 hour, basting occasionally.
Serves 4.
Mrs. C. L. Kolstad, III (Jill McPherson)

Pork Chops with Scalloped Potatoes

6	pork chops, ½ inch thick	¼	t. pepper
1	T. cooking oil	½	c. chopped green onion
5	c. sliced, pared potatoes	1	10¾ oz. can cream of
6	1 oz. slices processed		celery soup
	American cheese	1¼	c. milk
1	t. salt		

Brown pork chops on one side in hot oil. Remove chops as they brown; reserve drippings. Place half of potatoes in greased 13 x 9 x 2 baking pan. Top with cheese slices and remaining potatoes. Place pork chops, brown-ed side up, on potatoes. Sprinkle with salt and pepper. Cook onions in pan drippings in skillet until tender but not brown. Add soup and milk. Heat and pour over chops. Cover with aluminum foil. Bake in 350° oven 1 hour. Remove cover and continue baking 30 minutes or until meat and vegetables are tender.
Serves 4 to 6.
Mrs. Dennis E. Ward (Jamie Brown)

Ham and Artichoke Rolls

12	thin slices boiled or baked ham	½	t. nutmeg
			Paprika
2	16 oz. cans artichoke hearts, drained		Pinch of white pepper
4	T. butter	1⅓	c. Swiss and Parmesan cheese, grated and
4	T. flour		mixed together
2	c. warm milk	4	T. dry white wine
Dash seasoned salt		⅔	c. buttered bread crumbs
Dash cayenne pepper			

Wrap artichoke hearts in ham and place in buttered oblong 2 quart baking dish. (If hearts are large, cut in half and wrap 2 halves in a slice of ham.) Melt butter over medium heat; blend in flour until smooth. Gradually stir in milk and cook until thickened. Add seasonings and half of the cheese mixture. Heat until melted. Remove from heat and stir in wine. Pour sauce over ham and top with bread crumbs and remaining cheese. Bake at 350° for 25 to 30 minutes or until brown.
Serves 6. Freezes.
Mrs. David G. Bucher (Cynthia Westfahl)

Ham Muffins

1	egg, beaten	½	lb. boiled or baked ham, ground
1	c. milk		
12	crackers, crumbled	½	lb. sharp Cheddar cheese, grated

Add milk and crackers to beaten egg. Let stand a few minutes until crackers are soft. Add ham and cheese. Mix well. Place mixture in greased muffin pans. Bake in 350° oven for 25 minutes. Let cool for 5 minutes before removing from muffin pans. Serve on a nest of chow mein noodles, cooked rice, or toast points. Pour heated undiluted mushroom soup over each muffin. **Yields 12 muffins.**
Serves 8.
Mrs. Joe G. Laumen, Jr. (Nancy Simpson)

Ham Roll Ups

1	10¾ oz. can condensed cream of celery soup	1	c. small curd cottage cheese
1	c. sour cream	2	eggs
2	T. Dijon-style mustard	½	c. finely chopped onion
1	c. quick-cooking rice	¼	c. unsifted flour
1	10 oz. pkg. frozen chopped spinach, thawed and drained well	18	slices (1½ lbs.) boiled ham
			Parsley buttered bread crumbs
			Paprika

In a small bowl, mix soup, sour cream, and mustard. In a medium bowl, combine ½ cup soup mixture, rice, spinach, cheese, eggs, onion, and flour; mix well. Place about 2 heaping tablespoons spinach mixture on each ham slice. Roll up and place close together, seam-side down, in an 11 x 7 baking dish. Spoon remaining soup mixture over ham rolls. Top with crumbs and sprinkle with paprika. Bake uncovered at 350° approximately 30 minutes or until heated through.
Serves 8. Freezes.
Mrs. Max Alldredge (Martha Tettleton)

Sausage and Wild Rice Casserole

1   c. wild rice, washed well   1   10¾ oz. can cream of
1   lb. bulk sausage   mushroom soup
2   3 oz. cans sliced   1   medium onion, thinly
     mushrooms, drained   sliced

Cook rice until tender but not mushy. Drain. Cook sausage until crumbly.
Pour off fat. Stir in mushrooms and soup. Add to rice. Put half of rice mix-
ture in a 2 quart buttered casserole. Top with onion. Put remaining rice mix-
ture over the onion. Cover casserole and bake in 350° oven for 1 hour.
Serves 4.
Mrs. W. H. Shuller, Jr. (Mary Plemons)

Sausage Stuffed Onions

8   large Bermuda onions   1½ c. crumbled cornbread
      (white and flat)   3   T. chopped parsley
1½ lbs. bulk sausage   ¼   c. melted margarine
1½ c. chopped celery   Parmesan cheese

Peel onions; cut ½ inch off tops. Remove centers of onions leaving a shell
¼ to ½ inch thick. Brush inside and out with vegetable oil. Arrange in a
steamer 4 at a time. (A collander may be used as a substitute for the steamer.
Place collander into a cooking pot with about 4 inches of water in the bottom.) Steam until just fork tender. Remove from steamer, salt lightly, and
arrange in a shallow 2 quart casserole. Saute sausage and celery. Add bread
crumbs, parsley, and margarine. Drain off excess fat. Fill onions with sausage
mixture. Sprinkle with Parmesan cheese and bake uncovered in 425° oven
20 minutes or until sausage is browned.
Serves 8.
May B. Bachtel, M.D. (May Bradley)

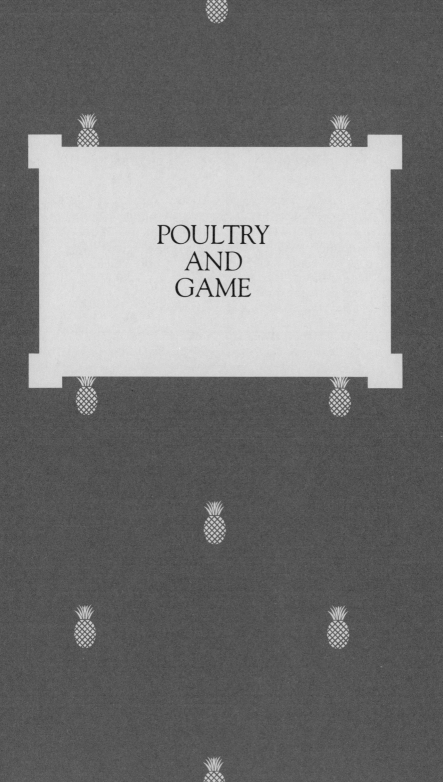

POULTRY
AND
GAME

Oven "Fried" Chicken

2	lb. frying chicken, quartered	1	t. onion powder
¾	c. plain pancake mix	1	t. MSG
1	t. celery salt	1	t. paprika
		⅔	c. hot water

Clean chicken, rinse, pat dry, and set aside. Combine remaining ingredients in a shallow 9 x 13 dish, stirring only until blended. Dip or roll chicken pieces in batter until lightly coated; the remaining batter may be spread on chicken. Place chicken, skin side up, in a nonstick roasting pan. Bake in a preheated 375° oven for 50 to 60 minutes, until chicken is brown and crispy and tender inside; turn twice during the cooking. Blot the chicken pieces in paper toweling and serve.
Excellent for the calorie counters.
Serves 4 to 6.
Mrs. Robert D. Harrell (Beverly Tucker)

Oven Fried Chicken with Coconut

4	chicken drumsticks	1	t. salt
4	chicken thighs	¾	c. flaked or shredded coconut
1	egg		
2	T. frozen pineapple or orange juice concentrate, thawed	½	c. dried bread crumbs
		¼	c. butter, melted

In shallow dish mix egg, undiluted pineapple or orange juice, and salt. In another shallow dish mix coconut, bread crumbs, and butter. With tongs, roll chicken in pineapple or orange mixture, then press into coconut mixture until well coated. Place in 13 x 9 baking pan. Bake at 400° for 40 to 50 minutes until chicken is fork tender.
Serves 4.
Mrs. Howard T. Winkler (Joyce Bell)

 For a brown crust on roasted chicken, rub mayonnaise over the skin before cooking.

Chicken Nuggets

3	whole boneless chicken breasts	1	t. salt
½	c. dried bread crumbs	1	t. dried thyme or ¼ t. powdered thyme
¼	c. grated Parmesan cheese	1	t. dried basil
2	t. MSG	½	c. melted margarine

Cut each breast into 6 to 8 pieces, about ½ inch in size. Combine bread crumbs, cheese, MSG, salt, and herbs. Dip chicken in melted margarine, and then in crumbs. Shape into nuggets. Place in single layer on foil-lined baking sheet. Bake at 400° for 15 to 20 minutes.
Serves 4 to 6 as main course or 12 hor d'oeuvres.
Mrs. W. Lamar Hamilton (Kitty Davey)

Chicken Elegante

4	chicken breasts	1	10¾ oz. can cream of chicken soup
½	c. flour	¾	c. milk
1	t. salt	1	c. mushroom buttons
1	t. paprika	¼	c. toasted slivered almonds
¼	t. pepper		
½	c. vegetable oil		

Sift together flour, salt, paprika, and pepper. Coat chicken in mixture. Heat oil in skillet. Brown chicken on all sides. Arrange chicken in 9 x 13 inch baking dish. Combine soup with milk and pour over chicken. Cover and bake in 325° oven for 45 minutes or until tender. Add mushrooms and almonds during last 15 minutes of baking.
Serves 4.
Mrs. John A. Fitzgerald (Thyra Prince)

Chicken Kiev

4	chicken breasts, halved	½	t. salt
½	lb. butter	¼	t. white pepper
2	T. chopped chives	¼	c. flour
2	T. chopped parsley	1	egg, beaten
1	minced clove garlic,		Dry bread crumbs
	optional		

Preheat deep fryer to 325°. Bone chicken breasts and remove skins. Place one breast at a time, boned side up, between pieces of plastic wrap. Using the flat side of a meat mallet or a rolling pin, flatten each until about ¼ inch thick; peel off wrap. Flatten remaining breasts in same way. Form butter into 8 balls. Roll butter balls lightly in a mixture of chives, parsley, salt, white pepper, and garlic. Place one of the seasoned butter balls in the center of each half breast and roll so that the butter is completely enclosed. Secure with a toothpick, if necessary. Dust with flour. Brush with beaten egg. Roll in dry bread crumbs. Fry in deep fat until golden brown, about 5 to 7 minutes. For hearty appetites or when light side dishes are planned, allow 2 per serving.
Serves 8.
Mrs. Alexander Nemer, II (Vicki Burke)

Chicken with Dried Beef

6	chicken breasts, boned	1	10¾ oz. can cream of
¾	lb. dried chipped beef		mushroom soup
6	strips lean bacon		Pepper to taste
		¼	c. sherry

Arrange dried beef in bottom of shallow casserole. Wrap a strip of bacon around each chicken breast and arrange over beef. Spread undiluted soup over chicken, cover with aluminum foil, and bake at 300° for 2 hours. Increase heat to 350° and bake for another 20 to 30 minutes, basting several times.
Serves 6.
Mrs. Ben Swinney (Linda Jenkins)

Chili Powder Chicken

6	chicken thighs		Salt
6	chicken breasts		Chili powder
2	T. salt	2	10¾ oz. cans golden
2	c. sifted flour		mushroom soup

Mix 2 tablespoons salt with enough cold water to cover chicken thighs and breasts. Soak chicken in water for 2 hours. Drain and clean. Roll chicken in flour and sprinkle each piece with salt and chili powder. Place chicken in two well oiled 13 x 9 inch baking dishes. Spread mushroom soup over chicken. Cover with foil, leaving about 1 inch open at one end. Bake at 375° for 1½ to 2 hours.
Serves 8.
Mrs. Wayne Walker (Katherine Cray)

Hawaiian Baked Chicken

1	8 oz. can sliced pineapple	2	to 2½ lbs. fryer pieces
⅓	c. Heinz 57 Sauce		Salt and pepper
2	T. honey		

Drain pineapple reserving 2 tablespoons juice. Mix juice with 57 sauce and honey. Season chicken with salt and pepper. Place in 12 x 7½ inch dish. Cover with sauce. Bake in 350° oven for 1 hour or until tender, basting occasionally. Arrange pineapple slices on top of chicken during last 5 to 10 minutes of baking.
Serves 4.
Mrs. Bob Stephenson (Sandra Durham)

Mandarin Chicken Breasts

1	11 oz. can mandarin oranges		Salt and pepper
6	boned chicken breasts	¼	c. melted butter or margarine
6	t. soft butter or margarine	1	T. chopped onion
6	t. minced onion	2	T. flour
¼	c. fine dry bread crumbs	½	c. sake or extra dry sherry
¼	c. flour		

Drain mandarin oranges, reserving syrup. Lay each chicken breast flat. Spread each with 1 teaspoon butter, several mandarin orange segments, and a teaspoon chopped onion. Sprinkle with salt and pepper. Roll up each breast and secure with toothpicks. Combine bread crumbs, flour, salt, and pepper. Roll chicken breasts in crumb mixture. Place in roasting pan, brush with melted butter, and bake at 500° for 15 minutes basting often. When chicken breasts are golden brown, remove to platter. Drain off all but 2 tablespoons of drippings from pan. Add remaining onion. Stir in 2 tablespoons flour, add sake or sherry, remaining orange sections, and syrup. Return the chicken breasts to roasting pan, and bake 5 more minutes.
Serves 6.
Mrs. Charles Palmer, Jr. (Inez Hawkins)

Party Chicken Bake

4	whole chicken breasts, may be deboned	1	0.8 oz. pkg. Italian salad dressing mix
3	T. melted butter	½	c. Sauterne or dry sherry
1	10¾ oz. can cream of mushroom soup, undiluted	1	8 oz. carton whipped cream cheese and chives

Brown chicken breasts in butter and place in a 9 x 9 baking dish. Stir remaining ingredients into browning butter and mix thoroughly. Pour over chicken and bake at 300° for 45 to 60 minutes. You may increase this for as many people as necessary. Allow a little more baking time. May be prepared ahead and baked later.
Serves 6 to 8.
Mrs. Ed Montgomery (Dorothy Meador)

Pollo Alla Cacciatore

¼	c. olive oil	1	t. salt
1	2½ to 3 lb. chicken, cut up	½	t. celery seed
		¼	t. pepper
2	onions, sliced	1	t. crushed dried oregano
2	garlic cloves, minced	2	bay leaves
1	16 oz. can Italian tomatoes	½	c. dry white wine
			Parmesan cheese
1	8 oz. can tomato sauce		

Heat oil in large, deep skillet. Brown chicken. Remove chicken and keep hot. Saute onions and garlic in oil in skillet until tender. Add other ingredients, except wine, and blend. Cook for 5 minutes. Return chicken to skillet. Cover and simmer 45 minutes. Add wine and cook uncovered for 15 minutes. Arrange on hot platter. Skim excess fat from sauce and remove bay leaves. Pour sauce over chicken. Serve over spaghetti, noodles, or rice with a sprinkling of cheese.
Serves 4 to 6. Freezes.
Mrs. Lucylle Pope MacNaughton

Chicken Casserole

1	c. diced, cooked chicken breast	½	c. slivered toasted almonds
½	c. mayonnaise	1	t. minced onion, or to taste
1	10¾ oz. can cream of chicken soup	½	c. cracker crumbs
2	hard-cooked eggs, diced	2	T. Worcestershire sauce
1	c. finely chopped celery		Crushed potato chips for topping

Mix and bake in 2 quart casserole about 20 minutes in 350° oven. If doubling recipe, add potato chips last 10 minutes.
Serves 6.
Mrs. John A. Fitzgerald (Thyra Prince)

Chicken Curry

1	4 to 5 lb. stewing chicken	2	medium onions, sliced
1	large onion, quartered	1	medium tomato, peeled,
4	whole cloves		seeded, and chopped
1	large carrot, diced	6	T. flour
	coarsely	2	T. curry powder
3	celery stalks with leaves,	½	t. ground cardamon
	coarsely chopped	½	t. ground ginger
2	T. chopped parsley	½	t. freshly ground pepper
8	peppercorns		Grated rind and juice of 1 lime
2	bay leaves	¼	c. seedless raisins
1½	t. salt	½	c. grated sweetened
½	c. dry white wine or as		coconut
	needed	½	c. light cream
½	c. butter	2	T. chopped chutney
2	cloves garlic, minced		
1	green apple, pared and		
	chopped		

Condiments

Chopped hard-cooked eggs	Quartered limes
Chopped peanuts	Crumbled crisp bacon
Coconut	Grated orange rind
Chutney	Freshly chopped mint
Chopped banana	Raisins
Chopped green onions	Chopped green peppers
Chopped almonds	

Place chicken in a large pot and cover with water. Stick a clove into each onion quarter; and add to pot with carrot, celery, parsley, peppercorns, bay leaf, and 1 teaspoon salt. Bring to a gentle boil and simmer for 2½ hours or until chicken is tender. Cool in stock. Remove chicken, skin and bone the meat, and cut into bite-size pieces. Strain enough stock to make 1½ cups. To that liquid add ½ cup white wine. (You may reserve another cup of the stock to adjust the consistency of the curry at the end.) Set these aside.

Melt butter in a large skillet and add garlic. When hot add apple, sliced onions, and tomato. Cover and simmer for 8 to 10 minutes or until tender. Combine flour, curry, cardamon, ginger, remaining ½ teaspoon salt, and pepper. Stir into vegetables, mixing well. Cook and stir for 3 minutes until well blended. Slowly add chicken stock and wine, grated lime rind, juice, and raisins. Add chicken, coconut, and chutney. Heat over low heat for 15 minutes. At this point mixture may be cooled and refrigerated for reheating the next day. Serve with rice and 6 or more condiments. If you like a hotter curry, season to taste with cayenne and black pepper.

This recipe is remarkably easy, tastes like real Indian curry, and doubles beautifully for a party.

Serves 8.

Mrs. John E. Presley (Lucinda Hanks)

Chelsea Chicken

2 young roasting chickens	Salt
1 carrot	2 to 4 peppercorns
A bouquet garni	Water and a little white wine to cover

Cream of Curry Sauce

1 T. oil	Salt, sugar, and a touch of pepper
¼ c. finely chopped onion	pepper
2 T. curry powder	1 or 2 slices lemon
1 t. tomato puree	A squeeze of lemon juice or more
5 oz. red wine	more
4 oz. water	1 to 2 T. apricot puree
1 bay leaf	¾ pt. mayonnaise
	2 to 3 T. lightly whipped cream

Poach the chickens with carrot, bouquet, salt, and peppercorns in water and a little wine to cover for about 40 minutes or until tender. Allow to cool in liquid. Joint the birds, and remove the bones with care.

Sauce Heat the oil, add onion, and cook gently for 3 to 4 minutes. Add curry powder and cook for 1 to 2 minutes. Add tomato puree, wine, water, and bay leaf. Bring to a boil; add salt, sugar, and pepper to taste. Add lemon and lemon juice. Simmer with the pan uncovered for 5 to 10 minutes. Strain and cool. Add the curry mixture by degrees to the mayonnaise with the apricot puree to taste. Adjust seasoning, adding a little more lemon juice if necessary. Finish with whipped cream. Mix chicken with a small amount of sauce (just enough to coat chicken). Arrange on a platter and coat with extra sauce.

Serves 6 to 8.

Mrs. B. T. S. Clarke, Chelsea, London, England

Chicken Chow Mein

⅓ c. vegetable oil
1 clove garlic, pressed
2 c. thinly sliced celery
1 small green pepper, thinly sliced
6 scallions, thinly sliced
1 c. thinly sliced water chestnuts
1 c. bamboo shoots
½ c. mushrooms

2 c. chicken stock
1½ t. sugar
2 c. cooked, diced chicken
3 T. soy sauce
3 T. cornstarch dissolved in 3 T. water
1½ t. salt
2 c. bean sprouts
2 3 oz. cans Chow Mein Noodles

Heat oil and add next 9 ingredients. Bring to a boil and cook for 10 minutes. Add remaining ingredients, heat, and serve over Chow Mein noodles. When preparing ahead, omit bean sprouts and add to heated mixture at serving time.
Serves 5 to 6. Freezes.
Mrs. Jack H. Hanks (Jackie Rayburn)

Herbed Chicken

2 chickens cut into pieces
1½ t. salt or to taste
Pepper to taste
Paprika to taste
½ c. margarine
1 8 oz. can sliced mushrooms and liquid

½ c. dry red wine or sherry
1 t. each rosemary, thyme, and marjoram
Water or chicken broth, optional

Wash and dry chickens. Sprinkle with salt, pepper, and paprika. Melt butter in skillet and brown chicken. Pour mushroom liquid and wine over chicken. Sprinkle with herbs, cover, reduce heat, and simmer for one hour or until tender. Baste several times during cooking period, adding water or chicken broth if necessary. Add mushrooms last 10 to 15 minutes of cooking time.
Serves 6 to 8.
Mrs. Daniel F. Rex (Emory Hill)

Chicken Delight

4 c. diced cooked chicken
1 6 oz. pkg. long grain and
 wild rice, cooked
1 onion chopped
1 c. chopped celery
1 T. margarine
1 10¾ oz. can cream of
 mushroom soup

1 4 oz. jar sliced pimiento,
 drained
1 8 oz. can sliced water
 chestnuts, drained
1 c. mayonnaise
1 16 oz. can French style
 green beans
2 t. lemon juice
1 or 2 dashes Tabasco
Salt and pepper to taste

Cook rice according to package directions. Saute onion and celery in margarine. Combine rice, onion, celery, and all other ingredients. Fold in chicken. Pour mixture into a 2½ or 3 quart casserole. Bake in 350° oven for 25 to 30 minutes. May sprinkle with Chinese noodles before baking.
Serves 12.
Cookbook Committee

Chicken Loaf

4 c. diced cooked chicken
1 c. cooked rice
1½ c. milk
1½ c. chicken broth
4 eggs, beaten

2 c. seasoned bread crumbs
2 T. pimiento
1 t. salt
¾ c. chopped celery

Mix chicken, rice, milk, broth, eggs, bread crumbs, pimiento, salt, and celery. Pour into a greased 9 x 5 inch loaf pan. Refrigerate overnight. Bake at 350° for 1 hour.

Sauce
¼ c. butter
4 T. flour
2 c. chicken broth
1 c. light cream

1 T. parsley
1 4 oz. can mushrooms,
 drained

Melt butter, add flour, and blend. Heat liquids and add to roux. Add parsley and mushrooms. Serve over chicken loaf.
Serves 12.
Mrs. Joe N. Davis (Marguerite Dellis)

Chihuahua Chicken

½ c. cottage cheese
3 oz. cream cheese
½ c. sour cream
1 10¾ oz. can cream of chicken soup
1 t. salt
⅛ t. garlic powder
1 4 oz. can diced green chiles

3 c. coarsely diced cooked chicken
3 c. cooked rice (cook in chicken broth)
1 c. grated Monterey Jack cheese
2 tomatoes, coarsely chopped
¾ c. crushed corn chips

Blend 3 cheeses until smooth. Add mixture to remaining ingredients except corn chips. Pour into shallow 2 quart baking dish. Sprinkle with corn chips. Bake in 350° oven for 25 to 30 minutes.
Serves 6. Freezes.
Mrs. R. L. Kenderdine (Daphne Dunning)

Chicken Ratatouille

¼ c. corn oil
2 chicken breasts, boned, skinned, and cut in 1 inch pieces
2 small zucchini, thinly sliced
1 small eggplant, peeled, cut in 1 inch cubes
1 large onion, thinly sliced

1 medium green pepper, cut in 1 inch pieces
½ lb. mushrooms, sliced
1 16 oz. can tomato wedges
1 t. each garlic salt, MSG, dried sweet basil, dried parsley
½ t. pepper

Heat oil, add chicken, and saute 2 minutes to a side. Add zucchini, eggplant, onion, green pepper, and mushrooms. Stir often during 15 minutes of cooking or until tender crisp. Then add tomatoes and seasonings and simmer 5 minutes until chicken is tender. Serve with rice.
Serves 4.
Mrs. Warren S. Emerson (Una Ramsey)

Company Chicken Casserole

2	c. diced cooked chicken	1	8½ oz. can English peas, drained
2¼	c. herb stuffing mix		
½	c. milk or broth	1	T. minced onion
		1	10¾ oz. can cream of celery soup

Butter a 9 x 11 inch casserole. Mix 1½ cups herb stuffing mix, milk or broth, chicken, peas, and onion and pour into casserole. Spread soup over this mixture, and top with remaining stuffing. Bake at 425° for 15 minutes. Serves 6.
Mrs. J. W. Sims (Lena Mae Roquemore)

Company Casserole

6	T. butter	2½	c. coarsely chopped cooked chicken
6	T. flour		
1	t. salt	8½	oz. can cooked sliced carrots
½	t. pepper		
2	c. chicken broth	8½	oz. can English peas
1	c. evaporated milk	2	T. chopped onions
		1	2 oz. jar pimiento

Melt butter and blend in flour, salt, and pepper. Gradually add chicken broth. Cook, stirring constantly until thickened. Remove from heat and gradually blend in milk. Add chicken, carrots, peas, onions, and pimientos. Pour in 13 x 9 inch casserole. Top with cheese whirls.

Cheese Whirls for Company Casserole

1½	c. sifted flour	6	T. shortening
¾	t. salt	½	c. milk
2	t. baking powder	1	c. grated sharp cheese

Sift dry ingredients and cut in shortening until it has the consistency of small peas. Stir in milk. Knead with enough flour until soft, not sticky. Roll out into large rectangle. Sprinkle with cheese to cover rectangle. Rollup, jelly roll fashion, and cut into 18 sections. Make three rows on top of casserole with 6 sections in each row. Place casserole on cooking sheet and bake at 450° for 30 minutes or until biscuits are brown. Freeze casserole separately from cheese whirls. Combine at baking time.
Serves 8 to 10.
Mrs. Clay Lockett (Jeanne Adcox)

Crepes Nicholas

Chicken
1   4 or 5 lb. chicken   1   qt. water
1   T. salt

Bring to boil in a stock pot and simmer until tender. Let the chicken cool in broth. Remove chicken; skin and debone. Cut up chicken for crepes. Strain broth for cheese sauce.

Crepes
2   eggs, beaten   ½   t. salt
1   c. milk   1   c. flour

Put all ingredients in bowl and stir until smooth. Cover and let stand at least ½ hour. The batter should be thin and just thick enough to coat a spoon dipped into it. If the batter is too thick, add a little milk. Heat a 5 or 6 inch frying pan (or use any type crepe pan), grease lightly with salad oil, and pour in just enough batter to cover the pan in a very thin layer. Tilt pan so batter spreads evenly. Cook on one side, turn with spatula, and brown the other side. Roll up or fold in quarters. Keep warm if you plan to serve immediately.
Yields 18 to 24 crepes.

Crepes Nicholas Put a tablespoon of chopped chicken on each crepe. Roll up and put close together in a shallow 2 quart (you will need two) baking dish. When ready to serve, pour piping hot cheese sauce over the crepes and brown slightly under the broiler.

Cheese Sauce
½   c. margarine   Salt and pepper to taste
⅔   c. flour   ½   c. sherry
3   c. chicken stock   ¼   c. Parmesan cheese
2   c. milk   ½   t. Worcestershire sauce

Melt margarine in saucepan. Blend in flour. Add milk and chicken broth gradually. Cook and stir constantly until well blended and thickened. Season with salt and pepper. Refrigerate overnight. Before serving crepes add sherry, Parmesan cheese, and Worcestershire to sauce. Pour over crepes by following directions above.
Serves 12. Crepes will freeze without cheese sauce.
Mrs. Grace Bremer Sheffield

Chicken Mushroom Filling for Crepes

24	medium sized fresh mushrooms, sliced	1⅓	c. sour cream
7	T. butter	2	T. chopped fresh parsley
2½	c. diced cooked chicken	¾	c. grated Parmesan cheese
6	hard-cooked eggs, chopped		Dash of cayenne pepper
			Salt to taste

Garnish
Sour Cream   Parsley
Parmesan cheese

Saute mushrooms in butter about 5 minutes. Combine mushrooms with rest of ingredients and heat in the top of a double boiler. Spoon about 2 tablespoons of chicken mixture in center of each crepe and roll. Place crepes in buttered 2 quart baking dish. Cover and bake in a 300° oven until heated. Remove from oven and place a dollop of sour cream on each crepe. Sprinkle with Parmesan cheese and garnish with parsley sprigs.
Yields filling for 30 crepes.
Mrs. Joe Ed Johnston (Marilyn Hardgrave)

Chicken a la King

2	T. butter	1	10¾ oz. can cream of mushroom soup
⅓	c. chopped green pepper	1	T. lemon juice
1	c. sliced mushrooms	2	T. sherry
1	t. chopped onion	½	t. paprika
3	T. butter	3	c. diced cooked chicken
5	T. flour	¼	c. chopped pimiento
¾	t. salt	3	or 4 drops yellow food color
2	c. light cream		

Cook green pepper, mushrooms, and onion in 2 tablespoons butter until lightly brown. Drain and set aside. Melt 3 tablespoons butter in saucepan, and blend in flour and salt. Gradually stir in cream and stir with wire whisk until sauce thickens. Stir in mushroom soup. Add lemon juice, sherry, and paprika. Stir in green pepper, mushrooms, and onion. Add chicken and pimiento. You may add a few drops of yellow food coloring to improve color of sauce. Serve in patty shells.
Serves 8 to 10.
Mrs. Gordon B. Broyles (Frances Dilley)

Chicken Hash

1	c. Bechamel sauce		2	c. diced white meat chicken
½	c. light cream		2	egg yolks
¼	c. sherry			Salt and pepper to taste

Bechamel Sauce

2	c. milk		¼	t. white pepper
2	T. flour			Dash Tabasco and
2	T. butter			Worcestershire sauce

Scald milk. Melt butter, add flour and stir with whisk for a few minutes. Gradually stir in milk. Add seasonings, and blend well.

In saucepan, combine Bechamel sauce and cream, whipping with whisk until fluffy. Add sherry and mix well. Stir in the chicken. Cook over low heat until mixture is hot. Season with salt and pepper, stir in egg yolks, and blend well. Serve over toast, waffle, baked potato shell, or wild rice; or use as stuffing for omelette or crepe.
Serves 4.
Mrs. Robert W. Wood (Martha Cook)

Creamed Chicken or Turkey and Eggs on Toast

4	hard-cooked eggs		1	c. cream of celery soup, undiluted
½	c. diced cooked chicken or turkey		¼	c. sour cream

Slice eggs. Combine with chicken or turkey and soup. Heat on low. Stir in sour cream. Serve hot over cheese toast. *Good for leftover chicken or turkey. Can also use ham.*
Serves 2.
Mrs. Jack Graves (Pauline Thompson)

Chicken and Dumplings

1	3 to 4 lb. hen, cooked and deboned	½	to 1 c. ice water
2	c. flour	2	c. chicken broth
1	t. salt	2	c. milk
½	c. shortening	½	c. butter
		Salt and pepper to taste	

Blend flour, salt, and shortening until mixture resembles corn meal. Slowly add cold water until it makes a dough. Roll dough thinly on a floured board and cut into strips. In a Dutch oven add equal amounts of broth and milk. Add butter, salt, and pepper. Bring to a slow boil, lower heat, and simmer. Add one strip of dough at a time to this liquid. Do not stir. Push down with a spoon. Cook for 15 minutes, then add meat carefully.
Serves 8.
Mrs. Joe Ed Johnston (Marilyn Hardgrave)

Chicken Spaghetti

2	large fryers, cooked and boned	1	7 oz. jar chopped pimiento
5	stalks celery, chopped	1	6 oz. can chopped ripe olives with juice
1	onion, chopped		
1	bell pepper, chopped	1	c. grated cheese
2	garlic cloves, minced	Salt to taste	
4	T. margarine	1	12 oz. box spaghetti cooked in broth and drained
1	10¾ oz. can cream of mushroom soup		
1	10¾ oz. can cream of chicken soup		

Cut chicken in bite size pieces. Saute celery, onion, bell pepper, and garlic in margarine. Mix soups, add pimiento, chopped olives and juice, and sauteed vegetables. Fold in chicken. Mix sauce with cooked spaghetti. Pour into two 2 quart casseroles. Top with cheese. Bake in 350° oven for 15 minutes or until bubbly.
Serves 12.
Mrs. Bob Burroughs (Thelma Andrews)

Chicken Tetrazzini

¼	c. butter	2	4 oz. cans sliced
4	T. flour		mushrooms, drained
2	c. light cream	3	c. diced chicken
¾	t. salt	1	T. lemon juice
1	10¾ oz. can cream of	½	t. paprika
	mushroom soup	1	c. thinly sliced slivers of
¼	c. chopped green pepper		ham
1	T. chopped onion	1	12 oz. pkg. thin spaghetti
1	T. margarine		Parmesan cheese to taste

Melt butter and add flour. Blend well. Add cream gradually and cook, stirring constantly, until mixture thickens. Add salt and mushroom soup. Saute green pepper and onion in margarine and add to sauce. Fold in mushrooms, chicken, and ham. Blend in lemon juice and paprika. Cook spaghetti. Drain and rinse with cool water. Spread spaghetti in a buttered 3 quart casserole. Pour sauce over and sprinkle well with Parmesan cheese. Bake at 350° for 20 to 30 minutes or until heated through.
Serves 12.
Mrs. W. M. Knowles (Jean Dilley)

After Christmas Casserole

3	T. chopped green pepper	3	T. chopped fresh parsley
3	T. chopped green onion	1	8 oz. can sliced
½	c. chopped celery		mushrooms, drained
2	T. chopped onion	2	6 oz. jars artichoke
½	c. butter		hearts, drained
1	10¾ oz. can cream of	4	c. chopped turkey
	mushroom soup		Dash of Worcestershire sauce
2	c. sour cream		Dash of Tabasco
1	c. grated Parmesan cheese		Salt and pepper to taste

In a large skillet saute green pepper, green onion, celery, and onion in butter. Add the remaining ingredients. Pour into a 3 quart casserole and bake at 350° for 45 minutes. *This recipe is great for using leftover turkey.*
Serves 8. Freezes.
Mrs. John Presley (Lucinda Hanks)

Turkey Enchiladas

2	4 oz. cans green chilies	15	corn tortillas
1	large clove garlic, minced	2	T. salad oil
1	12 oz. can tomatoes	2	t. salt
2	c. chopped onions	⅓	to ½ c. salad oil
3	c. shredded cooked turkey	½	t. oregano
2	c. grated Cheddar cheese	2	c. sour cream

Preheat 2 tablespoons oil in electric skillet with control set at 300°. Rinse seeds from chilies and chop; saute with minced garlic in oil. Drain and break up tomatoes; reserve ½ cup liquid. Add tomatoes, chopped onion, 1 teaspoon salt, oregano, and reserved liquid. Simmer at 200° uncovered until thick, about 30 minutes. Remove from skillet and set aside. Combine turkey with sour cream, grated cheese, and remaining 1 teaspoon salt. Heat ⅓ cup oil and dip tortillas until they become limp. Drain well on paper towels. Fill the tortillas with turkey mixture; roll up and arrange side by side, seam side down, in skillet. Pour the chili sauce over the top and heat at 250° until heated through, about 20 minutes.
Yields 15 enchiladas.
Mrs. Lawrence McWhorter (Elma Cornelius)

Elegant Quail

8	whole quail	½	c. unsalted butter
Salt and pepper to taste		4	T. cognac
2	T. lemon juice	Parsley for garnish	

Sprinkle quail with salt, pepper, and lemon juice. Heat butter until hot, not brown, in large heavy skillet. Brown quail evenly on all sides. Add cognac and cover, cooking over low heat 10 to 12 minutes. At this point quail can be left in the pan for up to 1 hour before serving. Remove quail to oven proof platter and place under broiler a few seconds to brown slightly. Garnish with parsley. You may or may not heat remaining cognac, light, and pour flaming over quail just before bringing to table. Serve with sauce and rice.
Serves 4.
Mrs. Frank McCreary (Irma Holland)

Rock Cornish Hens in Wine Sauce

3   Rock Cornish hens   1   10¾ oz. can cream of
2   c. flour   mushroom soup
3   T. butter   1   c. white wine
1   1.37 oz. pkg. onion soup   Parsley
     mix   Peach halves

Brown flour in dry skillet until toast color. I always brown 2 cups at a time
to use later in a roux. This takes about 2 hours to brown on low heat. Stir
occasionally. Thaw 3 Rock Cornish hens and halve. Discard giblets. Rinse
and wipe dry. DO NOT SALT. Place browned flour in paper bag and shake
hens ½ at a time, until well floured. Brown in skillet, using 3 tablespoons
butter. Transfer to shallow 7 x 12 baking dish, pouring pan drippings over
hens. Mix the package of onion soup well, stirring from bottom of package.
Sprinkle 3 tablespoons of the mix over hens. Pour cream of mushroom soup
over hens. Pour wine over hens. Do not stir soup and wine together. Cover
and cook at 350° for 1 hour. Arrange hens on platter. Garnish with parsley
and broiled peach halves. Serve sauce in gravy boat. Excellent served with
herbed long-grain and wild rice.
Serves 6.
Mrs. W. O. Smith (Marye Jo Green)

Quail for Two

2   quail   2   c. chicken stock
Salt and pepper   ½   c. dry white wine
½   c. butter   Dash of cayenne
2   T. flour

Salt and pepper birds. Pan-broil quail in butter until golden brown. Set aside.
In a saucepan, melt butter. Stir in flour and cook, stirring constantly, until
flour is blended. Add stock and simmer for 10 minutes. Add wine and seasonings. Return quail to pan. Cover and simmer for 15 to 20 minutes or until
tender.
Serves 2.
Mrs. Cad E. Williams (Francis Bailey)

Frying Pan Quail

6	to 8 whole quail	1	c. seedless green grapes
Flour		¼	c. chopped hazelnuts,
Salt and pepper			optional
½	c. butter	1	T. lemon juice
1	c. water		

Salt, pepper, and flour quail. In deep skillet brown quail in melted butter. Add water and simmer, covered, until tender. Add green grapes and cook 3 minutes. Stir in hazelnuts and lemon juice. *This recipe can also be used for 1 cut up pheasant.*
Serves 4.
Mrs. Stewart Kenderdine (Jane Kukar)

Sauteed Quail in Tea

2	T. butter	1	c. hot strong tea
6	quail	Salt and pepper	
3	scallions, chopped	1	T. lemon juice
1	t. flour	1	T. Worcestershire sauce

Melt butter in skillet and brown whole quail. Remove and stir-fry scallions for 2 minutes. Stir in flour. Add tea, salt, pepper, lemon juice, and Worcestershire sauce; and stir until bubbly. Reduce heat and add quail. Cover and cook over low heat for 30 minutes or until tender. Check liquid halfway through; if necessary, add 1 or 2 tablespoons water. Remove birds to a warm platter. Spoon gravy over each breast and serve.
Serves 4.
Mrs. R. D. Harrell (Beverly Tucker)

Doves for Company

12 doves	1 c. chopped green onions,
Salt and pepper	with tops
¼ t. MSG	1 c. beef consomme
½ c. margarine	½ c. dry white wine
¾ c. chopped parsley	1 to 2 T. flour

Season doves with salt, pepper, and MSG. After browning doves in margarine, lower heat and simmer slowly until tender, approximately 1 hour. Doves should be turned often. Add remaining ingredients in order given. Cover and cook slowly an additional 45 minutes. To thicken gravy, add flour.
Serves 4.
Mrs. Cad Williams (Francis Bailey)

Roast Venison

A haunch of venison

Marinade

1 c. brandy	1 t. allspice
1 c. Burgundy	6 whole cloves
1 c. vegetable oil	8 carrots, pared
1 T. freshly ground black	8 small onions, peeled
pepper	Butter
4 bay leaves	

Gravy

¼ c. butter	1 10¾ oz. can beef broth
¼ c. flour	Salt and pepper to taste
1 c. marinade	

Combine marinade ingredients and pour over venison. Let stand for 10 hours or overnight in refrigerator, turning haunch at least once. Venison keeps well in this mixture for 2 weeks, if well refrigerated. Remove venison to a roasting pan and arrange carrots and onions around meat. Dot meat with butter and cover with 1 cup marinade. Reserve remaining marinade for further basting. Bake in 375° oven for 15 minutes per pound, basting every 10 minutes and turning meat occasionally to prevent meat from drying out. Remove meat and vegetables and keep warm. To make gravy add butter, flour, marinade, beef broth, and seasonings to pan drippings. Simmer until thickened to gravy consistency, stirring constantly.
Mrs. Cad E. Williams (Francis Bailey)

Venison Chili

1	lb. ground beef	1	pod red pepper or ½ t.
3	lbs. ground venison		cayenne
¼	c. flour	3	cloves garlic, crushed
4	T. chili powder	1	t. onion powder
1½	T. ground cumin	2	15 oz. cans tomato sauce
		3¾	c. water

Brown beef. Remove from skillet and brown venison in fat from beef. Mix beef with venison, stir in flour and seasonings well. Add tomato sauce and water. Bring to a boil and simmer slowly for 2 hours or more. If thinner chili is desired, add more water. This is an excellent way to use venison. If desired, add 16 ounce can Ranch Style beans.
Serves 8 to 10.
Mrs. Frank McCreary (Irma Holland)

Venison Ham

First, the deer should be field dressed quickly after the kill and left to hang in cold weather (or cold storage) about 24 hours. It should then be skinned, butchered, and frozen.

To prepare ham, thaw and remove all fat, tendons, and as much membrane as possible. Make 3 or 4 slices, one inch deep, across the ham. Salt and pepper and push bacon strips into the slices. Cover other exposed meat with additional bacon strips. Smoke (not over live fire or coals) with pecan, hickory, blackjack, or mesquite (I prefer pecan) for 5 or 6 hours. Cover with foil, and bake at 300° for 2 hours.
John Cumby

Venison Stew

2	lbs. cubed venison, from shoulder or ham	2	10½ oz. cans beef bouillon
3	T. shortening	1	c. red wine
¼	t. pepper	12	small onions, peeled
½	t. salt	6	carrots, peeled and sliced
Dash of cayenne pepper		6	medium potatoes, quartered
1	bay leaf		

Brown meat in fat. Add seasonings, bouillon, and wine. Cover and simmer for 2 hours. Add vegetables and cook until vegetables are fork tender, about 30 minutes. You may thicken stew with a little flour. Delicious served with cornbread or French rolls, and your favorite red wine!
Serves 8.
Mrs. Frank McCreary (Irma Holland)

Venison Stroganoff

2	lbs. bottom round, shank, or ground venison. Equally good with elk.	2	c. diluted canned beef consomme (or, if using elk, fresh beef stock or canned broth)
¼	c. bacon drippings		
1	clove garlic or powder to taste	1	bay leaf
		8	peppercorns
1	c. diced celery	1	t. salt
½	c. chopped onion	4	T. butter
		4	T. flour
		1	c. sour cream

Cut meat in 2 inch cubes and brown in bacon fat along with garlic. Arrange in a 2 quart casserole. Cook celery and onion in same frying pan for two minutes, while stirring. Add canned consomme (or stock or broth for elk) bay leaf, salt, and pepper. Pour hot mixture over meat, cover and cook at 325° until meat is tender, 30 to 60 minutes. Melt butter in frying pan, stir in flour until well blended, slowly add liquid in which the venison cooked, stir until thick and smooth. Add sour cream and correct the seasoning, adding more sour cream if necessary. Pour over meat and serve with noodles and jellied cranberry sauce.
Serves 8.
Mrs. Lester Hamilton (Frances Edmunds)

Roast Wild Duck

6	ducks	2	medium onions
Salt and pepper		2	T. cooking oil
2	apples	1	c. red wine
2	ribs celery		

Rub duck cavities with salt and pepper. Chop next 3 ingredients, divide equally, and fill cavities. Heat oil in flat 9 x 13 baking dish. Roll ducks in oil, place side by side, breast up, and pour in red wine. Cover with foil and bake 1 hour. Remove foil, and bake 15 to 20 minutes, or until brown. Serve with your favorite rice and wine jelly sauce.

Wine Jelly Sauce

1	4 oz. jar currant or grape jelly	½	c. red wine
		½	c. butter

Melt together and serve with duck.
Serves 6.
Mrs. Frank McCreary (Irma Holland)

Wild Goose

1	young wild goose	Salt and pepper
¼	c. vinegar	2 oranges, thinly sliced
Juice of 1 lemon		Sliced bacon to cover goose
Juice of 1 orange		

Thaw goose in water with vinegar. Pat dry. Place in large roasting pan. Squeeze fruit juice generously inside and out. Season with salt and pepper. Place two thirds of orange slices inside goose. Cover breasts with bacon strips and place rest of orange slices over the bacon. Cover tightly and bake at 325° until tender, about 2 hours. If goose is not young, it may need more time to bake. Serve goose with the following sauce.

Sauce

¼	c. tart jelly (plum, currant, etc.)	2	T. sherry
		3	to 4 T. lemon juice
3	T. butter	Salt and pepper	

Heat sauce and serve. Goose may also be served with baked apples or apple sauce.
Serves 4.
Mrs. Daniel F. Rex (Emory Hill)

Venison Pot Roast

1	3 to 4 lb. venison roast	6	medium potatoes, peeled and cut into pieces
½	c. flour		
1	t. salt	6	carrots, peeled and sliced
½	t. pepper	6	medium onions, peeled and sliced
½	c. margarine		
½	c. dry red wine	3	or 4 fresh tomatoes, peeled and cut into pieces
1	t. dry mustard		
2	c. beef bouillon		

Roll venison in mixture of flour, salt, and pepper. Melt margarine in deep, heavy skillet and brown venison in the fat. Add wine, mustard, and one cup of bouillon. Cover and bake at 325° for 2½ hours. Add remaining bouillon, potatoes, carrots, and onions. Add extra bouillon if needed. Cook until potatoes are tender and add tomatoes for last few minutes to heat. Serves 6.
Mrs. Daniel F. Rex (Emory Hill)

Wild Turkey

1	10 to 12 lb. turkey	2	or 3 stalks of celery, chopped
Salt and pepper			
2	apples, peeled and cored	½	c. melted margarine
1	onion, chopped	½	lb. bacon

After cleaning the cavity of the turkey, rub it generously with salt and pepper. Mix the apples, onion, celery, and margarine. Stuff the cavity of the turkey with apple mixture. This dressing is for seasoning - not for eating. Place turkey in a roasting pan, and cover the breast with bacon strips. Roast at 325° for 25 minutes to the pound.
Serves 8 to 10.
Mrs. Frank McCreary (Irma Holland)

SEAFOOD

Crab Casserole

2	lbs. lump crabmeat	2	onions, finely chopped
¼	lb. crushed crackers	1	pt. light cream
1	c. margarine		

Saute onions in small amount of margarine. Cool. Add crabmeat and half of crushed crackers. Place in greased casserole. Top with remaining crackers. Melt butter and pour over everything; then pour cream over the casserole. Bake 20 minutes at 350°.
Serves 8.
Mrs. W. Lamar Hamilton (Kitty Davey)

Crabmeat Casserole

1	6 oz. pkg. cornbread mix	2	T. vegetable oil or
1	large rib of celery,		margarine
	chopped	2	lbs. lump crabmeat
1	large onion, chopped		Water to moisten
1	small bell pepper,		
	chopped		

Make own cornbread, if desired. Cool and crumble into 2 quart casserole. Saute celery, onions, and bell pepper in oil and pour into crumbled cornbread. Salt and pepper to taste. A bit of red pepper may be added, if desired. Add the crabmeat and a bit of water, if necessary. Mix and bake in 350° oven until lightly browned.
Serves 4.
Mrs. William George, Jr. (June Haddad)

Crabmeat Delight

1	c. crabmeat	1	c. bread stuffing mix
1	c. mayonnaise	3	hard-cooked eggs
1	c. cream		

Mix all ingredients together and pour into a buttered 1½ quart casserole. Bake in 375° oven for 30 minutes.
Serves 4 to 6.
Mrs. R. L. Kenderdine (Daphne Dunning)

Crab Imperial

1½ lbs. crabmeat, cooked and flaked	2 t. Worcestershire
½ c. chopped green pepper	2 t. prepared mustard
¼ c. chopped onion	½ t. salt
¼ c. butter	Freshly ground black pepper
¼ c. mayonnaise	3 T. butter
2 T. chopped parsley	Paprika

Saute pepper and onion in ¼ cup butter until tender. Combine all ingredients except paprika. Place mixture in 6 greased crab shells. Dot each with butter. Sprinkle with paprika. Bake at 350° for 20 minutes.
Serves 6.
Mrs. Robert Miller (Rosemary Hajenian)

Crab Lorenzo

½ c. butter	1 lb. fresh or frozen white crabmeat
2 cloves garlic, minced	1 c. coarse bread crumbs
½ bunch green onions or shallots, chopped	Salt and pepper to taste
1 bell pepper, chopped	Several dashes of Tabasco
1 T. flour	6 toast rounds
1 c. milk	12 anchovy strips, optional
6 sprigs parsley, chopped	4 T. grated Parmesan cheese
½ c. sherry	

Saute garlic in butter until lightly browned. Add green onions and bell pepper. Cook slowly until done but not brown. Add flour and mix well. Add milk and parsley, stirring until thick. Add the sherry and fold in crabmeat. Sprinkle in bread crumbs, season to taste with salt, pepper, and Tabasco, and form into 6 balls. Lay each ball on a crisp toast round and top each with two strips of anchovy. Sprinkle with grated Parmesan cheese and broil until lightly browned.
For a canape, smaller toast rounds with less Lorenzo is a great hit with cocktails.
Serves 6.
Mrs. Lamar W. Davis, Jr., Houston, Texas

Stuffed Crab

1	medium onion, chopped fine	2	bay leaves
½	c. green onions, chopped fine	½	t. salt
¼	c. butter	½	t. black pepper
1	c. coarse bread crumbs, dampened with oyster water or any kind of fish stock		Dash of cayenne
			Tabasco to taste
		1	lb. fresh or frozen white crabmeat
		1	T. fresh parsley, chopped

Saute onion in butter. Add dampened bread crumbs and cook 3 minutes. Add bay leaves, seasonings, crabmeat, and parsley. Mix thoroughly and heat through. Remove from heat and discard bay leaves. Pack stuffing into scallop shells and bake in shallow baking dish 15-20 minutes at 350°. *May be used to stuff mushrooms or artichoke bottoms.*
Serves 6. Freezes.
Mrs. Lamar W. Davis, Jr., Houston, Texas

Crabmeat Vermicelli

1	lb. vermicelli	¾	c. slivered toasted almonds
½	c. chopped green pepper		
2	c. chopped celery	3	to 4 c. ranch style creamy Italian dressing
10	to 12 green onions, chopped	1	to 1½ lbs. crabmeat or cooked shrimp
3	hard-cooked eggs, chopped		Garnish of toasted almonds and pimiento
2	oz. jar pimientos, chopped		

Break vermicelli into 2 inch pieces and cook. Drain and mix in the next 7 ingredients. Refrigerate overnight. Add crabmeat, toss, and garnish.
Serves 12.
Mrs. Harold Hunter (Frances Laughlin)

Baked Fish

1	cooking bag	Salt
2	lemons	Pepper
¼	c. white wine	Paprika
Butter		10 fish fillets

Put cooking bag in 9 x 13 baking dish. Lay fish in bag. Pour in wine. Squeeze juice of one lemon over fish. Slice other lemon and lay on fish. Sprinkle with salt, pepper, and paprika. Dot with butter. Punch holes in cooking bag. Bake 30 minutes at 350°.
Serves 5 or 6.
Mrs. C. L. Kolstad, III (Jill McPherson)

Cajun Fried Fish

2 lbs. fish filets
Salt and pepper to taste
½ c. prepared mustard
Tabasco to taste

1 c. yellow cornbread mix
(Pioneer is good
because it is not sweet.)
Cooking oil

If filets are frozen, thaw in milk to restore freshness. Sprinkle filets lightly with salt and pepper. In a pan mix mustard and Tabasco to taste. Coat filets lightly and transfer to a pan containing cornbread mix. Pat mixture firmly around each piece of fish. Set aside on waxed paper. These can be cooked immediately or can dry for up to ½ hour. In a deep fryer heat oil to 375°. Fry until golden brown and crisp, 3 to 4 minutes, making only a single layer. In a low oven keep fish warm on a baking dish lined with paper towels until all pieces are cooked. Serve immediately for top flavor. You will probably find that you do not need extra sauces when flavored this way. *Fish must be completely thawed or breading will not stick.*
Serves 4 to 6.
Mrs. Clyde Hanks (Howard Kolstad), Houston, Texas

Deviled Fish

Prepare day before serving.

2	lbs. fresh or frozen haddock	4	T. catsup
1	lb. fresh or frozen scallops	1	T. horseradish
		1	clove garlic, pressed
8	T. butter	1	t. prepared mustard
½	c. plus 1 T. flour	1	t. soy sauce
1	c. evaporated milk	2	t. MSG
1	c. consomme	½	t. salt
2	T. cornstarch	¼	t. cayenne pepper
1	T. lemon juice	4	T. chopped parsley
1	T. Worcestershire	¼	c. sherry
		1	c. bread crumbs, optional

Cover thawed fish with cold, salted water for 15 minutes. Put fish in top of greased double boiler. Cover and steam 20 minutes. Cool fish and cut into chunks. Melt butter; blend in flour. Heat the milk and consomme, and pour hot liquid into flour mix. Add the cornstarch blended with a little milk. Cook until there is no starchy taste, stirring constantly. Add remaining ingredients to sauce. Gently fold in fish. Pour into buttered 3 quart casserole. When cool, sprinkle with bread crumbs. Bake at 400° for 30 minutes. If desired, shrimp, lobster, or crab may be added or substituted.
Takes time but is not difficult.
Serves 8 to 10.
Mrs. R. L. Kenderdine (Daphne Dunning)

Filets of Sole Meuniere

6	filets of sole or 2 lbs. frozen sole		Salt and pepper
Flour		2	T. lemon juice
½	c. butter	2	T. chopped parsley

Wash sole filets, dry, and dip in flour. In a large frying pan, heat ¼ cup of butter until it is foaming. Saute the filets until golden brown on both sides. Remove to serving platter and sprinkle with salt and pepper. Melt remaining butter and cook to a light brown. Add lemon juice and parsley and pour over filets. Serve immediately with lemon wedges.
Serves 6.
Mrs. C. Gerald Joyce, Jr. (Jeanne Dunn)

Fish Filets Thermador

1	lb. fish filets	1	c. milk
½	c. dry white wine	1	c. cream
½	c. water	¼	c. sherry
4	T. butter	1	8 oz. can mushrooms,
4	T. flour		drained
1	t. salt	½	c. Parmesan cheese

In a skillet combine wine and water. When mixture boils, add fish filets; reduce heat *at once* and simmer the fish until done, about 5 minutes. Remove fish, drain well, and place fish in a buttered 1½ quart casserole. Melt the butter and add flour and salt. Cook until bubbly; then add milk, cream, and sherry. Cook until thick. Cover fish with mushrooms and the sauce. Sprinkle with cheese and bake in a 350° oven until brown and well heated.
Serves 4.
Mrs. Wayne Smith (Inez Murdaugh)

Oyster Spaghetti

3	doz. or more oysters	2	T. softened butter for
½	c. butter		each cup of liquid
¼	to ½ c. chopped green	½	c. white wine
	onions	1	c. heavy cream
4	T. chopped parsley	3	egg yolks
2	cloves garlic, minced	1	10 oz. pkg. spaghetti
2	T. flour for each cup of	Salt and pepper	
	liquid	Parmesan and Romano cheese	

Heat the butter in a Dutch oven, and saute onion and parsley until soft. Add garlic and oysters with their liquid. Cook over moderate heat until oysters are plump. Remove oysters to a bowl. After oysters have given off liquid, return liquid to pot. Let liquid reduce to 1½ cups. Add wine and reduce to 1½ cups again. Mix flour and butter; add some of the hot liquid slowly, and whisk until smooth. Return flour mixture to simmering liquid. Beat cream and egg yolks lightly and add to simmering liquid. Season to taste. Simmer slowly but do not boil. Return plumped oysters to Dutch oven and heat. Butter cooked spaghetti and mix with sauce (approximately 3 cups) and garnish with cheeses. If the sauce is too thick, thin by adding white wine.
Serves 8.
Mrs. J. E. Johnston (Marie Orgeron)

Oyster Macaroni Ring

1	12 oz. pkg. elbow macaroni	¼	c. chopped onion
1	c. grated cheese	2	slices white bread, broken up
1	c. milk	1	egg, beaten lightly
¼	c. chopped bell pepper		

Sauce

2	T. bacon drippings or margarine	2	pts. oysters, juice included
½	medium onion, chopped	1	T. Worcestershire sauce
½	bell pepper, chopped	1	to 2 T. flour mixed with 2 T. water
Salt and pepper to taste		½	c. catsup

Cook macaroni according to package directions. Drain well. Place macaroni into top of a double boiler; add grated cheese, milk, green pepper, onion, and bread. Cook over hot water until slightly thickened. Add a little more milk if needed. Remove from heat and add egg. Place mixture into a well greased ring mold. Place mold in a pan of hot water. Cook in 350° oven approximately 20 minutes or until macaroni begins to brown on top.

Sauce Melt bacon drippings in a large skillet. Add onion, bell pepper, salt, and pepper. Cook until vegetables are brown. Add oysters with juice and Worcestershire. Bring to a slow simmer. Add flour and water thickening. Increase thickening if necessary. Cook until creamy and oysters curl on ends. Add catsup and heat thoroughly.

On large round platter turn macaroni mold upside down and gently unmold. Pour oyster mixture into the center of the ring and serve.
Serves 6 to 8.
Luckett Kolstad, Jr.

Broiled Marinated Salmon

½	c. dry vermouth	½	t. marjoram
½	c. salad oil	¼	t. sage
2	T. fresh lemon juice	1	T. minced fresh parsley
¾	t. salt	4	salmon steaks
⅛	t. freshly ground pepper		Lemon wedges
½	t. thyme		Parsley sprigs

Make a marinade of vermouth, oil, lemon juice, and seasonings. Pour over salmon steaks and refrigerate for 2 to 3 hours. Place steaks on greased broiler rack or grill. Broil, basting frequently with marinade, for 7 to 8 minutes on each side or until salmon flakes easily with fork. Garnish with lemon wedges and additional parsley.
Serves 4.
Cookbook Committee

Oven Salmon Cakes

1¼	c. crushed Ritz crackers	⅛	t. Worcestershire
1	egg, slightly beaten	1	16 oz. can salmon,
2	T. snipped parsley		drained and flaked
2	T. sliced green onion	1	c. grated sharp cheese
2	T. milk	1	T. butter
⅛	t. pepper		

Combine ¾ cup cracker crumbs, egg, parsley, onion, milk, pepper, and Worcestershire. Add salmon and cheese; mix. Shape into 4 patties. Mix butter with remaining crumbs and coat patties with mixture. Place on lightly greased baking sheet. Bake 400° for 10 minutes.
Serves 4.
Cookbook Committee

Salmon Casserole

4	T. butter	½	c. sliced stuffed olives
4	T. flour	2	4 oz. cans sliced
¼	t. dry mustard		mushrooms
¼	t. paprika	1	8 oz. pkg. noodles,
1	t. salt		cooked and drained
3	c. milk		Buttered bread crumbs
1	t. Worcestershire	8	to 10 canned asparagus
1	T. lemon juice		tips
½	c. grated cheese		Parsley, pimiento, and paprika
1	16 oz. can salmon, drained and flaked		

Melt butter, blend in flour, mustard, paprika, and salt. Gradually add milk and cook, stirring until thickened. Add Worcestershire, lemon juice, and cheese, stirring until cheese is melted. Add salmon, olives, and mushrooms. Combine noodles and sauce. Spoon into lightly greased 2 quart casserole. Sprinkle with buttered bread crumbs, and bake at 375° for 30 minutes. Garnish with asparagus, parsley, pimiento, and paprika.
Serves 4 to 6.
Mrs. James W. Summers (Inez Thompson)

Salmon Loaf with Dill Sauce

1	16 oz. can salmon with liquid	2	eggs, slightly beaten
2	10¾ oz. cans cream of celery soup	½	c. chopped onion
		⅓	c. sour cream
1	c. dry bread crumbs	1	T. lemon juice
		1	to 2 t. dill weed

Debone and flake salmon. Mix with 1 can cream of celery soup, bread crumbs, eggs, chopped onion, and lemon juice. Place in greased 4½ x 8½ loaf pan, and bake at 350° for about 1 hour. Mix remaining can of soup and sour cream. Add dill weed and heat gently. Serve as sauce for salmon loaf.
Serves 4 to 6.
Mrs. Ed Montgomery (Dorothy Meador)

Seafood Casserole

1	c. chopped celery	1	c. mayonnaise
1	green pepper, chopped	1	t. lemon juice
1	T. butter	1	4 oz. can mushroom stems and pieces, drained
2	10¾ oz. cans cream of chicken soup or one 10¾ oz. can cream of celery soup and one 10¾ can cream of chicken	1	6½ oz. can white tuna, drained
		2	4¼ oz. cans shrimp, drained
		3	c. cooked rice
1	13 oz. can evaporated milk	½	c. crumbled potato chips

Saute celery and green pepper in butter. Combine soup, milk, mayonnaise, and lemon juice. Add celery, green pepper, and mushrooms. Fold in tuna and shrimp. Mix with rice and pour into greased 2 quart casserole, and bake at 350° for 20 minutes. Top with crumbled potato chips and continue to bake for 10 more minutes.
Serves 8.
Mrs. R. H. Hunter (Frances Laughlin)

Seafood Puffs

1	7 oz. can tuna	4	drops Tabasco
½	c. mayonnaise	2	egg whites, stiffly beaten
1	t. mustard	3	English muffins
1	t. lemon juice	**Butter**	

Drain tuna and mix with mayonnaise, mustard, Tabasco, and lemon juice. Fold in stiffly beaten egg whites. Lightly butter each half of muffin and spread with tuna mixture. Place on cookie sheet in center of 350° oven. Bake until puffy and lightly brown, approximately 10 to 12 minutes. *Makes a nice lunch with green salad.*
Serves 3.
Mrs. John W. Sims (Lena Mae Roquemore)

Seafood Wild Rice Supreme

2	c. cooked wild rice	3	10¾ oz. cans cream of
1	c. cooked white rice		mushroom soup
2	6 oz. cans crabmeat,	1	c. broken shrimp
	flaked	Butter	
1½	c. chopped celery	1	lb. fresh mushrooms or
1	green pepper, chopped		one 16 oz. can
1	medium onion, chopped		mushrooms
1	2 oz. jar pimiento,		
	chopped		

Combine first 7 ingredients. Add 1½ cans mushroom soup and ½ cup shrimp. Place mixture into buttered 3 quart baking dish. Bake at 350° for 1½ hours.

Sauce Brown mushrooms in small amount of butter. Add remaining 1½ cans of mushroom soup and remaining ½ cup of shrimp. Heat through. Serve crab and rice mixture with hot mushroom sauce.
Variation Substitute a thick white sauce for 3 cans of cream of mushroom soup.

Thick White Sauce
12	T. butter	4	c. light cream
16	T. flour	1	t. salt

Melt butter, add flour, stir, and cook over low heat until well blended. Add cream gradually, stirring constantly. Cook until thickened, then add salt.
Serves 6 to 8.
Mrs. W. H. Shuller (Mary Plemons)

Scallops and Shrimp Vermouth

1	lb. scallops	2	T. flour
1½	lbs. shrimp in shell, cooked and cleaned	¼	c. vermouth or dry white wine
½	c. chicken broth	½	c. light cream
¼	c. butter	½	t. salt
½	c. chopped green onions	⅛	t. pepper
1	4 oz. can sliced mushrooms, drained, reserving liquid	⅛	t. paprika
		2	t. lemon juice
		Buttered bread crumbs	

Wash scallops. Simmer in broth for 10 minutes. Drain, reserving liquid. If scallops are large, they may be cut in halves or fourths. Heat butter in saucepan. Add onions and mushrooms. Saute 3 minutes. Remove and set aside. Add flour to butter and stir until smooth. Gradually add reserved cooking liquid, mushroom liquid, cream, and wine. Cook slowly until thickened, stirring constantly. Add seasonings, onions, mushrooms, scallops, shrimp, and lemon juice. Let cook for 1 minute. May be served in chafing dish or poured into 3 quart casserole, individual ramekins, or shells. Top with buttered bread crumbs. Bake at 350° for about 15 minutes or until crumbs are brown.
Serves 6.
Mrs. John B. McDonald (Dorothy Crider)

Scampi

¼	c. butter	2	T. lemon juice
¼	c. olive oil	Dash cayenne	
2	T. chopped parsley	1	lb. large fresh shrimp with tails
2	t. garlic powder		
½	t. salt		

Preheat oven to 400°. In large ovenproof dish, melt butter; add oil, half the parsley, garlic powder, salt, cayenne, and lemon juice. Mix well. Add shrimp, tossing gently. Arrange in single layer. Bake 8 to 10 minutes or until just tender. Sprinkle with remaining parsley. Serve with or over rice. As an hors d'oeuvre, sliced French bread may be dipped in sauce and eaten with shrimp.
Serves 4.
Mrs. Stewart Kenderdine (Jane Kukar)

Creamed Shrimp

1	10¾ oz. can chicken gumbo soup	1	to 2 lbs. shrimp, scallops, or white fish cubes, cooked
1	10¾ oz. can cream of asparagus soup		Curry powder, optional
1	10¾ oz. can cream of mushroom soup		

In a 3 quart saucepan, combine undiluted soups; heat to blend. Add curry to taste. Add cooked shrimp, cooked scallops, cooked fish, or combination of the three. Serve over hot cooked rice. You may add water chestnuts, mushrooms, or artichoke hearts.
Serves 4 to 6.
To use as soup, add 1 quart of milk to basic ingredients.
Serves 10.
Mrs. R. L. Kenderdine (Daphne Dunning)

Nana's Green Eggplant and Shrimp

	Eggplant, 1 large or 2 average		Garlic to taste
1	lb. shrimp, raw and peeled	1	c. raw rice
4	T. butter	1	10¾ oz. can cream of mushroom soup
½	c. chopped green pepper	1	c. grated cheese
1	onion, minced	1	c. buttered bread crumbs
½	c. diced celery		Parsley

Peel eggplant, cut in cubes, and parboil in salted water until tender; drain well. Melt butter in skillet, and saute shrimp until pink. Remove from pan. Saute celery, onions, green pepper, and garlic until tender. Boil rice 10 minutes and drain. Add rice, onion, celery, green pepper, garlic, shrimp, and eggplant. Mix gently and pour into a greased 2 quart baking dish. Add soup and cheese. Sprinkle with bread crumbs, and garnish with parsley. Bake uncovered at 350° for 30 to 45 minutes and cheese is bubbly.
Serves 12. Freezes.
Mrs. John B. McDonald (Dorothy Crider)

Shrimp and Artichoke Casserole

5	T. butter	1	c. grated Parmesan cheese
1	lb. fresh mushrooms	Paprika	
1½	lbs. cooked shrimp		
2	14 oz. cans artichoke hearts, drained		

Sauce

9	T. butter	½	c. dry sherry or to taste
9	T. flour	2	T. Worcestershire
1½	c. milk	Salt and pepper to taste	
1½	c. heavy cream		

Melt butter and saute mushrooms. Layer the artichokes, shrimp, and mushrooms in 4 quart casserole. Melt 9 tablespoons butter. Add flour, then milk and cream. Cook and stir constantly with a wire whisk until slightly thickened. Add sherry, Worcestershire, salt, and pepper. Pour sauce over layered ingredients. Sprinkle with cheese and paprika. Bake at 350° for 1 hour. Serve over rice. May be prepared day before and refrigerated.
Serves 12. Freezes.
Mrs. Dan F. Rex (Emory Hill)

Shrimp and Scallop Gruyere

¾	c. plus 2 T. butter	¼	t. dry mustard
¾	c. flour	3	t. tomato paste
3	c. milk	3	t. lemon juice
8	to 12 oz. Gruyere cheese	1	lb. raw scallops
¼	t. garlic powder	1	lb. cooked shrimp
3½	t. salt	½	lb. mushrooms
¼	t. white pepper	2	T. green pepper
¼	t. MSG		

Make a cream sauce in top of double boiler with ¾ cup butter, flour, and milk. Cook until sauce thickens. Cut cheese into small pieces and add to sauce. Cook and stir until cheese melts. Add garlic powder, 3 teaspoons salt, pepper, MSG, mustard, tomato paste, and 2 teaspoons lemon juice. Poach scallops for about 10 minutes in water and remaining lemon juice and salt. Add ½ cup of the broth to the cream sauce. Saute mushrooms in 2 tablespoons butter and add to sauce. Add scallops and shrimp. Heat 10 to 15 minutes. Use green pepper as garnish.
Serves 8.
Mrs. Jackson R. Hanks (Helen Reeves)

Shrimp and Wild Rice

2	c. cooked wild rice	¼	c. chopped green onion
2	c. cooked and broken shrimp	1	4 oz. can mushrooms, drained
½	c. butter	1	t. soy sauce
¼	c. chopped bell pepper	3	eggs, well beaten

Melt butter and add pepper, onion, and mushrooms. Saute until transparent.
Add shrimp and rice. Cook on low heat until warm. Remove from heat;
add soy sauce and eggs. Pour into 1½ quart greased baking dish, and bake
at 350° for 20 to 30 minutes.
Serves 4 to 6.
Mrs. Bob Stephenson (Sandra Durham)

Shrimp Creole

2	medium onions, chopped	⅛	t. pepper
1	medium green pepper, chopped	1	t. celery seed
1	clove garlic, minced	¼	t. thyme
2	T. shortening	2	t. parsley
2	T. flour	2½	c. cut okra
3	c. tomatoes, mashed	2	c. whole shrimp, cleaned
½	t. salt	2	t. Worcestershire sauce
2	bay leaves	3	c. cooked rice

Saute onion, pepper, and garlic in shortening until tender. Blend in flour.
Gradually add tomatoes, stirring constantly. Add seasonings and cook slowly
30 minutes or until thickened, adding more water if needed. Add okra,
shrimp, and Worcestershire. Cook 15 minutes longer. Serve over rice.
Serves 6.
Mrs. Carl Kirk (Lela Mae Saunders)

 Place juice and rind of ½ lemon, plus few shakes of tomato catsup into water in which you boil shrimp. There will be no odor of shrimp in the kitchen.

Shrimp Orleans

1	T. butter	2	c. cooked shrimp
1	c. chopped onion	1	10¾ oz. can cream of
½	c. chopped green pepper		mushroom soup
1	clove garlic, crushed	1	c. sour cream
1	4 oz. can sliced	¼	c. catsup
	mushrooms, drained		

Saute onion and green pepper in butter. Add garlic, cook until tender, but not brown. Combine soup, sour cream, and catsup. Stir into onion mixture. Add shrimp and mushrooms. Cook over low heat. Serve over rice.
Serves 4.
Cookbook Committee

Shrimp Remoulade

1	T. minced parsely	1	T. chopped green onion
1	T. finely minced garlic		tops
1	T. paprika	½	c. sherry or Sauterne
1	c. Creole or horseradish		Dash of Worcestershire sauce
	mustard	½	t. salt
½	c. salad oil	½	t. pepper
½	c. white vinegar	3	lbs. shrimp - cooked,
2	T. minced celery		peeled, and deveined

Mix well parsley, garlic, paprika, and mustard. Alternate oil and vinegar as you add to mustard mixture. Blend well. Add celery, onion tops, and sherry. Season with Worcestershire sauce, salt, and pepper. Add cooked shrimp to sauce, and marinate in refrigerator at least 4 hours before serving. Serve on beds of shredded lettuce. This recipe may also be used as an hors d'oeuvre served with party crackers.
Serves 6 to 8.
Mrs. Paul R. Hable (Rose Turner)

Shrimp Tempura

3	to 4 lbs. large shrimp in shell	½	t. MSG
1	c. cornstarch	2	eggs
1	c. flour	1	c. water
1	t. salt		Vegetable oil

Shell and clean shrimp, leaving on tails. Split down back, cutting almost through. Open to butterfly shape. Combine cornstarch, flour, salt, and MSG in bowl. Add eggs and water. Beat batter until just smooth. Using deep-fat thermometer, heat oil to 375° in deep saucepan. Holding shrimp by tail, dip into batter, and drop gently a few at a time into hot oil. When shrimp rise to surface, turn and cook until golden brown. Serve with sauces.
Serves 6 to 8.

Shoyu Sauce

⅛	t. ground ginger	¾	c. water
⅓	c. soy sauce	2	T. dry sherry
½	t. sugar		Pinch of MSG

Combine all ingredients in pan. Heat to luke warm.
Yields 1¼ cups.

Apricot Sauce Honi

1	c. dried apricots, cut up	½	c. rum
1	c. water	⅓	c. vinegar
¼	t. salt	2	T. honey
¼	c. sugar	1	t. paprika

Cook apricots in water in covered saucepan until soft, about 30 minutes. Most of water should be absorbed; if not, drain. Puree apricots in blender, food processor, or put through a fine sieve; add remaining ingredients and beat until smooth. May be prepared ahead of time. Keeps well in refrigerator. *Sauces are delicious but children like catsup.*
Yields about 1 pint.
Mrs. Kendall West (Helen McCain)

Shrimp-Rice Casserole

1	10¾ oz. can cream of mushroom soup	1	c. diced celery
½	c. mayonnaise	2	T. parsley
⅓	c. milk	2	T. grated onion
1½	lbs. boiled shrimp	3	c. cooked rice
1	8 oz. can water chestnuts, sliced		Dash of Tabasco
		1½	c. bread crumbs
		3	T. butter, melted

Combine soup, mayonnaise, and milk. Add shrimp, water chestnuts, celery, parsley, onion, rice, and Tabasco. Pour mixture into a 2 quart casserole, and top with bread crumbs which have been tossed with melted butter. Bake at 350° for 25 to 30 minutes.
Serves 4 to 6.
Mrs. Dick Hartt (Dorothy Marshall)

Sweet and Sour Tuna

1	20 oz. can pineapple chunks	2	T. vinegar
2	c. green pepper strips	1	T. soy sauce
2	T. butter	⅓	c. sugar
1	chicken bouillon cube	2	6½ oz. cans white tuna, drained
1	c. boiling water	2	3 oz. cans chow mein noodles
2	T. cornstarch		

Drain pineapple and reserve liquid. Cook pineapple in butter 3 minutes. Measure ⅔ cup juice and pour half into pineapple. Add green pepper. Cover and simmer 10 minutes. Dissolve bouillon cube in water and add to pineapple mixture. Mix cornstarch with ⅓ c. syrup and add. Add soy sauce, vinegar, and sugar. Cook, stirring constantly, until clear and thick. Add tuna. Heat until tuna is hot. Serve over noodles heated in slow oven. *Water chestnuts may be added. Parsley for color.*
Serves 6 to 8.
Mrs. Regina May Thompson

Tuna Bake

2	T. butter	1	16 oz. can chop suey
¼	c. chopped green pepper		vegetables, rinsed and
¼	c. chopped onion		drained
1	T. flour	1	6½ oz. can tuna, drained
¼	t. pepper		and flaked
½	c. milk	2	medium tomatoes, cut in
1	egg, slightly beaten		wedges
¼	c. sour cream	2	T. butter
½	c. mayonnaise	½	c. crushed chow mein
			noodles

Melt 2 tablespoons butter in saucepan; add green pepper and onion; cook 2 minutes. Blend in flour, salt, and pepper. Gradually add milk. Cook and stir until slightly thickened. Blend together egg, sour cream, and mayonnaise; stir into sauce. Add vegetables and tuna. Turn into buttered 1 quart baking dish. Arrange tomato wedges on top. Bake at 375° for 25 minutes. Melt 2 tablespoons butter in skillet; add chow mein noodles; and heat until lightly browned. Sprinkle over top of Tuna Bake.
Serves 4 to 5.
Mrs. K. G. Johnson (Betty Fister)

Tuna-Spinach Bake

1	7 oz. can white tuna,	1	T. lemon juice
	drained	2	T. Parmesan cheese
⅓	c. fine, dry bread crumbs	¼	t. salt
1	10 oz. pkg. frozen		Dash of pepper
	spinach, cooked and	½	c. mayonnaise
	drained	½	c. grated sharp cheese

Blend tuna, bread crumbs, spinach, lemon juice, cheese, salt, and pepper; then fold in mayonnaise. Spoon into individual fish shells or a lightly greased 1 quart baking dish. Sprinkle with grated cheese. Bake at 350° for 15 minutes. *Children love this!*
Serves 6.
Mrs. Harold L. Kennedy (Helen Hancock)

VEGETABLES

Asparagus Chestnut Bake

1	15 oz. can asparagus, drained	1	10¾ oz. can cream of mushroom soup
1	17 oz. can English peas, drained	¾	c. grated Cheddar cheese
Salt to taste		3	or 4 slices white bread
1	6 oz. can water chestnuts, sliced	3	T. melted butter

In a buttered 2 quart casserole, layer vegetables in order given. Spoon and spread soup over top and sprinkle with cheese. Cut bread in strips and saturate with melted butter. Lay bread over top of casserole and bake uncovered in 350° oven for 30 to 40 minutes.
Serves 8.
Mrs. Curtis Mann (Jay Nemer)

Baked Beans

1	large onion, chopped	1	c. catsup
1	large bell pepper, chopped	½	c. brown sugar, packed
2	16 oz. cans pork and beans	1	t. prepared yellow mustard
1	15 oz. can Ranch Style beans	Bacon slices	

Combine all ingredients except bacon slices and pour into 2½ quart bean pot. Place bacon slices on top. Bake at 350° uncovered for 2 hours.
Serves 12.
Mrs. Ben W. Swinney (Linda Jenkins)

Red Bean Toss

2	c. red or kidney beans	½	t. salt
1	c. chopped celery	½	t. chili powder
⅓	c. chopped pickles (Polish variety)	½	t. Worcestershire sauce
		Few	drops Tabasco sauce
¼	c. finely chopped onion	½	c. salad dressing
1	c. diced sharp cheese (¼ lb.)	1	c. coarsely crushed corn chips

Drain beans and combine with next four ingredients. Blend seasonings with salad dressing. Add to bean mixture and toss lightly. Pour into shallow 1 quart baking dish. Sprinkle with chips. Bake in 450° oven for 10 minutes. Serves 4.
Mrs. E. Wayne Craddock (Alpha Boyett)

Fresh Shelled Peas
(Black-Eyed, Purple Hull, or Cream)

About 3 quarts peas, washed (may be frozen)
Water
Salt
2 to 4 thick slices bacon, salt pork, or ham cut in pieces

1 large onion, coarsely chopped
3 stalks celery with tops, chopped
Black pepper
Seasoned salt, optional
Seasoned pepper, optional
Parsley, optional

Place peas in a 5 quart deep cooking pot. Add water to come to within an inch or two of the top of the pot. Bring to a boil and skim off any foam until it stops forming. Add about a tablespoon and a half salt (this can be adjusted to taste as peas cook), the bacon pieces, onion, celery, and a good bit of freshly ground black pepper. You may add any other seasonings of your choice to taste such as seasoned salt and pepper or parsley. These may be added during the cooking period. Bring to a boil, reduce heat, cover, and simmer *slowly* about 2½ hours or until peas are tender. Add water if needed. Flavor improves each time the peas are reheated.
Serves 12. Freezes.
Mrs. Cad E. Williams (Francis Bailey)

Black-Eyed Peas Creole

2	strips bacon	½	t. sweet basil
1	c. chopped onion		Salt and freshly ground pepper
1	c. chopped bell pepper		to taste
1	c. chopped celery	2	pkgs. frozen black-eyed
1	20 oz. can tomatoes		peas or two 15 oz. cans
1	T. sugar		cooked dry black-eyed
1	large bay leaf		peas

Fry bacon until crisp and remove from grease. Saute onion, pepper, and celery in grease. Transfer vegetables to a 3 quart saucepan. Add bacon, tomatoes, sugar, bay leaf, sweet basil, salt, and pepper. Simmer 5 minutes. Add peas without thawing. Cook slowly for 1½ hours, adding water when necessary.
Serves 6.
Mrs. Curtis C. Mann (Jay Nemer)

Broccoli Crepes

1	10 oz. pkg. frozen	¼	c. milk
	chopped broccoli	½	c. coarsely grated
	Salt and pepper to taste		Cheddar cheese
1	hard-cooked egg, sliced	8	to 10 crepes
1	10¾ oz. can condensed		
	cream of asparagus or		
	cream of celery soup		

Cook broccoli until just tender, drain well, and season with salt and pepper. Divide onto crepes. Top with a slice of egg. Roll crepes and arrange seam side down in buttered shallow baking dish. Blend soup with milk, heat, pour over crepes, and sprinkle with cheese. Bake in 400° oven about 20 minutes or until the cheese browns. Fills 8 to 10 crepes.
Serves 4 to 6.
Mrs. J. R. Parker (Pat McCrary)

Broccoli Rice

1   6 oz. pkg. Uncle Ben's
    long grain and wild rice
1   10¾ oz. can cream of
    chicken soup, undiluted
1   8 oz. can sliced water
    chestnuts, drained

1   10 oz. pkg. frozen
    chopped broccoli,
    thawed
1   8 oz. jar cheese whiz

Cook the rice according to directions. Add remaining ingredients and pour into a 9 x 9 casserole and bake uncovered at 350° for 30 minutes. You may add diced chicken, mushrooms, etc.
Serves 6 to 8.
Mrs. J. M. Davenport (Almarine Allen)

Cabbage Noodles

2   T. butter
Caraway seed, as desired
1   small chopped onion
Generous ½ c. chopped
    cabbage

1½   c. thin egg noodles,
     cooked and drained
Salt and pepper to taste

Saute chopped onion and caraway seed in butter over medium low heat. Add chopped cabbage and saute. Add more butter, if needed. Season with salt and pepper and simmer until tender crisp. Cover while simmering. Cook noodles and add to cabbage.
Serves 4.
Mrs. J. E. Johnston (Marie Orgeron)

Glorified Cabbage

1	medium head cabbage	½	lb. Velveeta cheese
6	T. butter	1	c. bread crumbs
1	onion, finely chopped		Salt and red pepper to taste
1	10¾ oz. can cream of mushroom soup		

Boil chopped cabbage until tender in salted water and drain. Saute onion in butter; add cheese and stir until melted. Combine with mushroom soup and fold in cabbage. Add bread crumbs. Season to taste. Pour into 2 quart casserole. Bake in 350° oven 20 to 30 minutes.
Serves 6.
Mrs. Joe Ed Johnston (Marilyn Hardgrave)

Carrot Souffle

1	c. cooked mashed carrots	½	t. pepper
2	whole eggs, beaten	1	T. sugar
½	c. rolled cracker crumbs	6	T. melted butter
1	c. milk	1	c. grated Cheddar cheese
1	t. salt		

Preheat oven to 375°. Mix all ingredients together. Pour into a round 1½ quart casserole, and bake in 375° oven for approximately 50 minutes or until knife inserted into the center comes out clean.
Serves 4.
Mrs. Joe Ed Johnston (Marilyn Hardgrave)

Carrot Mushroom Stir-Fry

2	T. butter	5	medium green onions
2	T. oil		with tops, thinly sliced
1	lb. carrots, peeled and	1	T. lemon juice
	thinly sliced	½	t. salt
¾	lb. mushrooms, thinly	¼	t. freshly ground pepper
	sliced		

In a large skillet, heat the oil and butter until bubbly. Add carrots, mushrooms, and onions. Cook and stir vegetables until tender, about eight minutes. Stir in lemon juice, salt, and pepper.
Serves 4.
Mrs. A. Hugh Summers (Ahnise Varnell)

Creamed Cauliflower

1	medium head cauliflower	¼	t. pepper
2	T. butter	2	T. chopped pimiento
2	T. flour	1	c. chopped green onions
1½	c. milk	½	c. buttered bread crumbs
½	t. salt	¼	to ½ c. grated cheese

Cook cauliflower in boiling salted water for about 20 minutes. Drain and break cauliflower into flowerets and place in baking dish. Melt butter in small pan. Add flour and stir until blended. Gradually add milk, stirring until smooth and thick. Add salt, pepper, pimiento, and green onions. Blend well and pour over flowerets. Sprinkle with grated cheese and bread crumbs. Bake in 375° oven for 20 minutes or until slightly browned.
Serves 4 to 6.
Mrs. W. H. Shuller, Jr. (Mary Plemons)

Williamsburg Creamed Celery

4	c. celery cut diagonally in ½ inch pieces	2	c. milk
2	T. butter	1	t. salt
2	T. flour	¾	c. pecan halves
		½	c. buttered bread crumbs

Boil celery in a small amount of water until tender, then drain. Melt butter in saucepan. Stir in flour, milk, and salt. Cook stirring constantly until mixture thickens. Add well drained celery. Spoon into slightly greased 6 cup casserole. Top with pecan halves and cover with buttered bread crumbs. Bake at 400° for 15 minutes.
Serves 6.
Mrs. Harold L. Kennedy (Helen Hancock)

Corn Casserole

2	16 oz. cans whole kernel corn, drained	1	T. sugar
1	8 oz. pkg. cream cheese, softened	1	t. salt
		1	3 oz. can chopped green chilies, drained
2	T. butter, softened	1	T. chopped bell pepper
¼	c. milk	1	T. chopped pimiento

Mix all ingredients and pour into 1½ quart casserole and bake at 350° for 25 minutes.
Serves 6.
Mrs. Frank George (Jeanette Stephan)

Stuffed Mushrooms Parmesan

12	large mushrooms	12	Ritz crackers, crushed
2	T. butter	3	T. Parmesan cheese
1	medium onion, chopped fine	1	T. parsley
		½	t. seasoned salt
1	small green pepper, chopped fine	¼	t. dried oregano
		Dash of pepper	
1	small clove garlic, minced	⅓	c. chicken broth
2	oz. pepperoni, chopped		

Clean mushrooms; remove stems, chop, and reserve. Melt butter, add onion, pepper, garlic, pepperoni, and chopped mushroom stems. Cook until tender but not brown. Add crackers, cheese, parsley, salt, oregano, and pepper. Mix well; stir in chicken broth. Spoon stuffing into mushroom caps. Place in a shallow pan with ¼ inch water. Bake uncovered at 325° for 15 to 20 minutes. May be served as a vegetable or an appetizer.
Serves 6.
Mrs. R. L. Kenderdine (Daphne Dunning)

Corn Casserole Mexican

1	8 oz. box Chicken Rice-A-Roni	1	10¾ oz. can mushroom soup
1	12 oz. can Mexicorn, undrained	1	8 oz. jar jalapeno Cheese Whiz

Prepare Rice-A-Roni according to package directions. Add remaining ingredients and spoon into a 2 quart casserole. Cover and bake in a 350° oven for 30 minutes.
Serves 8.
Mrs. Gordon I. Thielen (Lavelle Mathis)

Corn Spoon

3	eggs, separated		2	T. butter
1¼	c. milk, scalded		1	17 oz. can cream-style
¾	c. corn meal			corn
¾	t. salt		¾	t. baking powder

Grease a round 2 quart baking dish. Beat egg whites until stiff but not dry; beat egg yolks until thick and lemon colored. Stir corn meal and salt into scalded milk, beating hard with wire whisk. Cook a few seconds over low heat, stirring until consistency of thick mush. Blend in butter and corn and then baking powder. Fold in yolks, then whites. Bake in 375° oven about 35 minutes or until puffy and golden brown. This may also be cooked in microwave.
Serves 4 to 6.
Mrs. Cad E. Williams (Francis Bailey)

Corn Puff

¼	c. margarine		1	scant T. sugar
1	17 oz. can yellow cream-style corn		2	eggs, beaten
½	c. yellow corn meal		1	4 oz. can chopped green chilies
1½	c. milk		1	c. grated sharp Cheddar cheese
1	t. salt			

Melt margarine in a 2 quart saucepan, and stir in the other ingredients in the order given. Cook over medium heat, stirring until thickened. Watch carefully so it won't scorch. Pour into a well buttered 2 quart casserole, and bake in a 350° oven for one hour. Goes well with baked ham and a tossed green salad. When doubling recipe do not increase the amount of salt and sugar.
Serves 8.
Mrs. Ben L. Slack (Alice Jeffrey)

Greens
(Collards, Mustard, or Turnip Greens)

2 to 2½ lbs. greens	2 slices bacon cut into
Water	pieces, optional
Salt	Pepper sauce vinegar

Use greens that have crisp, clean leaves with good color. Avoid seedy or woody stems. Discard ends, tough stems, and yellowed leaves. Wash 3 times, lifting greens out of water each time and shaking well so sand sinks to bottom of water. Cook in ½ inch boiling water, covered. If the greens are very young and tender, use no water; greens will cook in water clinging to leaves after washing. Add ½ teaspoon salt per pound of greens and bacon if desired. Cook 5 to 15 minutes or until tender. Collards usually take longer to become tender than do mustard or turnip greens. Serve with pepper sauce vinegar. *A combination of the greens is my favorite way to cook them.*
Serves 4. Freezes.
Mrs. Cad E. Williams (Francis Bailey)

Hominy

1 bell pepper, chopped	2 14½ oz. cans white
1 onion, chopped	hominy, drained
2 T. butter	1 16 oz. can whole tomatoes

Saute bell peppers and onion in butter. Add hominy and tomatoes. Simmer 25 to 30 minutes.
Serves 4.
Mrs. C. L. Kolstad, III (Jill McPherson)

Hominy Casserole

2	14 oz. cans white hominy, drained	1	c. chopped green pepper
2	T. margarine	1	10¾ oz. can cream of mushroom soup
1	c. chopped onion	1	8 oz. jar jalapeno Cheese Whiz
1	c. chopped celery		

Saute vegetables in margarine. Add hominy to vegetable mixture and combine with heated mushroom soup and Cheese Whiz. Place in greased 2 quart casserole and bake in 350° oven for approximately 30 minutes.
Serves 6 to 8.
Mrs. H. Green (Bennie Eubanks)

Savory Hominy Casserole

2	T. butter		Dash of cayenne
1	T. corn starch	1½	lbs. old English cheese, grated
1	c. milk or cream		
1	c. ripe olive juice	1	9 oz. can pitted ripe olives, chopped
1	t. Worcestershire		
5	drops Tabasco	2	28 oz. cans white hominy, drained
Salt and pepper to taste			

Melt butter and blend in corn starch. Add milk and cook, stirring constantly until thick. Mix in olive juice, seasonings, and grated cheese. Stir olives into sauce together with drained hominy. Place in greased 2 quart casserole and bake at 375° for 45 minutes.
Serves 8 to 10.
Mrs. Wright Matthews (Ruby Millhouse)

Baked Eggplant

1	large eggplant (1¼ to 1½ lbs.)	5	T. chopped green chilies
2	T. chopped green onion	1	large egg, well beaten
Salt and pepper to taste		¼	c. toasted bread crumbs
5	oz. cream cheese	2	T. butter, melted

Peel and cube eggplant. Boil in seasoned water to which chopped onions have been added. Boil until fork tender and drain thoroughly. While still hot mash, add cream cheese, and stir until well blended. Add well beaten egg and green chilies. Pour into a greased 1 quart baking dish. Top with bread crumbs and drizzle with melted butter. Set in a pan of hot water and bake at 350° for 30 minutes or until set.
Serves 4 to 6.
Mrs. Fred E. Felder (Jean Granger)

Eggplant au Gratin

4	small eggplants, peeled	2	eggs, beaten
2	large onions, sliced	Salt and pepper to taste	
1	lb. sharp Cheddar cheese, grated	1	stick butter, divided
		½	to 1 c. cracker crumbs

Boil eggplant in salted water until tender. Drain and mash. Drain again if necessary. Saute onion in half of butter. Combine eggplant, onions, cheese, eggs, salt, and pepper. Place in oiled 3 quart casserole. Top with crumbs and dot with remaining butter. Bake at 350° for 40 to 45 minutes.
Serves 10.
Mrs. A. J. Overton, Jr. (Lila May Morriss)

Eggplant Parmesan

2	large eggplants, peeled and cubed	1	c. grated Parmesan cheese
1	rib celery, chopped	1	c. cracker crumbs
2	onions, chopped	½	c. grated American cheese
2	green peppers, chopped	2	T. chopped parsley
2	T. olive oil	½	t. rosemary, optional
2	T. butter	½	t. sweet basil, optional
2	eggs, slightly beaten	1	t. garlic salt
		1	c. small shrimp, optional

Cook eggplant until tender in small amount of salted water. Drain and mash. Saute onions, pepper, and celery in oil and butter until tender but not brown. Mix all ingredients reserving ½ cup cracker crumbs and cheese. Place in 2 quart casserole. Cover with remaining crumbs and top with American cheese. Dot with butter and sprinkle with paprika. Bake in 350° oven 30 minutes.
Serves 8.
Mrs. Frank Hicks (Helen Davenport)

Eggplant Casserole

1	large eggplant	½	t. Worcestershire
1	T. flaked onions	2	eggs, beaten
18	crushed Ritz crackers		Lump of butter
¼	to ½ lb. Velveeta cheese		Salt and pepper to taste

Peel one large eggplant and cut into cubes. Boil in salted water until tender about 5 or 6 minutes. Drain well. Add remaining ingredients and place in a greased 3 quart casserole. Bake 30 minutes in a 350° oven.
Serves 8 to 10.
Mrs. W. A. Glass, Jr. (Sarah Kolstad)

Eggplant-Zucchini Casserole

1	large eggplant	1	4 oz. can chopped green
2	lbs. zucchini, sliced		chilies, drained
1	8 oz. pkg. cream cheese	1½	c. buttered bread crumbs

Pare eggplant. Dice and soak in salted water. Drain and cook briefly with zucchini in small amount of water. Drain. Add cream cheese to eggplant mixture. Stir gently until cheese melts and add green chilies. Pour into buttered 3 quart shallow baking dish. Top with bread crumbs and bake in 350° oven 30 minutes or until crumbs are brown.
Serves 8 to 10. Freezes.
Miss Thelma Anderson

English Pea and
Water Chestnut Casserole

½	c. margarine	1	4 oz. jar diced pimientos
1	small onion, minced	Salt and pepper to taste	
2	T. diced bell pepper	1	10¾ oz. can cream of
1	c. chopped celery		mushroom soup
2	17 oz. cans small English	1	c. buttered cracker
	peas, drained		crumbs
1	8 oz. can water chestnuts,		
	sliced		

Saute onion, pepper, and celery in margarine. Add peas, water chestnuts, and pimientos. Stir together and add salt and pepper to taste. Arrange in layers in a greased 2 quart casserole, alternating layers of vegetable mixture and soup, beginning and ending with vegetables. Top with buttered cracker crumbs. Bake in 350° oven 20 to 30 minutes.
Serves 8 to 10. Freezes.
Mrs. W. O. Smith (Marye Jo Green)

Sweet and Sour Beans

2	16 oz. cans cut green beans, drained	½	c. sugar
1	medium onion, thinly sliced	1 ½	t. salt t. MSG
½	c. vinegar	2	T. salad oil
		Black pepper to taste	

Alternate layers of beans and onion in 1½ quart dish. Combine remaining ingredients and heat. Pour over beans and refrigerate overnight. May be served hot or cold.
Serves 6.
Mrs. Gordon B. Broyles (Frances Dilley)

Sweet-Sour Green Beans

1	lb. green beans	½	c. water
4	slices bacon	⅓	c. cider vinegar
2	T. bacon drippings	2	T. sugar
1	medium onion, chopped	Salt and freshly ground pepper	
2	t. flour		to taste

Cover beans in boiling, salted water and cook until tender-crisp (6 to 8 minutes). Drain. In a large skillet, cook bacon until crisp, reserving 2 tablespoons drippings. Crumble bacon. Saute onion in drippings until tender. Stir in flour and cook until bubbly. Add water, sugar, and vinegar. Heat to boiling and continue to cook until slightly thickened. Add beans and heat thoroughly, tossing occasionally. May substitute two 16 oz. cans of green beans, drained, or two 10 oz. packages frozen cut green beans, cooked and drained.
Serves 6.
Mrs. A. Hugh Summers (Ahnise Varnell)

Green Beans Oriental

2	16 oz. cans whole green beans, drained	1	c. sour cream
		1	c. grated Cheddar cheese
1	8 oz. can water chestnuts, sliced		

Add water chestnuts to drained beans in 1½ quart casserole dish. Add sour cream to cover beans and sprinkle with grated cheese. Bake at 300° for 20 minutes or until cheese is melted.
Serves 6.
Mrs. Neilson Rogers (Bettie Tippit)

Green Bean Casserole

2	16 oz. cans French style green beans, well drained	½	t. pepper
		1	T. sugar
1	T. butter	1	T. grated onion
2	T. flour	1	c. sour cream
½	t. salt	½	lb. cheese, grated
		1	c. bread crumbs

Cover green beans with ice water and let stand while making sauce. To make sauce melt butter over low heat; add flour and stir; add remaining ingredients. Heat until well mixed and toss lightly over the well drained green beans. Place in a buttered 2 quart casserole. Sprinkle with bread crumbs. Bake at 325° for approximately 20 minutes.
Serves 6 to 8.
Mrs. Jeff D. Walker (Kathy Kolstad)

Honeyed French Green Beans

1	16 oz. can French style	1	T. Worcestershire sauce
	green beans	3	slices bacon
3	T. honey		

Pour undrained green beans into 1 quart casserole. Drizzle honey and Worcestershire sauce over the beans. Place bacon strips on top. Bake at 350° until bacon is crisp, approximately 30 minutes.
Serves 3 to 4.
Mrs. C. L. Kolstad, III (Jill McPherson)

Italian Bean Casserole

2	10 oz. pkgs. frozen Italian	2	T. toasted almonds
	beans	1	10¾ oz. can cream of
1	4 oz. can mushrooms,		mushroom soup,
	drained		undiluted
1	3 oz. can French fried	½	c. grated Cheddar cheese
	onion rings		

Place alternate layers of beans, mushrooms, and onion rings in 2 quart casserole. Mix soup and almonds and pour over layers. Sprinkle cheese on top and bake for 30 minutes at 350°.
Serves 6.
Mrs. J. W. Summers (Inez Thompson)

Blue-Cheesed Mushrooms

12	to 14 extra large fresh or canned whole mushrooms	¼	c. (1 oz.) crumbled blue cheese
¼	c. chopped green onions	⅓	c. fine dry bread crumbs
¼	c. butter		Salt and pepper

Remove stems from mushrooms; chop stems. Cook stems and onions in butter until tender but not brown. Add cheese, 2 tablespoons of the crumbs, and salt and pepper to taste. Fill mushroom crowns with mixture; sprinkle with remaining crumbs. Place on baking sheet. Bake in 350° oven for 12 minutes for fresh mushrooms or 8 minutes for canned. Serve as meat accompaniment.
Serves 6.
Mrs. N. C. Woolverton (Jettie Seagler)

Mushrooms Stuffed with Snails

8	T. soft butter	¼	t. salt, optional
1¼	t. minced shallots		Pepper to taste
2	large cloves garlic, finely minced	16	fresh mushrooms, each approximately 2 inches in diameter
1½	T. minced parsley		
½	T. grated celery	16	canned snails, drained

Preheat oven to 375°. Cream 6 tablespoons of the butter with the shallots, garlic, parsley, celery, salt, and pepper. Remove stems of the mushrooms. With a sharp knife, hollow out a ¾ inch depression in the top of each cap. Saute the mushrooms in the remaining 2 tablespoons of butter for 5 minutes, turning each over at least once. Place a small amount of the herbed butter in each mushroom cap; then add a snail and a little more butter. Place in shallow 3 quart baking dish and bake for 15 minutes. May be prepared ahead of time, covered and refrigerated until serving time. Then place in oven until butter is melted, cooking as stated above.
Serves 8.
Mrs. John E. Presley (Lucinda Hanks)

Stuffed Mushrooms Provencale

1	lb. large mushrooms	1	T. chopped parsley
3	T. grated Parmesan cheese	2	T. melted butter
1	clove garlic, chopped	4	to 6 T. olive oil
1	small onion, chopped		Salt and pepper to taste
1	c. bread crumbs		

Clean and remove stems from mushrooms. Mix the cheese, garlic, onion, bread crumbs, and butter. Add salt and pepper to taste. Fill the mushroom caps. Pour 2 tablespoons of oil in the bottom of a 2 quart baking pan. Place mushrooms in pan stuffed side up. Pour balance of oil equally over all mushrooms. Bake about 20 minutes in 350° oven. When mushrooms are tender and tops are brown, remove from oven. Serve hot.
Serves 4 to 6.
Mrs. Charles Stanton (Lisa Guarnieri)

Whole Baked Onions

4	large white onions	2	t. salt
4	T. butter	1	t. pepper
4	T. lemon juice	1	t. paprika

Remove outer peeling from onions and core small hole in top of each. Place each onion on individual sheets of foil and season each with the following: 1 tablespoon butter placed in hole on top, 1 tablespoon lemon juice, ½ teaspoon salt, ¼ teaspoon pepper, and ¼ teaspoon paprika. Fold foil over onion to seal, and bake at 375° for 1½ hours or until tender.
Serves 4.
Mrs. Jeff D. Walker (Katherine Kolstad)

Baked Potato Strips

4	baking potatoes	1	t. pepper
½	c. vegetable oil	1	t. paprika
2	t. salt		

Wash potatoes. Leaving skin on, cut each potato into 8 long strips. Dip potato strips in mixture of vegetable oil and seasonings. Place skin side down in foil-lined 9 x 13 baking dish. Bake at 450° for 20 minutes. Broil for 1 minute to crisp.
Serves 6.
Cookbook Committee

French Potato Balls

5	medium potatoes	2	eggs, separated
Salt and pepper to taste		Dry bread crumbs	
Freshly grated nutmeg to taste			

Peel potatoes, cut into quarters, and cook no more than 12 to 15 minutes in salted boiling water. Mash or quickly rice potatoes through food mill, add salt, pepper, nutmeg, and quickly fold in egg yolks. Mix well. Beat egg whites just until foamy. Form potato mixture into balls the shape of a small egg, dip into beaten egg white, and roll in dry bread crumbs. Fry until golden brown. You can make these a day ahead of time and fry when ready to serve.
Serves 6.
Mrs. Charles H. Stanton (Lisa Guarnieri)

  Combine ½ cup softened butter or margarine with 1 tablespoon grated fresh Parmesan cheese, 1 ½ teaspoons each basil and marjoram and ¼ teaspoon seasoned salt. Beat until light and fluffy. Melt this Parmesan Cheese Butter over grilled potatoes. Makes about ½ cup.

Mashed Potato Casserole

2	c. mashed potatoes (softer than you serve)	1	8 oz. pkg. cream cheese
1	medium onion, finely chopped	2	eggs
		1	3 oz. can French fried onion rings

Add onions, cheese, and eggs to hot mashed potatoes. Blend well with mixer. Pour into buttered 2 quart casserole and cover top with onion rings. Place covered casserole in 350° oven for 30 minutes. Left over mashed potatoes can be used.
Serves 4 to 6.
Mrs. P. A. Kolstad, Jr. (Dottie Ondus)

Pommes au Four
(Potatoes au gratin, French way)

2	t. instant beef broth	Butter
2	lbs. potatoes	1 clove garlic
¾	c. light cream	1 c. grated Swiss cheese

Pare potatoes, slice thinly, and cook in small amount of salted water until tender. Warm cream on low heat, and add instant beef broth and one clove crushed garlic. Place layer of potatoes in buttered 9 x 13 casserole, and cover with one half of the cream mixture. Repeat layers and top with cheese. Bake in 400° oven for 15 minutes or until cheese is golden.
Serves 4 to 6.
Mrs. Charles H. Stanton (Lisa Guarnieri)

Potatoes Romanoff

5 c. cooked diced potatoes	1 small clove of garlic,
2 t. salt	minced
2 c. creamed cottage cheese	½ c. grated Cheddar or
1 c. sour cream	American cheese
¼ c. finely minced green onions	Paprika

Sprinkle diced potatoes with 1 teaspoon salt. Combine cottage cheese, sour cream, onions, and garlic with remaining teaspoon salt; fold in potatoes. Pour into a buttered 2½ quart casserole; top with cheese and sprinkle with paprika. Bake in preheated 350° oven for 25 to 30 minutes or until heated through and bubbly. (Five medium potatoes will make 5 cups diced. You may cook the potatoes in the skin the day before, and store in the refrigerator for use the next day.)
Serves 8 to 10.
Mrs. Billy Gragg (Jackie Lockey)

Onion Pie

2 c. freshly sliced onion rings	1 9 inch unbaked pie shell
4 T. margarine	1 T. flour
½ c. sherry	1 c. sour cream
	2 egg yolks, well beaten

Saute onion rings in the margarine. Add sherry and steam 5 minutes. Remove onion rings from skillet and arrange in pie shell. Add flour, sour cream, and egg yolks to the sherry/margarine mixture remaining in the skillet. Mix well but do not cook. Pour over the onions in the pie shell. Bake in a 375° oven for 30 to 35 minutes. When done, the filling should be the consistency of custard. Serve immediately. Delicious with roast beef or fowl.
Serves 6 to 8.
Mrs. Daniel F. Rex (Emory Hill)

Refrigerator Mashed Potatoes

5	lbs. potatoes, pared and quartered	1	t. salt
2	3 oz. pkgs. cream cheese	¼	to ½ t. pepper
1	c. sour cream	4	T. butter
2	T. chopped green onion		Grated cheese

Cook potatoes in boiling salted water until tender. Drain well. Saute onion in butter. Whip potatoes until smooth. Add cream cheese, sour cream, onion and butter, salt, and pepper. Whip until fluffy. If mixture seems a bit stiff, add more sour cream. Place in airtight refrigerator container. Cool and cover. Recommended storage time is 10 days. To serve, place desired amount of potatoes in greased casserole. Dot with butter and cover with grated cheese, if desired. Bake in 350° oven for 30 minutes or until heated through. If you use full amount, heat in 2 quart casserole. Makes about 8 cups. Do not add milk to this recipe.
Mrs. Dennis E. Ward (Jamie Brown)

Pecan-Topped Sweet Potatoes

3	lbs. sweet potatoes, cooked and peeled	1	t. salt
½	c. light brown sugar	1	t. cinnamon
8	T. butter	½	to 1 c. fresh orange juice
1	egg	1	c. pecans

Mash potatoes (about 6 cups). Beat in egg, ¼ cup brown sugar, and 4 tablespoons butter. Add salt, cinnamon, and orange juice. Place in 1½ quart casserole. Arrange pecans on top, sprinkle with remaining brown sugar, and drizzle with remaining butter. Bake in 350° oven for 20 minutes until thoroughly heated.
Serves 6 to 8.
Mrs. A. J. Overton, Jr. (Lila May Morriss)

Green Enchiladas

1	10 oz. pkg. frozen spinach	1	pt. sour cream
2	10¾ oz. cans condensed cream of chicken soup, undiluted	¼	t. salt
		3	c. or more of grated Monterey Jack cheese
2	or 3 bunches of green onions, chopped	2	doz. corn tortillas
2	4 oz. cans chopped green chilies, drained		

Cook spinach in 1½ cups water. Drain thoroughly. Place cooked and drained spinach in blender. Add soup, 4 tablespoons chopped onion, 2 cans of chilies, and salt. Blend. Pour into mixing bowl and add sour cream and mix well. Soften tortillas in hot oil and drain on paper towels. Spread each tortilla with chopped onions and some grated cheese and roll. Place tortillas, seam side down, in a 2 quart baking dish. Pour sauce over tortillas and sprinkle remaining onions and grated cheese over top. Cover and bake at 350° for about 30 minutes. May be prepared several days in advance and refrigerated until ready to bake.
Serves 8 to 10.
Mrs. Ed Montgomery (Dorothy Meador)

Spinach-Artichoke Casserole

2	10 oz. pkgs. frozen chopped spinach	½	t. salt
½	c. finely chopped white onion	⅛	t. pepper
		¾	c. Parmesan cheese, reserving ¼ c. for topping
½	c. butter		
1	pt. sour cream	1	c. buttered bread crumbs
1	16 oz. can artichoke hearts, drained and cut in half		

Cook spinach as directed on box and drain well. Saute onions in butter. Mix first 8 ingredients together and put in buttered 2 quart casserole. Sprinkle a little Parmesan cheese on top. Cover with buttered bread crumbs. Bake in 350° oven 25 to 30 minutes. *Great dish for company!*
Serves 8 to 10.
Mrs. Elton Bomer (Ginny Roco)

Quick Spinach Casserole

2	10 oz. pkgs. frozen chopped spinach	½	c. bread crumbs
1	8 oz. pkg. cream cheese	¼	t. mace
½	c. margarine	¼	t. sage
		¼	c. margarine, melted

Cook spinach and drain. Mix cream cheese and margarine with spinach while it is hot. Put in unbuttered casserole. Mix bread crumbs with spices, then add melted margarine. Spread over casserole. Bake at 350° for 30 minutes until brown. *Quick and delicious!*
Serves 8.
Mrs. Willard W. Johnson, Jr. (Nancy Earle)

Spinach Madelaine

2	10 oz. pkgs. frozen chopped spinach	½	t. black pepper
4	T. butter	¾	t. celery salt
2	T. flour	¾	t. garlic salt
2	T. chopped onion		Salt and pepper to taste
½	c. evaporated milk	3	oz. jalapeno cheese
½	c. spinach liquor	3	oz. Old English cheese
		1	t. Worcestershire sauce

Cook spinach and drain, reserving ½ cup of the liquid. Melt butter in a saucepan over low heat. Add flour and blend until smooth. Add onion and cook until soft but not brown. Slowly add spinach liquor and milk. Stir until thick. Add seasonings and grated cheese. Mix cooked spinach with sauce. Spoon into a 2 quart casserole; top with bread crumbs; and bake in a 350° oven for 30 to 45 minutes. This is better prepared a day ahead.
Serves 6 to 8.
Mrs. J. E. Johnston, Sr. (Marie Orgeron)

Spinach Casserole

2   10 oz. pkgs. frozen
     chopped spinach
1   10¾ oz. can cream of
     mushroom soup

1   12 oz. carton small curd
     cottage cheese
1   3 oz. can French fried
     onions
½   c. bread crumbs

Cook and drain spinach; heat the soup and cheese and add spinach and onions. Place in buttered 2 quart casserole and top with bread crumbs. Bake in 350° oven until heated through. This is good for buffets. Even men like it!
Serves 6 to 8.
Mrs. Robert Cox (Louise Spreen)

Baked Squash Casserole

2½   lbs. yellow squash
1   small onion, chopped
1   egg, beaten
½   c. cubed Velveeta cheese
2   to 3 T. sugar
½   t. Worcestershire
2   T. butter

Salt and pepper
Small amount milk to moisten
8   to 10 Ritz crackers,
     crushed
Pinch oregano
½   c. grated cheese

Cook squash until tender; drain and add all ingredients except grated cheese. Pour into a 1½ quart casserole and top with grated cheese. Bake at 350° until brown about 25 to 30 minutes. Zucchini squash may be substituted for yellow squash.
Serves 6.
Mrs. Luckett C. Kolstad, Jr. (Katherine Taylor)

Corn Squash Casserole

6	large yellow squash, sliced	1	16 oz. can cream-style corn
1	large white onion, chopped		Salt and pepper to taste
		1½	c. grated Cheddar cheese

Boil squash and onion until tender; drain. Mix with cream-style corn. Pour into 2 quart casserole, top with cheese, and bake in 350° oven until cheese is melted and bubbly.
Serves 8.
Mrs. Harry Brown (Carol Albright)

Cream Cheese Squash Bake

3	lbs. yellow squash	Salt and pepper to taste
½	c. butter	Ritz crackers
1	8 oz. pkg. cream cheese	Sliced almonds
1	T. sugar	

Cook squash until tender. Drain all liquid. Cook until remaining liquid is gone. Add butter, sugar, and cream cheese. Mix well. Add salt and pepper. Put in greased 2 quart casserole. Crush Ritz crackers and spread over squash. Top with almonds. Cover casserole and bake in 350° oven for about 20 minutes until almonds are lightly browned. If freezing, omit cracker crumbs until ready to bake.
Serves 6 to 8.
Mrs. Norman Bonner (Susan Beyette)

Squash Casserole

2	to 3 lbs. yellow squash, sliced	2	onions, finely chopped
	Salt and pepper to taste	1	8 oz. can sliced water chestnuts, drained
½	c. butter, melted	1	2 oz. jar pimientos, drained
1	c. sour cream		
1	10¾ oz. can cream of chicken soup, undiluted	1	8 oz. pkg. herb-seasoned stuffing mix, divided

Cook squash in boiling water until tender; drain, reserving 1½ cups liquid. Season to taste with salt and pepper; mash. Combine reserved liquid and remaining ingredients except ½ cup stuffing mix. Stir in squash. Pour mixture into 2½ quart casserole. Top with reserved stuffing mix. Bake at 350° for 30 minutes.
Serves 12.
Mrs. Max Alldredge (Martha Tettleton)

Skillet Squash

2	T. butter	⅛	t. sugar
8	medium yellow squash	1	t. lemon juice
2	zucchini squash	2	T. water
3	T. coarsely chopped onion		Plain salt
	Seasoned salt	½	c. frozen English peas
	Freshly ground black pepper	2	strips crisp-fried bacon

Melt butter in large skillet over very low heat. Slice squash ⅓ inch thick. With small pancake turner, stir into butter. Stir in onions. Sprinkle lightly with seasoned salt, sugar, pepper, and lemon juice. Add water and cover. Cook over low heat. After 10 minutes sprinkle lightly with plain salt, turn, and stir. Recover skillet loosely. Cook until tender crisp, stirring occasionally. Add peas the last 5 minutes. Stir in bacon just before serving.
Serves 6 to 8.
Mrs. Lester Hamilton (Frances Edmunds)

Zucchini Pie

4	c. thinly sliced unpeeled zucchini	¼	t. sweet basil leaves
1	c. coarsely chopped onion	¼	t. oregano leaves
4	T. margarine	2	eggs, well beaten
½	c. chopped parsley or 2 T. parsley flakes	8	oz. (2 c.) grated Mozzarella cheese (or cheese of your choice)
½	t. salt	1	9 inch deep dish pie shell
½	t. pepper	2	t. Dijon or prepared mustard
¼	t. garlic powder		

Heat oven to 375°. In 10 inch skillet cook zucchini and onion in margarine until tender, approximately 10 minutes. Stir in parsley and seasonings. Blend eggs and cheese, and stir into vegetable mixture. Spread pie shell with mustard. Pour vegetable mixture evenly into pie shell, and bake in 375° oven for 18 to 20 minutes or until knife inserted near center comes out clean. Let stand 10 minutes before serving. To reheat, cover loosely with foil; heat at 375° for 12 to 15 minutes, or cover with plastic and heat in microwave oven for 1 to 2 minutes.
Serves 6.
Mrs. Cad E. Williams (Francis Bailey)

Heavenly Vegetable Casserole

1	10 oz. pkg. frozen French style green beans	1	8 oz. can sliced water chestnuts, drained
1	10 oz. pkg. frozen baby lima beans	1	4 oz. jar sliced pimiento, drained
1	10 oz. pkg. frozen small English peas	1	c. sour cream
Salt and pepper to taste		1	c. mayonnaise
3	green peppers, sliced	1	c. grated Parmesan cheese

Barely thaw vegetables; drain. In a greased 3 quart casserole layer vegetables, water chestnuts, and pimiento. Salt and pepper each layer to taste. Mix sour cream and mayonnaise. Spread over vegetables. Top with Parmesan cheese. Bake in 350° oven for 30 to 35 minutes.
Serves 10 to 12.
Mrs. R. L. Kenderdine (Daphne Dunning)

Mixed Vegetable Casserole

1	10 oz. pkg. frozen green peas	1	c. grated onions
1	10 oz. pkg. frozen French style green beans	1	T. oil
		1	t. Tabasco
1	10 oz. pkg. frozen baby lima beans	3	hard cooked eggs, chopped
1	c. mayonnaise	½	c. buttered bread crumbs

Precook vegetables; drain. Mix together mayonnaise, onion, oil, and Tabasco; combine with vegetables and eggs. Place in 2 quart casserole. Sprinkle with buttered bread crumbs. Bake 30 minutes at 350°.
Serves 6 to 8.
Mrs. J. B. Bellican (Lucile Beasley)

Noodle Pudding

My grandmother knew this as "Lokchen Kugel". It is a dish that can be varied with fruit, nuts, cottage cheese, from plain to sweet. The recipe can be a compliment to meat or poultry, or can be served as a dessert. We prefer it served hot, but I have seen my husband eating some of the left-overs directly from the refrigerator. This is an ethnic dish - Jewish in origin.

8	oz. wide noodles	½	c. raisins
2	T. corn oil	2	or 3 eggs, well beaten
1	small onion, chopped	2	apples, peeled and sliced, optional
¼	T. cinnamon		
½	to 1 T. salt	½	c. sugar

Cook noodles in salted boiling water, 10 minutes or until tender. Drain. Pour cold water over noodles and drain thoroughly. Place noodles in deep bowl and fold in 2 tablespoons of corn oil. Saute onion and add cinnamon, salt, raisins, sugar, and eggs. Fold in apples and add to noodles; mix well. Place in well buttered 1½ quart casserole. Bake uncovered in 350° oven about 30 minutes. Cover and continue cooking for additional 15 to 30 minutes.
Serves 6 to 8.
Mrs. Henry Leon (Diane Minck)

Ratatouille

⅓	c. olive oil	3	c. zucchini, ½ inch slices
¾	c. onion, thinly sliced	2	c. tomatoes, peeled,
2	cloves garlic, minced		seeded, quartered
4	green peppers, slivered	¼	c. dry red wine
2½	c. eggplant, peeled and		Salt and pepper to taste
	diced		Pinch of basil

Saute onion and garlic in oil until golden. Add remaining ingredients and simmer covered over very low heat 35 to 45 minutes. Uncover and continue to cook 10 minutes more to reduce liquid. Serve with Parmesan if desired. Freezes well.
Serves 4 to 6.
Mrs. Stewart Kenderdine (Jane Kukar)

Vegetable Casserole

1	16 oz., can French style green beans	1	c. grated cheese
1	12 oz. can shoe peg corn	1	10¾ oz. can cream of celery soup
1	8 oz. can sliced water chestnuts	1	c. sour cream
½	c. chopped onions		Salt and pepper to taste
		1	c. Ritz crackers

Drain beans, shoe peg corn, and sliced water chestnuts. Mix onions, cheese, celery soup, sour cream, salt, and pepper. Add vegetables to sauce. Place in buttered 2 quart casserole; top with crushed Ritz crackers; and bake in 350° oven for 25 minutes.
Serves 10 to 12.
Mrs. John Wagnon (Helen Hammer)

SWEETS

Apricot Brandy Pound Cake

3	c sugar	½	t. rum flavoring
1	c. margarine	1	t. orange extract
6	eggs	¼	t. almond extract
3	c. cake flour	½	t. lemon extract
¼	t. baking soda	1	t. vanilla extract
½	t. salt	½	c. apricot brandy
1	c. sour cream		

Grease and flour 10 inch tube pan. Cream sugar and margarine. Add eggs, one at a time, beating thoroughly after each addition. Sift together flour, baking soda, and salt. Combine sour cream, flavorings, and brandy. Add alternately flour and sour cream mixtures to the sugar mixture and mix well. Pour into pan and bake in 325° oven about 70 minutes or until done.
May B. Bachtel, M.D. (May Bradley)

Buttermilk Pound Cake

1	c. shortening	1	c. buttermilk with ½ t. soda
2	c. sugar		
4	eggs	1	t. vanilla extract
¼	t. salt	1	t. lemon extract
3	c. flour with 1 t. baking powder	1	t. almond extract

Cream sugar and shortening, add eggs, and beat well. Combine dry ingredients and sift together. Add buttermilk with soda to creamed mixture. Add dry ingredients and mix well. Add extracts and stir thoroughly. Bake in greased and floured tube pan at 325° for 1 hour and 10 minutes.
Serves 14.
Mrs. Arch C. Murray (Acie Graham)

Chocolate Pound Cake

1½	c. butter or margarine	2	c. unsifted flour
3	c. sugar	¾	c. unsweetened cocoa
3	t. vanilla	1	t. salt
5	eggs	¼	t. baking powder
2	t. instant coffee granules	1	c. buttermilk
¼	c. boiling water		

Cream butter, gradually add sugar, beating until light and fluffy, about 15 minutes at medium speed in mixer. Stir in vanilla. Add eggs one at a time, beating well after each addition. Dissolve coffee granules in boiling water. In a separate bowl combine flour, cocoa, salt, and baking powder. Add alternately with coffee and buttermilk to creamed mixture, beating at low speed just until mixture is blended. Pour into greased and floured 3 quart bundt pan or 10 inch tube pan. Bake at 325° for one hour and 15 minutes. Cool in pan 15 minutes. Remove from pan and cool completely. Sprinkle with powdered sugar.
Serves 12.
Mrs. Marley P. Styner (Martha Hunter)

Potato Chocolate Cake

1	c. hot unseasoned mashed potatoes	½	c. cocoa
2	c. sugar	3	t. baking powder
⅔	c. shortening	1	t. each cinnamon and nutmeg
4	eggs, unbeaten	½	t. salt
1	t. vanilla	½	c. milk
2	c. sifted all-purpose flour	1	c. chopped walnuts

Heat oven to 350°. Line bottom of two 9 inch layer pans or a 13 x 9 oblong pan with wax paper cut to fit. Prepare mashed potatoes. An easy way is to follow directions for 2 servings on packaged instant mashed potatoes. Measure and set aside. Gradually beat sugar into shortening, beating until fluffy. Add eggs 1 at a time, beating well. Add vanilla and potatoes. Add sifted dry ingredients and milk alternately, about ¼ of each at a time, beating until smooth. Stir in walnuts. Bake layers 40 to 45 minutes; loaf about 50 minutes or until done when tested. Let stand 5 minutes. Turn out on rack and peel off paper. Cool; frost with butter cream or other frosting. Sprinkle with walnuts.
Mrs. Jack Conboy (Evelyn Manczak)

Miss Georgia McMean's Chocolate Cake

Custard

1	c. grated chocolate or 3 one oz. squares unsweetened chocolate

1	c. light brown sugar
2	egg yolks
½	c. milk
1	t. vanilla

Mix chocolate, sugar, egg yolks, and milk. Cook in double boiler, or over very low heat, stirring constantly, until it thickens. To thicken custard 2 teaspoons arrowroot may be added. Add vanilla and cool.

Cake

½	c. butter or shortening
1	c. light brown sugar
2	egg yolks
2	c. flour
½	c. milk

4	egg whites, beaten to form soft peaks
1	t. soda dissolved in 1 T. warm water

Cream butter and sugar. Add egg yolks and beat. Add flour and milk, alternately. Add custard. Fold in egg whites. Add soda and warm water. Stir until blended. Bake in two 9 inch greased and floured cake pans in 350° oven for about 25 minutes or until center is firm and sides move away from pans. Ice with favorite frosting or the following recipe.

Icing

1½	c. sugar
½	c. water
3	or 4 egg whites, stiffly beaten

Pinch of baking powder	
½	t. vanilla

Boil sugar and water until it begins to thread or reaches the soft ball stage. Pour gradually into egg whites, beating constantly. Beat in baking powder and vanilla. Beat until frosting stands in peaks. Ice cooled cake.
Mrs. Edwin W. Link (Ann Seymour)

Coconut Cake

1	box white cake mix	3	large eggs
¼	t. baking powder	1	c. sour cream
¼	c. salad oil	1	8½ oz. can coconut cream

Icing

1	lb. powdered sugar	1	t. vanilla
1	8 oz. pkg. cream cheese	1	c. freshly grated or angel
2	T. evaporated milk or		flake coconut
	cream		

Combine all cake ingredients and beat on medium high speed for 2 minutes. Pour into a greased 9 x 13 pan and bake at 350° for 30 to 40 minutes. Beat all icing ingredients, except coconut, with electric mixer until smooth and creamy. Spread over surface of cake. Sprinkle desired amount of coconut on top.
Serves 18.
Mrs. Gordon B. Broyles (Frances Dilley)

Coconut Sour Cream Cake

1	18½ oz. pkg. butter flavor cake mix	1	12 oz. pkg. frozen coconut, thawed
2	c. sugar	1½	c. whipped cream or frozen whipped topping, thawed
1	8 oz. carton sour cream		

Prepare the cake according to directions, making two 8 inch layers. Split both layers horizontally after they have cooled. Blend together the sugar, sour cream, and coconut, and chill. Spread all but 1 cup of the sour cream mixture between the four layers. Blend the remaining cup of the mixture with the whipped cream, and spread on the top and sides of the cake. Seal in an airtight container and refrigerate for three days before serving. Keep refrigerated after cutting.
Serves 12.
Mrs. E. C. Stallcup (Evelyn Riddle)

Devil's Food Cake

2	c. sugar	2⅔	c. flour
⅔	c. shortening	1	t. salt
2	eggs	1	t. vanilla
4	T. cocoa	1	c. boiling water
2	t. soda in 1 c. buttermilk		

Icing

1¼	c. sugar	1	6 oz. pkg. semi-sweet
2	T. light corn syrup		chocolate morsels
¼	c. margarine	1	t. vanilla
⅓	c. cream or milk		

In a large mixing bowl, place 2 cups sugar, shortening, eggs, and cocoa. Stir soda into buttermilk, add to bowl, and beat well. Sift flour with salt and blend into mixture. Add vanilla and pour in boiling water. Beat just enough to mix. Bake in a greased 13 x 9 x 2 sheet pan at 350° for 40 minutes. In a saucepan blend 1¼ cups sugar, corn syrup, margarine, and cream. Heat until boiling; boil for *one* minute. Remove from heat, add chocolate morsels and vanilla, and whisk just until morsels have melted. Pour icing over cake *quickly* as it will set fast. The icing may be poured on a hot cake. *Cake is moist and keeps well.*
Mrs. Cad E. Williams (Francis Bailey)

Orange Angel Cake

1	angel food cake, about 20 oz.	½	c. lemon juice
		1½	c. sugar
6	large or 8 small eggs, separated	2	T. gelatin dissolved in ½ c. water
1½	c. orange juice	½	pt. heavy cream, whipped

Break cake into small pieces. Beat yolks until thick, then add lemon juice, ¾ cup sugar, and ½ cup orange juice. Cook in a double boiler. Add gelatin mixture, stir until dissolved, and add 1 cup orange juice. Cool. Beat egg whites until stiff and dry, and add ¾ cup sugar. Fold whites into cooled yolk mixture. Add cake. Pour into buttered angel food pan or loaf pan and set in refrigerator for 24 hours. Ice with stiffly beaten whipped cream. Top each slice with additional whipped cream if desired.
Serves 12.
Mrs. Vernon Fritze (Kathy Duderstadt)

Mocha Angel Food Cake

1   box angel food cake mix   1   T. instant coffee

Frosting
2   sticks butter or margarine   4½ c. sifted powdered sugar
½   t. salt   2   t. vanilla
4   T. instant coffee dissolved 1   2¼ oz. pkg. sliced
    in 6 to 8 T. milk   almonds, toasted

Make cake according to directions on box. Add instant coffee dissolved in the water added with the package of egg whites in the mix. For baking follow directions on box. When done set aside to cool.
For frosting, melt butter, add salt, and sugar. Mix as much coffee milk as needed to make icing light and fluffy. Ice cake on top and sides *generously.* Sprinkle sides and top of cake with toasted sliced almonds. Recipe for frosting may be halved.
Serves 12 to 15.
Miss Holli Gragg

Angel Custard Royale

¾   c. sugar   ¾   c. sugar
6   egg yolks   3   drops yellow food
¾   c. fresh lemon juice   coloring, optional
1½ t. grated lemon rind   1   10 inch fresh bakery angel
1   T. unflavored gelatin   food cake
¼   c. cold water   Sweetened whipped cream
6   egg whites, stiffly beaten

In top of double boiler beat egg yolks well. Add sugar, lemon juice, rind, and stir well. Cook over hot, not boiling, water until mixture coats spoon. Remove from heat. Soften gelatin in cold water and add to hot custard. Set aside. Beat egg whites until stiff with remaining ¾ cup sugar. Trim crusts from cake and tear it into small pieces. Arrange ⅓ of cake pieces loosely in bottom of a 10 inch oiled tube pan. When custard is cooled and slightly set, fold in egg whites and food coloring. Pour ⅓ of custard mixture over cake in pan, letting it run between cake pieces. Add two more layers of cake and custard. Chill until firm. Turn out and frost with sweetened whipped cream.
Serves 12.

Ice Cream Cake

20	ladyfingers	1	t. rum flavoring
2	qts. vanilla ice cream	6	maraschino cherries, chopped
1	6 oz. can frozen orange juice concentrate	3	T. chopped blanched pistachio nuts
2	10 oz. pkgs. frozen raspberries	½	pt. sweetened whipped cream
2	9 oz. cans crushed pineapple		Sugared strawberries
1	T. lemon juice		Mint leaves, optional
1	t. almond flavoring		

Line the bottom and sides of a 9 inch spring form pan with ladyfingers, split in half. Mix one quart of ice cream with the frozen undiluted orange juice. Pour into mold over bottom of laydyfingers. Work quickly to prevent ice cream from becoming too soft. Freeze firm. Meanwhile, buzz raspberries and pineapple in a blender with lemon juice or puree through food mill. Strain to remove seeds and freeze until partially frozen. Place in bowl and beat slightly. Spoon over orange layer and refreeze. To other quart of ice cream, add almond and rum flavorings, cherries, and nuts. Pour this over raspberry layer and freeze overnight. Remove to refrigerator two hours before serving. Final frills: garnish with sweetened cream, sugared fresh strawberries, and if you like mint. This recipe can be cut in half or made in two parts and used later.
Serves 12.
Mrs. J. G. Crook (Maxine Schultz)

Banana Split Cake

1	stick margarine	1	20 oz. can crushed pineapple, well drained
2	c. graham cracker crumbs		
2	8 oz. pkgs. cream cheese	1	12 oz. carton whipped topping
1	lb. box powdered sugar		
1	t. vanilla	1	6 oz. jar maraschino cherries, halved
5	bananas, sliced lengthwise		
		1	c. chopped nuts

Melt margarine and stir in crumbs. Put in 13 x 9 x 2 inch pan and pat down to form crust. Set aside. In mixer beat cream cheese, sugar, and vanilla until creamy. Spread over crust, cover with layer of bananas, then layer of pineapple, and cover with whipped topping. Sprinkle nuts and cherries on top. Cover with plastic wrap and chill well.
Serves 10 to 15.
Mrs. Francis M. Huffman (Mary Catherine Cooper)

Chocolate Sheet Cake

2	c. flour	2	eggs
2	c. sugar	1	t. soda
1	c. water	½	c. buttermilk
2	sticks margarine	1	t. vanilla
3	T. cocoa		

Frosting

½	c. margarine	½	c. chopped pecans
3	T. cocoa	1	t. vanilla
6	T. evaporated milk	½	c. coconut, optional
1	16 oz. box powdered sugar		

Sift together flour and sugar in a large mixing bowl. Bring to a boil in a saucepan the water, shortening, and cocoa. Pour this over flour mixture and mix. In a medium mixing bowl, beat eggs thoroughly, then add soda, buttermilk, and vanilla, mixing well. Add this to the other ingredients and blend. Pour into a greased and floured 13½ x 10½ x 1½ pan. Bake at 350° for 25 to 30 minutes. Mix margarine, cocoa, and milk in a saucepan. Heat over low heat, but do not boil. Remove from heat and add remaining ingredients, mixing well. Frost cake.
Serves 18.
Mrs. Walter E. Johnston (Lottie Mae Griffith)

Pineapple Fluff Cake

2	c. flour	1	t. vanilla
2	c. sugar	1½	c. sugar
2	eggs	1	5.33 oz. can evaporated milk
½	t. salt		
¾	c. vegetable oil	½	c. margarine
1	15¼ oz. can crushed pineapple and juice	1	c. pecans
2	t. soda	1	c. coconut, optional
		1	t. vanilla

Combine first eight ingredients using electric mixer. Pour into greased 9 x 13 pan, and bake 1 hour and 15 minutes in 300° oven. During last 15 minutes in a saucepan mix sugar with the milk and margarine and boil for 3 minutes. Remove from heat and add pecans, coconut, and vanilla. Pour on hot cake. *This is a delicious and rich cake.*
Serves 20 to 24.
Mrs. Elton L. Bomer (Ginny Roco)

Italian Cream Cake

1	stick margarine or butter	1	t. soda
½	c. shortening	1	c. buttermilk
2	c. sugar	½	c. chopped nuts
5	egg yolks	1	3½ oz. can grated coconut
1	t. vanilla	5	egg whites
2	c. flour		

Icing

1	8 oz. pkg. cream cheese	1	t. vanilla
¼	c. butter	½	c. chopped nuts
1	1 lb. box powdered sugar		

Cream margarine and shortening and gradually add sugar. Beat until light and fluffy. Add egg yolks and vanilla. Sift flour with soda and add alternately with buttermilk. Stir in nuts and coconut. Beat egg whites and fold into mixture. Pour batter into a greased and lightly floured 13 x 9 x 2 pan and bake at 325° for 30 minutes.

Icing Cream cheese and butter; add sugar, vanilla, and nuts; and mix well. Ice cake in pan. Cut into squares to serve.
Serves 20.
Mrs. Weldon Bynum (Opha Gilbreath)

Gooey Butter Cake

1	18.5 oz. pkg. yellow cake mix	1	stick margarine, softened
		1	egg

Topping

1	8 oz. pkg. cream cheese, softened	2	eggs
1	lb. box powdered sugar, reserving ¼ c.	1	t. vanilla

Combine margarine, egg, and cake mix thoroughly. Put into greased 13 x 9 x 2 pan.

Topping Combine ingredients and beat with mixer for 3 minutes. Pour on cake mixture. Bake at 350° for 40 minutes. Let cool slightly and sprinkle with powdered sugar. Cut into cookie-size squares or bars.
Yields approximately 50 pieces.
Mrs. Gerald G. May (Oleta Henderson)

Mandarin Cake

1	11 oz. can mandarin oranges	4	eggs
1	box butter cake mix	¼	c. corn oil

Frosting

1	9 oz. carton whipped topping	1	15¼ oz. can crushed pineapple and juice
1	3¾ oz. instant vanilla pudding	1	8 oz. pkg. grated coconut

Drain juice from mandarin oranges. Chop oranges and set aside. Put cake mix in large mixing bowl. Add juice, eggs, and corn oil. Beat 4 minutes on medium speed in electric mixer. Fold in oranges by hand. Bake in a 9 x 13 greased cake pan or 3 layer cake pans at 350° for about 30 to 35 minutes. Cool completely before icing.

Icing Place whipped topping in mixing bowl. Fold in dry instant pudding, pineapple, and juice. Spread over cake. Sprinkle with grated coconut. Refrigerate.
Serves 15.
Mrs. Walter E. Johnston (Lottie Mae Griffith)

Strawberry Cake

1	18 oz. box white cake mix	½	c. frozen sliced strawberries
1	c. salad oil		
4	eggs	½	c. milk
1	3 oz. pkg. strawberry gelatin		

Icing

4	T. butter or margarine	½	c. sliced strawberries
1	16 oz. box powdered sugar		

Combine ingredients for cake and mix on moderate speed in mixer until well blended. Pour into 3 greased and floured 9 inch cake pans or one oblong pan 13 x 9 x 2 and bake at 350° for 25 to 30 minutes. Cool.
Icing Melt butter, add powdered sugar, and strawberries. Stir until well blended and spread on cooled cake.
Serves 18.
Mrs. Wayne Lawrence (Evelina Martin)

Carrot Cake

2	c. sugar	¼	t. salt
2	c. sifted flour	1½	c. salad oil
1	t. soda	4	eggs
1	t. baking powder	2	c. grated carrots
1	t. cinnamon		

Frosting

½	c. butter	1	lb. box powdered sugar
1	8 oz. pkg. cream cheese	1	c. chopped pecans
1	t. vanilla		

Mix sugar, flour, soda, baking powder, cinnamon, salt, and oil. Add eggs, one at a time, mix by hand or moderate speed in mixer. Add carrots last. Dough will be of lumpy consistency. Pour into a greased and floured tube pan and bake at 350° for 1 hour. You may use two loaf pans and bake about 45 minutes. For frosting, cream together butter and cream cheese. Add vanilla and sugar and beat well. Mix in pecans and spread over cake. Serves 12.
Mrs. Dick Gragg (Nell Thomason)

Date Cake

1	16 oz. pkg. dates	2	eggs, well beaten
1	c. water	1¼	c. sifted flour
1	t. soda	1	t. baking powder
1	c. sugar	1	c. finely chopped nuts
3	T. butter	½	t. vanilla extract

Cut dates fine. In boiling water dissolve baking soda. Pour over dates and let stand until cool. Cream sugar and butter. Add eggs. Sift flour before measuring and stir into mixture along with baking powder. Add nuts, vanilla, and cool date mixture; and stir until thoroughly blended. Pour into greased and lightly floured bundt pan. Bake at 350° for 45 minutes or until done. Cool 15 minutes before turning out. Serve with sweetened whipped cream if desired. Serves 12.
Mrs. Oliver B. McReynolds, Jr. (Ellen Roueche)

Dutch Apple Cake

1	c. sugar	2	T. hot water
½	c. salad oil	1	c. chopped nuts
2	eggs	1	t. vanilla
1½	c. flour	2	c. chopped apple
½	t. salt	½	c. brown sugar
1	t. baking soda	½	c. chopped nuts

Mix sugar and oil; add eggs and beat well. Sift together flour, salt, and soda. Add to the oil mixture with hot water. Mix well. Add nuts, vanilla, and apples. Mix again and pour into a greased and floured 10 x 14 pan or two loaf pans. Make a topping of brown sugar and nuts mixed together and sprinkle on top of the batter. Bake at 325° for 35 or 40 minutes.
Serves 12 to 15.
Mrs. Vernon V. Fritze, Jr. (Kathy Sue Duderstadt)

Orange Slice Cake

4	eggs	1	11 oz. pkg. orange slice candy
2	c. sugar		
4	c. flour	2	T. orange rind
1	c. butter	1	t. soda
1	8 oz. pkg. dates	1⅓	c. buttermilk
		2	c. pecans

Glaze
2	c. sugar	1½	c. orange juice

Mix all the cake ingredients well and bake in a tube pan for 1 hour and 30 minutes at 300°.

Glaze Bring the two ingredients to a boil, then pour over the cake and allow to set in the pan overnight. Good substitute for fruitcake at Christmas.
Mrs. Jack Graves (Pauline Thompson)

  When using glass baking pans, always lower oven temperature by 25°.

Black Fruitcake

This recipe is of English origin and is known variously as Dark Fruitcake, English Fruitcake, Black Fruitcake, and Merry Christmas Cake.

¼   **lb. candied citron**
⅛   **lb. candied lemon peel**
⅛   **lb. candied orange peel**
½   **lb. candied cherries**
1   **lb. candied pineapple**
1   **lb. golden raisins**
½   **lb. seeded raisins**
¼   **lb. currants**
½   **c. dark rum, cognac,
     sherry, or Madeira**
¼   **lb. blanched shelled
     almonds**

¼   **lb. shelled walnuts or
     pecans**
2   **c. sifted all-purpose flour**
½   **t. mace**
½   **t. cinnamon**
½   **t. baking soda**
½   **c. butter**
1   **c. sugar**
1   **c. dark brown sugar,
     firmly packed**
5   **eggs**
1   **T. milk**
1   **t. almond extract**

Garnish
¼   **lb. red candied cherries**
¼   **lb. green candied cherries**
Whole almonds

Whole pecans
Corn syrup

The fruits and nuts should be prepared a day ahead as follows. Sliver the citron, lemon, and orange peel into very thin strips; cut the cherries in half and the pineapple in thin wedges. Set aside. Pick over the raisins and currants to eliminate stray stems or seeds; add rum, cognac, sherry, or Madeira; and soak overnight or longer. Chop the almonds and the walnuts or pecans coarsely. Set them aside, too. The following day, or later, prepare the pan or pans. Grease a 10 inch tube pan, four 1 pound coffee cans, or 2 bread pans, measuring 9 x 5 x 3. Line with brown paper.

To make the cake, mix ½ cup of the sifted flour with all the fruits and nuts in a large bowl. Sift remaining flour with spices and baking soda. Cream butter until soft, then work in granulated sugar and dark brown sugar, a little at a time, until mixture is smooth. Stir in the fruit and nuts and work together, with your hands or an electric mixer with a dough hook, until batter is very well mixed. Lift the batter into the pan or pans and press it down firmly to make a compact cake when cooked. Bake in a preheated 275° oven. A tube pan that uses all the batter will take 3¼ hours; the bread pans, which will each hold half the batter, 2¼ hours; the coffee cans, which each hold one-fourth the batter, 2 hours. Remove from oven, let stand half an hour, then turn out onto cake racks. Peel off the brown paper very carefully. The four small, round cakes make attractive Christmas presents.

(Continued on next page)

To garnish the fruitcakes, use ¼ pound red candied cherries, ¼ pound green candied cherries, whole almonds, and pecans. To decorate, before wrapping to age, brush the tops of the cakes with hot corn syrup, and trim in a design with fruit and nuts. When this is set, brush with a second coat, fairly thickly, of hot corn syrup. Let dry several hours.

To age fruitcakes, allow at least four weeks. Wrap each cake in several layers of cheesecloth well soaked in rum, cognac, sherry, or Madeira. Place in an airtight container, such as a large crock or kettle, and cover tightly. If cheesecloth dries out, moisten it with a little of the wine or spirits. Do not overdo it. The cakes should be firm, not soft, at the end of the aging period. This will make them easy to slice in neat, compact slices.

Mrs. Lamar Davis, Houston, Texas

Pecan Cake

1	lb. butter, softened	1	T. baking powder
2	c. sugar	1	2 oz. bottle lemon extract
6	eggs	1	lb. white or dark raisins
4	c. flour	4	c. pecan pieces

Cream butter and sugar, mixing well. Add eggs one at a time, beating well after each addition. Mix flour with baking powder and add to creamed mixture. Blend well and add lemon extract. Fold in raisins and pecans. Butter and flour two 8 ½ x 4 ½ x 2 ½ pans. Equally spread batter in the two pans. Bake in 250° oven for 2 ½ hours. Wrap and store in refrigerator several days before serving. *Flavor inproves with age.*

Jack W. Meeker

Texas Pecan Cake

1	lb. butter or margarine	1	lb. glazed pineapple,
3	c. sugar		chopped
7	eggs, separated	½	lb. candied cherries,
2	T. lemon extract		finely chopped
4	T. whiskey	1	qt. chopped pecans
		5	c. sifted cake flour

Cream butter and sugar together thoroughly. Beat egg yolks and add to creamed mixture. Blend in lemon extract and whiskey. Dredge fruit and nuts in 1 cup of the flour. Gradually add flour, fruit, and nuts, stirring by hand. Beat egg whites until stiff and fold into mixture. Pour into a greased and floured 10 inch tube pan. Place foil on rack to set pan on and place sheet of foil on top of pan. Bake 4 hours at 250°. Cool overnight and turn out of pan.

Mrs. Leland McReynolds (Annita Verzal)

Caramel Icing

2	c. sugar	½	c. buttermilk
1⅓	sticks margarine	1	t. soda
12	large marshmallows	1	c. chopped pecans,
1	T. light corn syrup		optional

Combine first 6 ingredients in heavy saucepan. Cook slowly until it forms soft ball when dropped into cold water. Beat until cloudy. Spread on cooled cake. Will frost a 2 layer cake.

Mrs. W. Lamar Hamilton (Kitty Davey)

Chocolate Icing

2	c. sugar	1	stick margarine
2	1 oz. squares bitter	2	T. light corn syrup
	chocolate	1	t. vanilla
⅔	c. milk	1	c. chopped nuts, optional
¼	t. salt		

Mix ingredients in a heavy saucepan. Bring to boil, stirring constantly. Boil 1½ minutes. Add vanilla and nuts if desired. Beat until thick. Spread on cake. Will cover two 9 inch layers.

Easy White Icing

1	c. light corn syrup	¼	t. cream of tartar
¼	c. sugar	¼	t. salt
2	egg whites	1	t. vanilla
8	or 10 large marshmallows		

Mix and cook in double boiler over boiling water. Beat constantly with an electric beater until thick, about 5 to 7 minutes. Food coloring and 1 cup chopped pecans may be added after cooking, if desired. Spread on cool cake. It is enough for a two-layer cake or a tube cake.
Mrs. David J. Dial (Margery Hombs)

Easy Pie Crust

| ½ | c. salad oil | ½ | t. salt |
| ¼ | c. milk | 1½ | c. flour |

Pour all ingredients in pie pan or mixing bowl and stir by hand. Press dough out and up on sides of pie pan to form shell. Makes one pie crust. Recipe may be doubled and frozen to use when needed.
Yields one 9 inch pie crust.
Mrs. John Ballard McDonald (Linda Cole)

Hot Water Pastry

1	c. shortening	½	t. baking powder
½	c. boiling water	1	t. salt
3	c. flour		

Melt shortening in hot water. Add flour, baking powder, and salt. Chill. Use as needed. Store in refrigerator. Practically foolproof. Take out of refrigerator for awhile before rolling out. This is best used for pies or tarts that are to be cooked in the shell rather than baking the crust separately.
Yields two 10 inch pie shells or 36 miniature tarts.
Mrs. Lester Hamilton (Frances Edmunds)

Tiny Tart Shells

2 c. all-purpose flour,	⅓ c. butter or margarine
measured before sifting	⅓ c. shortening
1 t. salt	Ice water

Sift flour and salt into bowl; cut in butter and shortening with pastry blender until mixture resembles coarse meal. Add ice water sparingly while tossing with fork, using only enough for dough to hold together. Roll thin on floured board, cut in circles and press over bottom of tiny muffin tins. Prick all over with fork. Place tin on cookie sheet and bake at 425° for 5 minutes. Now place a flat cookie sheet over top of pastry to keep bottoms flat; reduce heat to 350°, and bake until lightly browned. Allow to cool before removing from pans. May be prepared ahead and frozen.
Yields 24.
Mrs. John B. McDonald (Dorothy Crider)

Lemon Custard Tarts

Tart Shells

3 c. sifted flour	1 c. shortening
1½ t. salt	6 T. cold water

Sift flour and salt and cut in shortening. Sprinkle water over mixture, mixing thoroughly until smooth. Roll on floured board to ⅛ inch thickness. Cut into rounds, place in small muffin tins, and bake at 400° for 12 to 15 minutes. Fill with lemon custard.
Yields 17 miniature tarts.

Lemon Custard

3 eggs, well beaten	⅓ c. lemon juice
1 c. sugar	½ pt. heavy cream, whipped
Grated rind of one lemon	Whipped cream and grated
	lemon rind for topping

Mix eggs, sugar, lemon juice, and grated rind and cook in double boiler until thick, about 15 to 20 minutes. Cool and add whipped cream. Pour into tart shells. Top with a bit of whipped cream and grated lemon rind.
Mrs. Thomas B. Bailey (Sue Simmons)

Strawberry Cream Tarts

1	8 oz. pkg. cream cheese, softened	6	pastry shells
1	c. powdered sugar	1	pt. strawberries, washed and sliced
½	pt. heavy cream, whipped		Additional whipped cream
1	t. vanilla		

Mix softened cream cheese and sugar. Whip. Fold in vanilla and whipped cream. Spoon into baked pastry shells. Cover each tart with fruit and garnish with whipped cream.
Serves 6.
Cookbook Committee

Black Bottom Cup Cakes

1	8 oz. pkg. cream cheese	¼	c. cocoa
½	c. sugar	1	t. soda
1	egg, beaten	½	t. salt
⅛	t. salt	1	c. water
1	6 oz. pkg. chocolate chips	⅓	c. salad oil
1½	c. flour	1	T. vinegar
1	c. sugar	1	t. vanilla

Combine cream cheese, sugar, egg, and salt. Stir in chocolate chips and set aside. This is topping for batter. Sift flour, sugar, cocoa, soda, and salt. Add water, salad oil, vinegar, and vanilla. Fill muffin pans ⅓ full of cocoa batter. Top with 1 tablespoon of cream cheese mixture. Bake at 350° for 20 to 25 minutes.
Yields 18 cup cakes.
Mrs. Joe Ed Johnston (Marilyn Hardgrave)

Jelly Tarts

1	c. sugar
½	c. butter
3	eggs

1   c. jelly (Tart plum is good. If using apple, add a little cinnamon or a few drops of lemon flavoring.)

Cream sugar and butter. Beat eggs lightly. Mix with sugar and butter. Stir in jelly. Fill unbaked tart shells in muffin tins. Place in 450° oven 3 or 4 minutes, then lower to 350° and bake until firm, 30 to 35 minutes. These are easily made with Hot Water Pastry, page 245.
Yields about 16 tarts.
Mrs. Lester Hamilton (Frances Edmunds)

Black Bottom Pie

1	10 inch pie shell, baked
1	c. sugar
1	T. cornstarch
2	c. milk, scalded
4	egg yolks, beaten
1	t. vanilla
1	6 oz. pkg. chocolate chips
1	oz. unsweetened chocolate

1	T. unflavored gelatin
¼	c. rum (or water)
4	egg whites
½	c. sugar

Topping

1	c. heavy cream
1	T. powdered sugar

1   t. vanilla
Shaved chocolate

Combine sugar and cornstarch in top of double boiler. Slowly add milk to beaten egg yolks and stir into sugar mixture. Cook and stir in double boiler until custard coats spoon. Add vanilla. To one cup of the custard, add the chocolates. Stir until it melts. Pour chocolate mixture into pie shell. Chill. Soften gelatin in rum. Add to remaining hot custard. Chill until slightly thick. Beat egg whites, adding sugar gradually until peaks form. Fold into custard. Pour over chocolate layer. Chill. Whip cream with a tablespoon of powdered sugar and a teaspoon of vanilla. Layer on pie and garnish with shaved chocolate.
Serves 6 to 8.
Mrs. C. L. Kolstad, III (Jill McPherson)

Banana-Blueberry Cream Pie

2   9 inch pie shells, baked
2   large bananas, sliced
2   envelopes Dream Whip
4   3 oz. pkg. cream cheese

1½ c. sugar
Juice of one lemon
1   21 oz. can blueberry pie
    filling

Line bottom of crusts with bananas. Prepare Dream Whip according to package directions. Combine cream cheese, sugar, and lemon juice. Fold in Dream Whip. Spread over bananas. Top each pie with blueberry pie filling. Chill.
Yields 2 pies.
Mrs. Reo Stolzenburg (Tommie Lou Nicholson)

Chocolate Meringue Pie

1   9 inch pie shell, baked
3¾   T. cornstarch or ⅔ cup
     flour
1½   c. sugar
1½   c. milk
3   T. butter or margarine
3   eggs, separated

3   1 oz. squares unsweetened
     chocolate, melted
¼   t. salt
1   t. vanilla
½   t. cream of tartar
⅛   t. salt
3   T. sugar

Mix cornstarch or flour with sugar, add milk and cook in double boiler for 20 minutes, stirring frequently. Remove from heat, cool 2 or 3 minutes, add butter, and well beaten egg yolks. Return to heat and cook for 15 minutes or until thickened. Add melted chocolate the last 5 minutes of cooking. Stir until thickened and smooth. Cool 5 to 10 minutes and pour into baked pie shell. Beat egg whites until stiff, adding cream of tartar and salt. Gradually beat in sugar. Spread meringue completely over filling so it will not pull away from crust. Brown in 350° oven for approximately 12 to 15 minutes.
This is a delicious, rich, creamy, very chocolate pie!
Mrs. David J. Dial (Margery Hombs)

Daiquiri Pie

1	3¾ oz. pkg. lemon pudding and pie filling	½	c. light rum
1	3 oz. pkg. lime gelatin	1¾	c. thawed non-dairy whipped topping
⅓	c. sugar	1	9 inch graham cracker crust, baked and cooled
2½	c. water		
2	eggs, slightly beaten		

Combine pudding mix, gelatin, and sugar in a saucepan. Stir in ½ cup water and eggs; blend well. Add remaining water, cook and stir over medium heat until mixture comes to a *full* boil. Remove from heat; stir in rum. Chill. Thoroughly blend thawed topping into chilled mixture. Spoon into pie crust and chill until firm, approximately 2 hours. Garnish with additional whipped topping and lime slices. Keeps well.
Serves 6.
Mrs. Wayne Craddock (Alpha Boyett)

Mocha Cream Pie

1	9 inch pie shell, baked	1	T. instant coffee
½	c. sugar	1	t. vanilla
1	c. milk	3	T. flour
½	t. salt	1	c. heavy cream
1	oz. unsweetened chocolate	1	t. cornstarch
		6	to 10 marshmallows

Combine sugar, chocolate, instant coffee, flour, cornstarch, milk, and salt. Cook over low heat, stirring constantly. Allow to cool — mixture cools and thickens quickly. Stir in vanilla. Whip cream until stiff. Fold approximately two-thirds of whipped cream into the chocolate mixture. Partially fold in the remaining cream to achieve a marbled effect. Pour into baked shell. Place marshmallows on top for poka dot effect.
Serves 6.
Mrs. Joe Moore (Veda Walters)

Old-Time Buttermilk Pie

1	9 inch unbaked pie shell	3	eggs, beaten
½	c. butter, softened	1	c. buttermilk
2	c. sugar	1	t. vanilla
3	T. flour		Dash of nutmeg

Cream butter and sugar together by hand. Do not use electric mixer. Add flour and eggs. Stir in buttermilk, vanilla, and nutmeg. Pour into unbaked pie shell. Bake 45 to 50 minutes at 350°. Cool before serving.
Serves 6.
Mrs. Julian Hunt (Doris Leathers)

Pineapple Chess Pie

1	9 inch pie shell, unbaked	6	T. margarine
1¼	c. sugar	2	eggs
3	T. fresh lemon juice or 1	¼	t. salt
	T. lemon crystals	1	8 oz. can crushed
3	T. sifted flour		pineapple, undrained

Cream sugar, lemon juice, flour, and margarine. Add whole eggs and beat by hand or mixer. Add salt and pineapple. Bake in pastry shell for 10 minutes at 400°; then 30 minutes at 300°. If center is not firm, leave in oven 10 minutes more with oven turned off. May be served warm.
Freezes.
Mrs. Guy Keeling (Lucile DuPuy)

Pecan Cheese Cake Pie

1	9 inch pie shell, unbaked	2¾	oz. pkg. pecans, chopped
1	8 oz. pkg. cream cheese	3	eggs
¼	c. sugar	2	T. sugar
1	egg	¾	c. white corn syrup
1	t. vanilla	1	t. vanilla

Cream together cheese, ¼ cup sugar, 1 egg, and 1 teaspoon vanilla and pour into pie shell. Pat chopped pecans evenly over cheese mixture. In another bowl blend 3 eggs, 2 tablespoons sugar, syrup, and 1 teaspoon vanilla. Pour carefully through a fork over pecans. Bake 35 minutes in 375° oven or until pie is firm.
Serves 6.
Mrs. Lester Hamilton (Frances Edmunds)

Rum Cream Pie

38	to 40 vanilla wafers,	Dash of nutmeg
	crushed	Dash of salt
⅓	c. melted butter	½ c. dark rum
1	T. unflavored gelatin	1 t. vanilla
½	c. cold water	1 pt. heavy cream, whipped
6	egg yolks	Garnish of bittersweet
1	c. sugar	chocolate and walnuts

Mix wafers and butter and press into a deep dish 10 inch pie plate. Soak and bring to a boil gelatin and water; cool slightly. Beat eggs until light colored, adding sugar, nutmeg, and salt. Gradually combine gelatin mixture with egg mixture, beating constantly. Refrigerate 2 hours until thick, but not jelled. Whip cream, adding rum and vanilla. Fold this into jelled mixture, blending well. Chill again and pour into pie shell. Refrigerate overnight. Garnish with bittersweet chocolate curls and chopped walnuts, if desired.
Serves 8 to 10.
Mrs. Lester Hamilton (Frances Edmunds)

Special Cheese Cake

1	4 oz. box Zwieback,	1 c. sugar
	crushed into crumbs	1 t. vanilla
½	c. sugar	½ t. pineapple extract
1	t. cinnamon	1 16 oz. carton sour cream
⅓	c. butter, melted	3 T. sugar
5	medium eggs, room	½ t. salt
	temperature	½ t. vanilla
4	8 oz. pkg. cream cheese	

Mix Zwieback, ½ cup sugar, cinnamon, and butter. Pack the mixture in the bottom of a 9 inch spring form pan. In large bowl of electric mixer, beat eggs for about 20 minutes. When they have foamed up almost to the top of the bowl, start adding bit by bit the cream cheese. This will take about 20 minutes. Whip to a smooth paste. Continue beating and add 1 cup sugar, 1 teaspoon vanilla, and pineapple extract. Pour this mixture on top of the crust in the pan and bake in a 325° oven for 45 minutes. Mix together sour cream, 3 tablespoons sugar, salt, and ½ teaspoon vanilla and pour over the cheese cake. Bake 5 minutes longer at 325°. Cool in pan on wire rack. Then refrigerate for at least 5 hours before serving. May be frozen.
Serves 18 to 20.
Mrs. C. F. Sizer (Mary Cordray)

Godiva Cheese Cake

1½	c. crushed chocolate wafers	½	t. cinnamon
½	c. chopped nuts	¼	c. margarine, softened

Filling

1	12 oz. pkg. cream cheese	4	oz. Godiva dark chocolate or 3 oz. German chocolate plus 1 oz. bitter chocolate
½	c. sugar		
1	t. grated lemon rind		
2	eggs		Whipped cream
1½	c. sour cream		Walnut halves
			Maraschino cherries

Combine margarine, cinnamon, nuts, and wafer crumbs. Press into a lightly greased 10 inch pie plate.

Filling Blend first 5 filling ingredients with electric beater. Melt chocolate slowly over warm water, not hot. Drizzle into cheese mixture. Both mixtures should be at room temperature. Chocolate will harden if hot and not mix well. Put into crust and bake at 350° for 35 minutes. Chill. Serve with whipped cream, walnut halves, and maraschino cherries on top.
Serves 6.
Mrs. Cecil W. James (Fern Laine)

Sweet Potato Pecan Pie

Pastry for 9 inch pie shell, unbaked			Dash of mace
1½	c. cooked, mashed sweet potatoes	3	eggs, beaten
		1½	c. scalded milk
1	c. brown sugar, divided	¼	c. margarine, melted
¼	t. salt	¾	c. chopped pecans
1	t. cinnamon		Whipped cream

Line 9 inch pie plate with pastry. Combine potatoes, ½ cup sugar, salt, cinnamon, and mace. Add eggs; mix well. Stir in milk. Pour into pie shell. Bake in preheated 350° oven for 20 minutes. Combine remaining ½ cup sugar, butter, and pecans and mix well. Sprinkle over partially cooked pie. Bake for about 25 minutes longer or until set. Serve topped with whipped cream.
Mrs. Gerald G. May (Oleta Henderson)

Date Nut Pie

2	c. sugar	2	c. chopped dates
2	T. margarine	2	c. chopped pecans
6	eggs, beaten	2	9 inch pie shells, unbaked

Blend sugar and margarine. Add eggs, mixing well. Stir in dates and nuts. Pour into pie shells. Bake at 400° about 40 minutes or until center is firm. Cool before cutting. Garnish with ice cream or whipped cream.
Mrs. Robert B. Bristow (Jimmie Reta Inmon)

Crunchy Nut Mince Pie

1	9 inch pastry shell, unbaked	28	oz. jar mincemeat

Topping

½	c. margarine, softened	⅓	c. shredded coconut
1	c. sifted flour	½	c. brown sugar
		½	c. chopped pecans

Spoon mincemeat into pie shell. Cut margarine into flour until crumbly. Add coconut, sugar, and pecans. Toss together. Sprinkle evenly on top of mincemeat. Bake at 400° about 20 to 25 minutes or until crust is golden brown.
Serves 6.
Mrs. Bruce Barber (Brenda Wilson)

Apple Pie

10	inch deep dish pie shell and top crust	¼	t. cinnamon
6	green apples	⅜	t. nutmeg
1	c. sugar	⅛	t. mace
1	T. flour	2	T. butter
Dash salt		1	T. milk
		2	T. sugar

Peel and slice apples. Arrange in pie shell. Mix sugar, flour, salt, cinnamon, nutmeg, and mace. Sprinkle over apples. Dot apples with butter. Put on top crust and crimp edges. Brush top crust with milk and sprinkle with sugar. Bake at 400° for about 40 minutes or until crust is brown.
Serves 8.
Mrs. C. L. Kolstad, III (Jill McPherson)

Pear Praline Pie

5	fresh pears	¾	t. ground ginger
¾	t. grated lemon peel	1	9 inch pie shell, unbaked
⅔	c. sugar		Garnish of fresh pear slices,
¼	c. flour		optional
	Dash of salt		Whipped cream

Praline Topping

½	c. brown sugar	½	c. chopped pecans
⅓	c. flour	¼	c. butter

Core and slice pears. Toss with lemon peel, sugar, flour, salt, and ginger. Combine brown sugar, flour, and pecans. Cut in butter until mixture is crumbly. Sprinkle ¼ cup of topping in bottom of pastry shell. Add sliced pears. Sprinkle with remaining topping. Bake at 400° for 40 minutes. Garnish with fresh pear slices, and serve warm with whipped cream.

Mrs. Lawrence McWhorter (Elma Cornelius)

Meringues

4	egg whites	1	12 oz. pkg. chocolate
1	c. sugar		chips
1	t. vanilla		

Separate eggs carefully and let whites come to room temperature (1 hour or more). Beat whites on high speed until stiff. On lowest speed, add sugar slowly. When all sugar has been added, beat a few seconds on high speed. Add vanilla. Mix with a spoon. Fold in chocolate chips. Drop by tablespoons on brown paper on a cookie sheet. Bake at 325° for 25 to 30 minutes. **Yields 60 meringues.**

Mrs. R. L. Kenderdine (Daphne Dunning)

Blackberry Deep Dish Pie

6	c. blackberries	3	T. butter
2	c. sugar	¼	t. salt
8	T. flour		Pastry for double crust pie
4	T. lemon juice		

Line 2 quart round deep casserole with pastry. Mix above ingredients and pour half into crust. Cover with thin strips of pastry as dumplings. Pour in remaining mixture and cover with top crust. Slit top crust and bake 1 hour at 425°.
Serves 6 to 8.
Mrs. C. F. Sizer (Mary Cordray)

Peach Cobbler

1	29 oz. can peach halves in heavy syrup	¾	c. flour
2	c. sugar, separated	2	t. baking powder
½	c. margarine		Pinch of salt
		¾	c. milk

Cut peach halves into small slices. Add 1 cup sugar and let stand while preparing batter. By hand, thoroughly mix 1 cup sugar, flour, baking powder, salt, and milk. In a 10 inch iron skillet melt margarine. Pour batter mixture into skillet. Spread peach mixture evenly over batter. *Do not sitr.* Place skillet on cookie sheet and bake in 350° oven for 1 hour. Serve while warm.
Serves 6 to 8.
Mrs. Horace W. Shelton (Dollie Rogers)

Brownies

½	c. butter	1	t. vanilla
2	1 oz. squares unsweetened chocolate	¾	c. flour
		½	t. baking powder
2	eggs	¾	t. salt
1	c. sugar	1	c. nuts, chopped

Melt butter and chocolate together. Let cool. Beat eggs, sugar, and vanilla. Sift flour, baking powder, and salt. Stir into egg mixture. Fold in butter and chocolate and add nuts. Pour into greased 8 inch square baking pan. Bake in 350° oven for 30 to 35 minutes. Do not over cook. Frost brownies when cool.

Cooked Fudge Frosting

1	c. sugar	¼	c. milk
⅛	c. light corn syrup	¼	c. butter
1	1 oz. square unsweetened chocolate	1	t. vanilla

Cook sugar, syrup, chocolate, milk, and butter over low heat until chocolate melts. Bring to a boil and cook 1 minute. Add vanilla, beat slightly by hand until cool, and frost brownies. *Sinfully rich!*
Yields 16 squares.
Mrs. Robert D. Harrell (Beverly Tucker)

Brown Sugar Brownies

1⅓	c. sifted flour	1	c. light brown sugar, firmly packed
1	t. baking powder		
½	t. salt	1	egg
½	c. soft butter	1	t. vanilla extract
		½	c. chopped nuts

Grease 9 inch pan. Sift flour, baking powder, and salt. Beat together butter, sugar, egg, and vanilla until smooth. Stir in flour mixture and nuts. Bake at 350° for 25 to 30 minutes. Cut while warm.
Yields 2 dozen brownies. Freezes.
Mrs. Bruce Barber (Brenda Wilson)

Butterscotch Brownies

½	c. margarine, melted	1	t. salt
2	c. brown sugar	2	t. vanilla
2	eggs	1	c. pecans, chopped
1½	c. flour	1	6 oz. pkg. chocolate chips
2	t. baking powder		

Combine margarine and brown sugar. Add eggs and mix well. Sift together flour, baking powder, and salt; and add to margarine and brown sugar mixture. Mix in vanilla and pecans, and pour into a 9 x 12 pan. Sprinkle chocolate chips over mixture. Bake at 325° for 25 minutes or until brownies pull away from side of pan.
Yields 24 brownies. Freezes.
Mrs. Mike Wright (Patti Alexander)

Three-Layer Brownies

Your favorite brownie recipe		Green food color	
3	c. powdered sugar	2	T. butter
4	T. softened butter	2	squares unsweetened
3	T. milk		chocolate
2	t. peppermint extract		

Prepare your favorite brownie recipe and bake in a 13 x 9 pan. Turn out on wire rack and cool. For the second layer: cream the butter and powdered sugar. Mix well. Add milk, extract, and green food color. Spread on brownies. For third layer: melt 2 tablespoons of butter and the unsweetened chocolate. Spread on top of other two layers. Refrigerate. Cut into small squares to serve.
Yields approximately 2 dozen.
Mrs. Harold Hunter (Frances Laughlin)

 If you break an egg on the floor, sprinkle heavily with salt and leave it for 5 to 10 minutes. Sweep dried egg into dustpan.

Brownie Icing

1½ c. sifted powdered sugar	2 T. butter
2 T. cocoa	2 to 3 T. hot coffee
Pinch of salt	½ t. vanilla

Mix sugar, cocoa, and salt in a medium size bowl. In a teacup mix butter and coffee. Make a well in the middle of the sugar and cocoa mixture. Pour in the melted butter, a small amount at a time, and stir just enough for icing to be at spreading consistency. Add vanilla and spread icing on brownies.
Miss Maurine McMahan

Fudge Squares

2 eggs	2 1 oz. squares unsweetened
⅛ t. salt	chocolate
1 c. sugar	½ c. sifted flour
½ c. butter or margarine	1 t. vanilla
	1 c. chopped pecans

Beat eggs with salt until they are lemon colored. Add sugar and mix well. Melt butter and chocolate in top of double boiler over hot water; stir gradually into egg mixture. Add flour, vanilla, and pecans. Pour into a greased 9 inch square pan. Bake in 325° oven for 25 minutes.
Yields approximately 20 squares.
Mrs. David J. Dial (Margery Hombs)

Christmas Goodies

1 14 oz. can sweetened	1 12 oz. pkg. chocolate or
condensed milk	butterscotch chips
1½ c. graham cracker crumbs	1 3½ oz. can angel flake
1 c. chopped nuts	coconut

Mix ingredients well. Pat into buttered 9 x 11 baking dish. Bake at 325° for 30 minutes. Cut into squares.
Yields 24 squares.
Mrs. Weldon Bynum (Opha Gilbreath)

Cheese Cake Cookies

⅓	c. butter	1	8 oz. pkg. cream cheese
⅓	c. brown sugar	1	egg
1	c. flour	2	T. milk
½	c. chopped walnuts	1	T. lemon juice
¼	c. sugar	½	t. vanilla

Cream butter and brown sugar. Add flour and nuts; mix to make a crumb mixture. Set aside 1 cup crumb mixture and press remainder into bottom of an 8 inch square pan. Bake at 350° for about 15 minutes or until lightly browned. Blend sugar with cream cheese until smooth. Add egg, milk, lemon juice, and vanilla; and beat well. Spread over baked crust. Sprinkle with reserved crumb mixture. Bake at 350° for 25 minutes. Cool. Cut into 2 inch squares.
Yields 16 squares. Freezes.
Mrs. Bob Stephenson (Sandra Durham)

Coconut Butterscotch Bars

½	c. butter, softened	1	c. brown sugar, firmly
½	c. light brown sugar,		packed
	firmly packed	1	t. vanilla
1	c. sifted flour	2	T. flour
2	eggs, unbeaten	½	t. baking powder
⅛	t. salt	1	c. chopped nut meats
		1	c. shredded coconut

Mix first 3 ingredients and beat until well blended, about 2 minutes. Press mixture firmly into a greased 8 x 12 pan. Bake at 325° for 20 minutes. Do not brown. In a small bowl mix eggs, salt, sugar, vanilla, flour, and baking powder. Beat until light, about 2 minutes. Add nuts. Mix well and spread over partially baked batter. Sprinkle with coconut. Bake at 325° about 25 minutes or until lightly brown. Cut into small bars while warm. Cool in pan.
Yields 2 dozen bars. Freezes.
Mrs. Lester Hamilton (Frances Edmunds)

Lemon Bars

1 c. margarine, softened	½ c. lemon juice
2¼ c. flour, divided	Dash of salt
½ c. powdered sugar	1 t. baking powder
4 eggs, beaten	Powdered sugar
2 c. sugar	

Combine margarine, 2 cups flour, and ½ cup powdered sugar; blend until smooth. Pat dough into a lightly greased 13 x 9 pan. Bake at 300° about 30 minutes or until lightly browned. Combine eggs, sugar, and lemon juice; mix well. Add ¼ cup flour, salt, and baking powder; blend well. Pour over pastry. Bake at 300° for 30 to 40 minutes or until done. Sprinkle with powdered sugar and cut into large bars.
Yields 1½ to 2 dozen bars.
Mrs. N.C. Woolverton (Jettie Seagler)

Praline Cookies

24 graham crackers	1 c. light brown sugar
1 stick margarine	1 c. pecans

Place graham crackers on a 5 x 10 cookie sheet with sides. Mix margarine, brown sugar, and pecans. Bring mixture to boil and cook *only* 2 minutes. Spread mixture over crackers evenly. Bake at 350° exactly 10 minutes. Cool a short time and cut into 1 inch squares.
Yields 2 dozen cookies. Freezes.
Mrs. Maurice Price, Jr. (Carol Cleveland), Dallas, Texas

Scotch Shortbread

1 c. butter	2½ c. flour
½ c. sugar	Pinch of salt

Cream butter and sugar. Add flour gradually. Add salt. Roll ¼ inch to ½ inch thick. Cut dough with biscuit cutter, then quarter each round, and prick with fork. Bake on ungreased cookie sheet at 300° for 25 to 30 minutes. Do not brown.
Yields approximately 2 dozen. Freezes.
Mrs. W. M. Knowles (Jean Dilley)

Three-Layer Cookies

First layer
½   c. butter
¼   c. sugar
⅓   c. dry cocoa
1   t. vanilla extract

1   egg, slightly beaten
1½   c. graham cracker crumbs
1   3½ oz. can coconut
½   c. chopped nuts

Combine butter, sugar, cocoa, and vanilla in double boiler. Cook until blended; add egg. Cook 5 minutes. Add crumbs, coconut, and nuts. Press into buttered 9 x 13 pan. Let stand.

Second layer
½   c. butter
3   T. milk

2   T. vanilla pudding
2   c. powdered sugar

Cream butter until light and fluffy. Mix milk and pudding and add to butter. Beat while adding sugar until fluffy. Spread over first layer and refrigerate.

Third layer
¾   of 12 oz. pkg. semi-sweet
      chocolate chips

6   T. butter

Melt chocolate chips and butter in double boiler. Cool slightly. Spread over second layer. Refrigerate. To cut, let stand at room temperature for 20 to 30 minutes.
Yields about 50.
Mrs. C. L. Kolstad, III (Jill McPherson)

Sugar Puffs

1   c. sugar
½   c. brown sugar, firmly
      packed
1   c. shortening
1   egg, beaten

2   c. flour
2   t. soda
½   t. salt
2   t. cream of tartar
1   t. vanilla

Cream sugars and shortening well. Add beaten egg and mix thoroughly. Stir flour, soda, salt, and cream of tartar together. Add to creamed mixture. Stir in vanilla. Roll into small balls, dip top in sugar, and place on lightly greased cookie sheet. Bake at 350° approximately 10 minutes.
Yields 7 dozen cookies.
Mrs. Robert E. Jordan (Margaret Haygood)

Chocolate Chip Cookie Mix

Mix

4	c. vegetable shortening	4	t. baking soda
3	c. granulated sugar	2	t. salt
3	c. dark brown sugar	4	12 oz. pkgs. semi-sweet
9	c. flour		chocolate chips

Cream shortening and sugars together. Sift together flour, baking soda, and salt; add to shortening-sugar mixture. Stir in chocolate chips. This mix can be stored in an air-tight container up to 6 months.

One recipe

6	c. mix	2	eggs, slightly beaten
1	t. vanilla		

Combine mix, vanilla, and eggs. Stir until blended. Drop by teaspoon onto greased cookie sheet. Bake in 375° oven about 8 to 10 minutes. *One cup chopped pecans may be added to cookie dough.*
Yields approximately 8 dozen.
Cookbook Committee

Pumpkin Cookies

3	c. flour	¾	c. shortening
1	t. soda	1½	c. sugar
½	t. salt	1	egg, beaten
½	t. allspice	1	c. pumpkin
¼	t. cloves	¼	c. milk
1	t. cinnamon	1	c. chopped pecans

Mix dry ingredients and set aside. Cream sugar and shortening. Add egg and pumpkin. Stir in dry ingredients and milk. Drop on ungreased cookie sheet and bake 15 minutes at 350°.

Icing

2	c. sifted powdered sugar	½	t. cinnamon
¼	c. margarine, softened	½	t. vanilla
			About 1 T. milk

Mix sugar, margarine, cinnamon, and vanilla. Add milk to obtain spreading consistency. Ice cookies.
Yields 5 to 7 dozen cookies. Freezes.
Mrs. David Bratz (Marjorie Braly)

Thimble Cookies

1	c. margarine	2	t. vanilla
½	c. sugar	½	lb. pecans, finely chopped
2	eggs, separated	Jelly	
2	c. flour		

Cream margarine and sugar. Add well beaten egg yolks and thoroughly mix. Add vanilla and flour. Shape cookies into walnut size balls. Roll in unbeaten egg whites and then in finely chopped pecans. Place on greased cookie sheet and mash centers nearly all the way through with thimble. Bake in 350° oven for 5 minutes; then mash cookie again with thimble. Continue cooking for 12 more minutes. Put jelly in hole while cookie is still hot. Strawberry jelly makes these cookies pretty at Christmas or on Valentine's Day. Chocolate chips or candied cherries may be substituted for the jelly.
Yields approximately 3 dozen. Freezes.
Mrs. Mike Wright (Patti Alexander)

Sugar Crisps

¾	c. shortening	1	t. vanilla
½	c. brown sugar, firmly packed	2	t. soda
		½	t. salt
½	c. white sugar	2	c. flour
¼	c. light corn syrup	½	c. chopped pecans
1	egg		

In large saucepan, melt shortening over low heat. Remove and let cool. Add sugar, syrup, and egg; beat well and add vanilla. Sift together dry ingredients and add to first mixture. Blend well and add nuts. Chill dough in covered container or wrap in wax paper. Place rounded teaspoons of dough on greased cookie sheets. Bake at 350° for 8 minutes or until lightly browned.
Yields 4½ dozen cookies.
Mrs. John Ballard McDonald (Linda Cole)

Butterscotch Icebox Cookies

1	c. butter	1	t. soda
2	c. light brown sugar, packed	1	t. cream of tartar
		1½	t. vanilla
2	eggs, beaten	1	c. well-chopped nuts
4	c. unsifted flour		

Cream together the butter, brown sugar, and eggs. Sift flour, soda, and cream of tartar twice; and add to egg mixture beating until stiff. Add vanilla and chopped nuts. Knead in any remaining flour mixture. Shape into 2 loaves or more if you want smaller cookies. Wrap in waxed paper and place in refrigerator at least 2 hours. Better yet, freeze. They are more easily sliced while frozen. Cut into thin slices, place on greased cookie sheets, and bake at 375° about 8 to 10 minutes or until golden brown. Watch closely last few minutes. Remove cookies from pan quickly. Cool thoroughly before packing in tin container. These freeze well but also keep well for 10 days or more in a tight container.
Yields 60 cookies.
Mrs. Lester Hamilton (Frances Edmunds)

Icebox Cookies

1	c. butter	1	c. chopped pecans
1	c. powdered sugar	1	t. vanilla
2	c. sifted flour		Pinch of salt

Cream butter and sugar. Add flour, pecans, vanilla, and salt. Mix and roll in wax paper. Store in refrigerator. To bake cut into thin slices, place on lightly greased cookie sheet, and bake at 350° about 10 minutes or until edges are lightly browned. Cookies freeze well either before or after baking.
Yields 6 dozen.
Mrs. David J. Dial (Margery Hombs)

Oatmeal Icebox Cookies

1	c. shortening	1½	c. sifted flour
1	c. brown sugar, firmly packed	1	t. salt
		1	t. soda
1	c. sugar	3	c. oatmeal
2	eggs, beaten	½	c. nuts
1	t. vanilla		

Cream shortening and sugars. Add eggs and vanilla. Sift together flour, salt, and soda. Combine with the sugar egg mixture. Stir in oatmeal and nuts. Mix well, shape into rolls, wrap in wax paper, and chill. Slice thin and bake on ungreased baking sheet at 350° for 10 minutes.
Yields 5 dozen cookies. Freezes.
Mrs. K. G. Johnson (Betty Fister)

Roll Out Cookies

1	c. butter	2	t. vanilla
⅓	c. shortening	½	t. lemon juice
1	c. white sugar	3½	c. flour, sifted 4 times
¼	t. salt	1	t. soda
1	egg	1	t. cream of tartar
3	T. milk		

Cream together butter and shortening. Add remaining ingredients, mix well, and chill. Roll out on lightly floured board. Cut into desired shapes. Place on greased cookie sheet and bake in 350° oven 10 to 12 minutes until lightly browned. *Good for making decorative cookies.*
Yields about 3 dozen cookies.
Mrs. C. L. Kolstad, III (Jill McPherson)

  When creaming butter and sugar together, rinse the bowl in very hot water first. The two will cream faster.

Candied Orange Peel

5	oranges	2	c. sugar
1	c. water	2	T. light corn syrup

Cut five oranges in quarters and remove edible part. In a heavy 3 quart saucepan, cover peel with water and simmer for 30 minutes. Cool and with a spoon remove most of the inner white part. Cut in strips, place in pan with water, sugar, and corn syrup. Simmer until partly transparent. Cover and let set overnight. On following day, heat to simmer again. Do this until liquid is mostly used up and liquid will form a soft ball. Strain peel and spread on crinkled aluminum foil. Leave until fairly dry and sprinkle with sugar. At Christmas time you may want to add a few drops of red or green food color to syrup. Very pretty. May use grapefruit peel.
Serves 20.
Jack W. Meeker

Caramel Fudge

6	c. sugar	¼	lb. butter
1	pt. light cream	1½	lbs. nuts
¼	t. soda		

Caramelize 2 cups sugar in heavy skillet. When almost melted, in large pan start the other 4 cups of sugar and cream to boil. Combine slowly with caramelized sugar. Cook to soft ball stage, 238° on candy thermometer. Remove from heat. Add soda and butter and stir until melted. Let set 25 minutes. Beat until smooth and glossy. Add nuts. Pour into a buttered 9 x 12 dish. Cut into squares while still warm. *Difficult to make but well worth it.*
Yields approximately 50 pieces.
Mrs. Ben W. Hearne (Esther Johnson)

Chocolate Fudge Candy

1½ c. sugar	2 6 oz. pkgs. chocolate
1 5.33 oz. can evaporated	chips
milk	1 small piece bitter
1 7 oz. jar marshmallow	chocolate
creme	1 t. vanilla
¼ c. margarine	Pecan halves

Mix together sugar, milk, marshmallow creme, and margarine; and heat slowly. Bring to a boil and cook 5 minutes or until mixture reaches 240° on candy thermometer. Remove from heat and add the chocolate chips, bitter chocolate, and vanilla. Whip vigorously until mixture is ready to pour into buttered 9 inch pan. Cool and then cut into squares. Decorate with pecan halves.
Yields 36 pieces.
Mrs. Ben J. Walker (Miriam Stevens)

Chocolate Nuts

1 6 oz. pkg. German sweet	2 10 oz. pkgs. shelled
chocolate	walnuts or equivalent
1 6 oz. pkg. butterscotch	amount of pecans or
morsels	almonds
	Pinch of salt

Melt chocolate and butterscotch in top of double boiler. Add pinch of salt and remove from heat. Stir in nuts and drop by teaspoon on wax paper. Cool.
Mrs. Ed Montgomery (Dorothy Meador)

Date Loaf Candy

2 c. sugar	½ lb. dates, chopped
1 c. milk	1 c. chopped pecans

Boil sugar and milk until it forms a firm soft ball, 240° on candy thermometer. Remove from heat, add dates and work until softened. Add pecans and stir until cool. Turn out on buttered board, form into a roll, and wrap in a damp napkin. Refrigerate. Slice to serve. Stores indefinitely.
Mrs. W. O. Smith (Marye Jo Green)

Divinity

2	c. sugar	2	egg whites
¾	c. light corn syrup	½	c. chopped pecans
½	c. water		

Mix sugar, syrup, and water in a saucepan and cook until it forms a soft ball when you drop a spoonful in water, 238° on candy thermometer. Beat egg whites until stiff. Then pour syrup over egg whites. Add pecans and beat until ready to drop on waxed paper.
Mrs. Ben J. Walker (Miriam Stevens)

Peanut Brittle

2	c. shelled peanuts	½	c. water
1	c. light corn syrup	½	t. baking soda
1	c. sugar		

Combine first 4 ingredients in a 2 quart saucepan. Stir and cook until mixture reaches the hard crack stage, 290° to 300° on a candy thermometer. Remove pan from heat and quickly stir in baking soda. Mixture will immediately bubble and fizz. Quickly spread a thin layer of mixture on a large greased cookie sheet. When cool crack into desired size pieces.
Mrs. Harvey Bell (Virginia Kimball)

Peanut Patty

3	c. sugar	2	T. butter
3	c. raw peanuts	1	c. milk
⅔	c. light corn syrup	1	t. vanilla

Combine all ingredients in a large saucepan. Boil until mixture reaches stiff ball stage, 245° on a candy thermometer. Remove from heat and beat with wooden spoon until mixture begins to thicken. Spoon candy onto wax paper to form patties or you may pour into greased pan and break into pieces when cool.
Mrs. J. D. Glenn (Marguerite Mullins)

Pralines

½   c. sugar, caramelized   2   c. pecans
5   T. boiling water   Lump of butter
2   c. sugar   1   c. hot water

Caramelize ½ cup sugar in heavy skillet. Heat the sugar on low heat, stirring constantly until light brown. Add 5 tablespoons of water and stir until well blended and smooth. Then mix together sugar, pecans, butter, and hot water. Cook this mixture until it reaches the soft ball stage, 238° on candy thermometer. Add caramelized sugar to this and beat until creamy. Drop by spoonfuls onto waxed paper.
Mrs. Howard Winkler (Joyce Bell)

Raisin Peanut Butter Bon Bons

1   c. creamy peanut butter   ½   c. chopped pecans
2   T. soft butter   1   6 oz. pkg. semi-sweet
1   c. sifted powdered sugar   chocolate pieces
1½   c. seedless raisins   2   T. shortening

Combine peanut butter, butter, and powdered sugar, mixing until smooth. Stir in raisins and nuts. Shape into small balls. Melt chocolate with shortening over warm, not hot, water. Dip balls, one at a time, into chocolate. Place on waxed paper until set.
Yields 3 dozen bon bons.
Mrs. W. G. Darsey, Jr. (Roberta Deerman)

Ice Cream — The Best

2   14 oz. cans sweetened   1   c. heavy cream, whipped,
     condensed milk   or one 8 oz. carton non-
2   qts. whole or skim milk   dairy whipped topping
                                   1   T. vanilla

Combine all ingredients in a blender and mix well. Freeze in ice cream freezer.
Yields 1 gallon.
Mrs. Dick Hartt (Dorothy Marshall)

Lemon Ice Cream

Juice of 7 lemons	1	pt. cream
3 c. sugar	2	t. gelatin
1½ qts. milk	½	c. water

Mix lemon juice and sugar. Set aside for a while to dissolve sugar. Place milk and cream in freezer and turn until chilled. Dissolve gelatin in water and add to sugar mixture. Combine with milk and cream and freeze. *A light and refreshing dessert.*
Serves 8.
Mrs. Marion Boyd (Lucile Sutton)

Three-Fruit Ice Cream

3	large bananas	2	13 oz. cans evaporated
¾	c. lemon juice		milk
1	c. orange juice	2	qts. plus 1 c. milk
3	c. sugar		

In a large bowl mash the bananas, and stir in the orange and lemon juices. Add the sugar and evaporated milk. Stir until well mixed. Pour into gallon freezer container. Fill up with milk to fill line and freeze.
Yields 1 gallon.
Mrs. Haskell Adcox (Eleanor Tilley)

Bananas Flambe

½	c. butter	½	c. rum
½	c. brown sugar	Vanilla ice cream	
6	bananas		

Melt butter in saucepan or chafing dish. Add brown sugar, stirring just until the sugar melts and a caramel sauce is made. Lemon juice may be added, if desired. Peel bananas and slice in half. Add to the caramel sauce and simmer about 5 minutes. Add rum; flame and serve over vanilla ice cream.
Serves 6.
Mrs. Gordon B. Broyles (Frances Dilley)

Charlotte Russe

1	T. gelatin	6	stale coconut macaroons, rolled
¼	c. cold water		
½	c. boiling water	12	marshmallows, cut in small pieces
½	c. sugar		
1	pt. heavy cream, stiffly beaten		Peeled green seedless grapes
		¼	t. salt
¼	lb. chopped pecans or almonds	1	t. vanilla

Soak gelatin in cold water. Add boiling water and stir until dissolved. Add sugar and chill. When cool, add remaining ingredients and chill until firm. Serves 8.
Mrs. David J. Dial (Margery Hombs)

Cherry Berries on a Cloud

6	egg whites	2	c. miniature marshmallows
½	t. cream of tartar		
¼	t. salt	1	21 oz. can cherry pie filling
1¾	c. sugar		
2	3 oz. packages cream cheese, softened	1	t. lemon juice
		2	c. fresh strawberries, sliced or one 10 oz. pkg. frozen strawberries
1	c. sugar		
1	t. vanilla		
1	c. heavy cream, whipped		
1	c. sour cream		

Preheat oven 275°. Grease a 13 x 9 x 2 inch pan. Beat egg whites, cream of tartar, and salt until frothy. Gradually beat in the 1¾ cups of sugar. Beat until very stiff and glossy, approximately fifteen minutes. Spread in prepared pan and bake 60 minutes. Turn off oven and leave meringue in until cool. Mix cream cheese with the remaining sugar and vanilla. Gently fold in whipped cream, sour cream, and marshmallows. Spread over meringue; refrigerate overnight. Combine pie filling, lemon juice, and strawberries for topping. Cut into serving pieces and top with berries.
Serves 12 to 15.
Mrs. Robert E. Jordan (Margaret Haygood)

Chocolate Dessert

1	13 oz. angel food cake	2	eggs, separated
1	12 oz. pkg. chocolate chips	2	T. sugar
¼	c. hot water	1	12 oz. carton whipped topping
1	c. miniature marshmallows		Pecans
			Coconut

Tear cake into small pieces and place in a 9 x 13 inch pan. Melt chocolate chips with hot water in top of double boiler. Add marshmallows. Mix well. Beat egg yolks and add to chocolate mixture. Pour over cake pieces and pat down to saturate. Beat egg whites stiff with sugar. Fold in topping and cover chocolate mixture. At serving time garnish with coconut and chopped pecans. At Christmas time substitute chopped green and red candied cherries for pecans and coconut.
Serves 15 to 16.
Mrs. Joe N. Davis (Marguerite Dellis)

Creme Brulee

5	egg yolks	1	T. vanilla extract
2	c. heavy cream, scalded		Dark brown sugar
¼	c. superfine sugar	½	c. brandy

Beat the egg yolks together with the cream in an electric mixer. Add the sugar and vanilla and beat on lower speed until blended. Preheat oven to 400°. Pour the mixture into a shallow baking dish, preferably circular. Place the dish in a pan with hot water to come about ½ way up the sides of the dish. Reduce the oven temperature to 300° and bake for about 1 hour or until a knife inserted into the center comes out clean. Refrigerate at least 6 hours. About 1 to 2 hours before serving the brulee, remove from refrigerator and sprinkle evenly with a layer of dark brown sugar, ⅛ to ¼ inch thick. Set the dish under a broiler, but not so close that the sugar will burn readily. Watch very carefully, and as soon as sugar gets to be crusty and dark, remove from oven. It should be very slightly burned, but not too crisp. Return to the refrigerator for about 1 hour. When ready to serve, top with brandy. The baking of the custard for the creme brulee can be done the day before, and the dessert completed the hour or so before you serve it. *It is rich, but so delicious.*
Serves 4.
Mrs. John E. Presley (Lucinda Hanks)

Jay's Glory

1½ c. crumbled almond macaroons	½ c. Cognac or Tia Maria
½ c. sugar	1 pt. heavy cream, stiffly whipped

Mix first 3 ingredients and fold in whipped cream. Place in dessert or custard cups and put in freezer for at least 3 hours. Mixture stiffens, but will not freeze. Add a drop or two of food coloring for whatever season or reason. Serves 8.
Mrs. Curtis C. Mann (Jay Nemer)

Pavlova

8 egg whites	4 t. malt vinegar (found in grocery gourmet section)
2 c. granulated sugar	1 t. vanilla

Beat egg whites until stiff. Add sugar and continue beating until well mixed. Add vinegar and vanilla. Pour into a flat 9 x 13 baking dish lined with foil. Cook in 250° oven for 1½ hours. Remove from oven and turn upside down onto a plate and peel off foil. When cool, cover with whipped cream and "decorate" (cover) with fresh fruits.
Serves 10 to 12.
Sir John and Lady Paget, Haygrass House, Taunton, Somerset, England

 To store leftover egg yolks, cover with cold water and keep in refrigerator. Drain and use within 3 days. Whites will keep in refrigerator, covered, for about 10 days.

Lemon Bisque

1	3 oz. pkg. lemon gelatin	1	c. sugar
1½	c. boiling water	1	13 oz. can evaporated
⅛	t. salt		milk, *very cold*
3	T. lemon juice	2	c. graham cracker crumbs
Rind of 1 lemon, grated			

Dissolve gelatin in boiling water. Add sugar, salt, lemon rind, and juice. Chill until syrupy. Beat canned milk (that has been in freezer for at least 30 minutes) until thick. Add to gelatin mixture. Beat until well mixed. Spread graham cracker crumbs in bottom of 9 x 13 inch pan. Pour in lemon mixture; top with more crumbs and chill.
Serves 12.
Mrs. Charles Stanton (Lisa Guarnieri)

Toffee Delight

Sponge cake cut to size		1	qt. vanilla ice cream,
2	T. instant coffee		softened
1	T. boiling water	1	8 oz. carton whipped
5	toffee candy bars, frozen		topping, softened
		3	T. creme de cacao

Cut sponge cake to fit bottom of 8, 9, or 10 inch spring form pan. Dissolve coffee in boiling water. Cool. Crush 4 of the frozen toffee bars by pounding with a mallet. Combine crushed candy bars with softened ice cream and dissolved coffee. Spoon mixture on top of sponge cake and freeze until firm. Mix creme de cacao into topping. Spread over ice cream layer. Crush remaining candy bar and sprinkle over topping. Freeze until firm. Cut into wedges to serve.
Serves 10 to 12.
Mrs. C. L. Kolstad, III (Jill McPherson)

Strawberry Royale

Crepes

1⅓ c. milk	2 eggs
3 T. butter	¾ c. pancake mix

Heat milk and butter in small saucepan just until butter melts. Cool to lukewarm. Beat eggs until light in medium bowl. Blend in milk mixture and pancake mix. Beat with rotary beater just until smooth. Do not overbeat. Batter will be very thin. Let set about 30 minutes. Heat griddle very slowly until drops of water bounce. Lightly grease griddle. Ladle 2 tablespoons batter onto heated griddle to make 5 inch crepes. They should be very thin. Tilt pan to spread batter. Cook until top appears dry. Turn and brown. Arrange crepes in stacks of 3 or 4 on plate. Cover with waxed paper and keep moist until ready to fill.

Filling

4 3 oz. pkgs. cream cheese	1½ T. grated lemon rind
¼ c. sugar	3 T. lemon juice

Soften cream cheese to room temperature. Mix in sugar, lemon juice, and rind. Beat until fluffy. Spoon about 2 tablespoons filling across middle of each crepe. Roll crepe around filling. Place folded side down in shallow oven proof dish. These can be frozen at this point.

Topping

1 10 oz. pkg. frozen sliced strawberries	1 T. lemon juice

Heat strawberries and lemon juice. Just before serving, heat filled crepes in 400° oven for 10 minutes or just until hot. Pour heated sauce over rolled crepes and serve at once.
Yields 16 crepes.
Mrs. Gordon B. Broyles (Frances Dilley)

Cream Puffs

¼	c. butter	½	c. flour
½	c. boiling water	2	eggs, beaten

Add butter to water and melt. Add flour all at once and stir until a ball forms. Remove from heat and let cool at least 10 minutes. Beat 1 egg at a time into mixture. Drop by tablespoons on lightly greased cookie sheet. Bake at 400° for 20 minutes.
Yields 6 or 7.

French Custard Filling

¾	c. sugar	3	c. milk
3	T. flour	2	egg yolks
¾	t. salt	1	t. cold water
3	T. cornstarch	2	t. vanilla

Combine dry ingredients. Stir in 1 cup cold milk and 2 cups hot milk. Stir constantly over medium heat until thick. Add 1 teaspoon cold water to 2 egg yolks. Add to custard and bring to a boil. Add vanilla and mix well. Cool and fill cream puffs.

Chocolate Topping

2	1 oz. squares unsweetened chocolate	⅔	c. powdered sugar
		2	T. milk
1½	T. butter or margarine		

Melt chocolate with butter. Cool slightly. Add sugar and milk and beat until smooth. Pour over filled cream puffs.
Serves 6 or 7.
Mrs. Leo F. Mizell (Muriel Murphy)

Paradise Pudding

Fresh berries of your choice	White bread
Sugar to taste	Whipped cream

Stew fresh fruit with sugar for 5 minutes. Line a dish with slices of white bread and cover with stewed fruit; bread should be *well soaked* in juice. Refrigerate overnight. At serving time cover with whipped cream.
Mrs. David Rasch, Heale House, Woodford near Salisbury, Wiltshire, England

Creamy Apple Delight

1	pkg. yellow cake mix	3	green apples, sliced
½	c. butter	1	c. sour cream
¼	c. brown sugar	1	egg
½	t. cinnamon		

In a separate bowl stir together ⅔ cup of cake mix, ¼ cup brown sugar, and ½ teaspoon cinnamon. Set aside for the topping. In another bowl blend the remaining cake mix with butter. Pat this mixture in an 11 x 9 x 3 inch baking dish. Place sliced apples over the cake mixture. Blend sour cream and egg and spread over sliced apples. Sprinkle topping over this mixture and bake in 350° oven for 25 to 30 minutes.
Serves 8.
Mrs. James N. Parsons, III (Karen Hawkins)

Dutch Apple Torte

½	c. butter	3	apples, peeled and diced
1	c. sugar	½	c. chopped pecans
1	egg		Juice of ½ lemon
1	c. flour	½	t. salt
¼	t. cinnamon		Whipped cream
½	t. baking soda		

Cream butter and sugar. Add egg and flour and mix well. Add remaining ingredients and pour into a greased 9 inch pan. Bake at 350° for 45 minutes. Top with whipped cream.
Serves 6.
Mrs. Frank C. Hicks (Helen Davenport)

 Heavy cream will whip faster if a pinch of salt is added.

Bread Pudding

2	c. bread cubes	¾	c. sugar
4	c. milk, scalded	4	eggs, slightly beaten
2	T. margarine	1	t. vanilla
½	t. salt		

Soak the bread in milk for 5 minutes. Add butter, salt, and sugar. Pour slowly over the eggs and add the vanilla. Mix well. Pour into greased 2 quart casserole. Place in pan of hot water. Bake in oven at 350° until firm, about 50 minutes.
Serves 6 to 8.
Mrs. W. Lamar Hamilton (Kitty Davey)

Cup Custard

3	eggs, separated	1	t. vanilla
½	c. sugar	5	t. brown sugar
2	c. milk		

Beat egg whites until stiff and set aside. Beat yolks and sugar together. Add milk and vanilla. Fold in egg whites until well mixed. Put one teaspoon brown sugar in five custard cups. Fill cups with custard. Set cups in baking pan with 1 to 2 inches of water. Bake in a 350° oven about 45 minutes or until custard is set.
Serves 5.
Mrs. O. L. Gragg (Inez Hardin)

Blueberry Dessert

1	c. graham cracker crumbs	2	eggs
¼	c. butter	1	21 oz. can blueberry pie filling
¼	c. sugar		
1	8 oz. pkg. cream cheese	½	pt. heavy cream, whipped
½	c. sugar		

Mix first 3 ingredients and press into a 9 inch square pan. Combine cheese, sugar, and eggs and mix well. Pour over cracker mixture and bake in 300° oven about 25 or 30 minutes. Cool. Pour blueberry pie filling over mixture and refrigerate. Serve with whipped cream. Can be made a day ahead.
Serves 10 to 12.
Mrs. Henry Jordan (Evelyn Davis)

Blueberry Kuchen

1 c. flour plus 2 T.	1 T. white vinegar
Pinch salt	Dash cinnamon
1 c. sugar plus 2 T.	3 c. fresh blueberries
½ c. butter	Powdered sugar

Combine flour, salt, and 2 tablespoons sugar. Work in butter with pastry blender. Mix in vinegar. Spread crust mixture evenly in the bottom of a 9 inch spring form pan and thinly around sides to height of 1 inch. Combine 1 cup sugar, 2 tablespoons flour, and the cinnamon. Add 2 cups blueberries. Pour into crust. Bake at 400° for 1 hour. Remove from oven. Spread remaining berries on top. Cool. Remove rim of pan and dust with powdered sugar. May be served with hard sauce.
Serves 6.
Mrs. Bruce Barber (Brenda Wilson)

Spicey Boiled Apples

12 apples	6 cloves
3 c. water	¼ t. vanilla
1 c. sugar	Red food coloring
½ t. or 2 sticks cinnamon	

Peel and core apples. In a saucepan combine remaining ingredients, add apples, and bring to a boil. Boil uncovered for 20 minutes in mixture. Let set in juice 30 minutes. *Nice as a light dessert or served as an accompaniment to meat.*
Yields 12.
Mrs. Bob Burroughs (Thelma Andrews)

PICKLES, JELLIES
AND
SAUCES

Easy Sweet Pickles

2	qts. sour pickles, sliced	5	c. sugar
1	clove garlic	½	c. vinegar
		4	T. pickling spice

Slice 2 quarts sour pickles. Add 1 clove garlic and 5 cups sugar. Mix gently, cover, and let stand 24 hours. Drain juice from pickles, add ½ cup vinegar, and simmer for 10 minutes. Pack 4 pint jars with sliced pickles. Pour juice over pickles. Seal. Chill before serving.
Yields 4 pints.
Mrs. Howell Mitchell (Kathryn Willis)

Crunchy Oil Pickles

2	qts. sour pickles	8	garlic cloves
4	c. sugar	4	T. pickling spices
4	T. vegetable oil		

Drain pickles. Slice into desired thickness and place in a crock with the other ingredients. Cover and allow pickles to set at room temperature for three days, stirring daily. On the fourth day put in jars and refrigerate. Serve cold.
Yields 2 quarts.
Mrs. C. G. Joyce, Sr. (Lottie McDonald)

Watermelon Sweet Pickles

3	lbs. rind (about 3 qts. of small pieces)	½ of a 1.25 oz. box whole all spice
3	t. powdered lime (found at drugstore) to 1 gallon water	½ of a 1.12 oz. box whole cloves
4	lbs. sugar	½ of a 1.25 oz. box cinnamon sticks
1	qt. white vinegar with a little water added	

Soak rind in lime water for 24 hours. Pour off water and rinse several times. Tie spices in cloth bags. Cook sugar, vinegar, and spices about 1 hour to make a syrup. Cook rind in clear water about 1 hour or until tender. Drain and put in hot syrup and cook 1 hour.
Yields about 6 pints.
Mrs. Gordon B. Broyles (Frances Dilley)

Pickled Beets

1	c. sugar	2	16 oz. cans small whole beets
1	c. vinegar		
1	c. beet juice	5	or 6 whole cloves, optional

Bring sugar, vinegar, and beet juice to boil and pour over beets. Refrigerate.
Yields approximately 4 cups.
Mrs. W. H. Shuller, Jr. (Mary Plemons)

Pickled Onions

4	qts. small onions	2	qts. vinegar
1	c. salt	¼	c. pickling spice
2	c. sugar		

Cover onions with boiling water. Let stand 2 minutes. Drain, cover with cold water, and peel. Cover with cool water and 1 cup salt. Let stand overnight. Put in colander, rinse, and drain. Tie spices in bag and boil with sugar and vinegar about 15 minutes. Remove spices, add onions, and bring to a boil. Pack while hot in sterilized jars. Seal immediately. Chill before serving.
Yields 4 quarts.
Mrs. Curtic C. Mann (Jay Nemer)

Pickled Pigs' Feet

4	pigs' feet, split	2	bay leaves
3	c. vinegar	6	whole cloves
1	onion, sliced	1	T. salt
12	peppercorns		

Scrub pigs' feet. Place in a pot and cover with water and vinegar. Bring to boil and skim foam. Add remaining ingredients and simmer for 3 hours or until fork tender. Serve cold.
Serves 4.
Mrs. Curtis C. Mann (Jay Nemer)

Caddo Green Tomato Relish

1	gal. green tomatoes, cut in chunks	4	large green sweet peppers
1	qt. onions, cut in pieces	1	qt. white vinegar
3	hot peppers or to taste	¼	c. salt
		2	c. sugar

In a large pot combine ingredients, bring to a boil, and simmer 15 minutes or until tender.
Yields 5 pints.
Miss Rose Nemer

Pickled Garden Relish

½	small head cauliflower broken into flowerets	1	3 oz. jar stuffed green olives, drained and sliced
2	carrots, pared and cut in 2 inch strips	¾	c. apple cider vinegar
1	c. tender celery, cut in 1 inch pieces	½	c. vegetable oil
1	green pepper, cut in 1 inch pieces	2	T. sugar
1	2 oz. jar pimiento, drained and sliced	1	t. salt
		½	t. dried oregano leaves
		¼	t. pepper
		¼	c. water

In a large skillet combine ingredients with ¼ cup water. Bring to boil and stir occasionally. Reduce heat, cover, and simmer for *5 minutes*. Do not overcook! After cooling refrigerate at least 24 hours before serving. Drain well.
Yields approximately 1 quart.
Mrs. Ben L. Slack (Alice Jeffrey)

Canning jars may be sterilized in the microwave by filling glasses or jars ½ full with water and heating with microwave energy until the water boils rapidly.

Pimientos

Sweet red peppers   **Salt**

Select ripe unblemished red peppers. Plunge peppers into boiling water for 10 to 15 minutes. Remove skins, stems, and seeds. Flatten peppers and pack into hot, sterilized ½ pint jars. Add ¼ teaspoon salt to each jar. Adjust lids and process in a water bath for 45 minutes. *Do not add any other liquid.*
Jack W. Meeker

Pear Relish

15	pears	6	medium onions
6	large green peppers	2	c. sugar
3	red bell peppers, optional	2	c. vinegar
12	hot peppers	2	T. salt

Do not peel pears. Wash and core. Grind pears, peppers, and onions. Add sugar, vinegar, and salt. Bring to a boil, lower the heat, and simmer for 30 to 45 minutes. Fill sterilized jars and seal while hot.
Yields 10 pints.
Cookbook Committee

Thunder & Lightnin'

1	20 oz. can firmly packed tomatoes, chopped and drained	1	t. salt
		4	T. vinegar
		2	t. sugar
1	4 oz. can green chilies, chopped and drained	1	t. pepper
		½	t. oregano
1	large onion, chopped	1	clove garlic, crushed

Mix together and cook slowly for 20 to 30 minutes. Nice as a dip served with chips. Fresh tomatoes can be substituted for the canned.
Yields approximately 3 cups.
Mrs. Cad E. Williams (Francis Bailey)

Orange Jelly

2	6 oz. cans orange concentrate, thawed	1	1¾ oz. box Sure-Jell
		4½	c. sugar
2½	c. water		

Thoroughly mix Sure-Jell, concentrate, and water in large saucepan. Stir constantly over high heat until bubbles form around edge. Immediately add all sugar and stir. Let come to a full rolling boil. Boil hard for 1 minute, stirring constantly. Remove from heat, skim, and pour into sterilized jars. Cover with paraffin.
Yields 6 cups.
Mrs. Jack H. Hanks (Jackie Rayburn)

Mint Jelly

2	c. water	1½	c. mint leaves
1	c. vinegar	1	6 oz. box liquid fruit pectin
6½	c. sugar		
Green food coloring			

Combine water, vinegar, and sugar. Heat, stirring occasionally, until sugar is dissolved. Stir in food coloring and add mint leaves. Bring to a boil. Add liquid pectin and return to a boil. Boil 1 minute, skim, and remove leaves. Pour into hot, sterilized jars. Seal.
Yields 12 to 14 four oz. jars.
Mrs. Jack H. Hanks (Jackie Rayburn)

Peach Honey

3   c. peeled peaches, blended   2   c. sugar

Bring the above to a boil, reduce heat, and cook 5 minutes. May be stored in sealed jars. *Very good over ice cream or toast.*
Mrs. J. E. Johnston, Sr. (Marie Orgeron)

Creme de Menthe Jelly

1   6 oz. can frozen lemonade   1¾ oz. pkg. Sure-Jell
       concentrate, undiluted   2½ c. sugar
1   c. water   ½ c. creme de menthe

Combine lemonade, water, and Sure-Jell in a large saucepan. Bring to a rapid boil, add sugar, and boil 1 minute. Remove from heat and stir in *green* creme de menthe. Pour into hot sterilized jars and seal with paraffin.
Yields approximately 2 cups.
Cookbook Committee

Wine Jelly

3   c. sugar   1   3 oz. pkg. liquid fruit
2   c. wine, Sauterne or   pectin
       Burgundy

Measure sugar and wine into top of double boiler; mix well. Place over rapidly boiling water and stir until sugar is dissolved. Remove from heat. At once stir in fruit pectin and mix well, skimming foam. Pour quickly into jars. Cover with melted paraffin.
Yields 5 cups.
Cookbook Committee

To sterilize jars in the oven, fill the jars with 2 inches of boiling water, and place the jars on a shallow pan or cookie sheet. Place the pan on the oven rack in 250° oven. Sterilize at least 15 minutes or until ready to use.

Horseradish Jelly

3 ¼   c. sugar   ½   c. cider vinegar
½   c. prepared horseradish   ½   c. liquid pectin

In a large saucepan, heat and stir sugar, horseradish, and vinegar until sugar
dissolves. Bring to boil, then stir in pectin all at once. Bring to full rolling
boil while stirring. Remove from heat and skim foam. Pour into hot sterilized
jars and seal with paraffin. *Good with beef or chicken.*
Yields 3 half pints.
Mrs. Jack H. Hanks (Jackie Rayburn)

Barbecue Sauce

3   T. water   1   6 oz. bottle
1   pt. vinegar   Worcestershire sauce
1   lb. margarine, melted   Garlic salt to taste
1   6 oz. jar prepared
       mustard

Mix thoroughly. Sauce will store indefinitely in refrigerator. *Good on any
type of barbecued meats, especially chicken.*
Mrs. P. A. Kolstad, Jr. (Dottie Ondus)

Sauce Mousseline

3   yolk of eggs   Black pepper
Plenty of lemon juice to taste   ¼   large carton of thick
6   oz. butter   cream
Salt (if you are using unsalted
    butter)

Break egg yolks into a bowl over a bain marie (double boiler). Beat,
preferably with an electric beater, until yolks go pale in colour. Gently add
melted butter (not too hot or it will curdle), season and add lemon juice
and cream.

Serve fairly quickly to the table but it's delicious anyway so don't worry.
Delicious with any fish or fresh asparagus or globe artichokes in season.
**The Countess of Guildford, Waldershare Park, near Dover, Kent,
England**

Raisin Sauce

½	c. seeded raisins	1	t. cornstarch
¼	c. chopped citron	1	T. butter
1	c. boiling water	½	t. lemon juice
¾	c. sugar		

Simmer raisins and citron in boiling water until tender. Sift sugar and cornstarch together, and add to raisin mixture. Mix well and continue cooking 10 minutes. Stir in butter and lemon juice, mixing well. Serve warm. *Delicious with baked ham. Even good without the citron!* **Yields 2½ cups.**
Mrs. Curtis Mann (Jay Nemer)

Sweet and Sour Sauce

Black currant jelly   **Prepared mustard**

Mix equal parts jelly and mustard, and melt in top of double boiler. Serve with baked ham or use in Chinese dishes.
Mrs. W. O. Smith (Marye Jo Green)

College Inn Remoulade Sauce

4	hard-cooked eggs, sliced	2	T. Worcestershire sauce
4	cloves garlic, crushed		Dash of Tabasco
3	T. Creole mustard	4	T. vinegar
3	c. mayonnaise	4	T. finely chopped parsley
2	T. paprika	3	T. horseradish

Salt and pepper to taste

Blend all ingredients well. Let stand in refrigerator 12 hours before using. To thin sauce, add small amount of vinegar.
Mrs. Everett Hutchinson (Elizabeth Stafford)

Red Cocktail Sauce

1	c. chili sauce	3	t. Worcestershire sauce
1	c. catsup	4	T. lemon juice
½	c. horseradish or to taste	2	or 3 dashes Tabasco sauce

Mix ingredients and chill. Serve with cold, boiled shrimp or crab.
Yields 2½ cups.
Mrs. Curtis Mann (Jay Nemer)

Heavenly Hot Fudge Sauce

½	c. butter or margarine	½	t. salt
4	1 oz. squares unsweetened chocolate	1	13 oz. can evaporated milk
3	c. sugar		

Melt butter and chocolate in top of double boiler over boiling water. Stir in sugar gradually, about 4 tablespoons at a time, being sure the sugar is completely moistened after each addition. Mixture will become very thick and dry. Add salt and slowly stir in milk a little at a time. Serve hot.
Yields 1 quart.
Mrs. Julian M. Hunt (Doris Leathers)

Hard Sauce

¼	lb. butter	2	T. whiskey
2	c. powdered sugar		Pinch salt

Have butter at room temperature. With electric mixer blend in sugar, salt, and whiskey. Refrigerate.
Mrs. Gordon B. Broyles (Frances Dilley)

Metric Conversions

It should be pointed out that two distinct factors complicate the process of converting cookery recipes from one set of units to another. In general we may specify the "amounts" of the various ingredients used, either by weight or by volume. In those regions of the world where English and U.S. customs dominate, amounts are usually specified by volume, *e.g.* — 1 cup or 1 teaspoon; whereas measures by weight are commonly used in other parts of the world.

A more serious problem arises in converting a French recipe to its equivalent for use in the United States. The difficulty arises as a result of variations in the "strength and purity" of the food stuffs available in different parts of the world.

Experimentation will in all probability be required in order to successfully convert the recipes contained in this book to their metric equivalents, particularly if the ingredients available are not of North American origin.

Table of Equivalents

Temperature:
$\quad$ F = Farenheit $\qquad$ C = Celsius (Centigrade)

Weight:
$\quad$ 1 kilogram = 1,000 grams = 2.2 pounds = 35 ounces (avdp.)
$\quad$ 1 pound = 454 grams
$\quad$ 1 ounce (avdp.) = 28 grams

Volume (or Capacity):
$\quad$ 1 liter = 10 deciliters = 1.1 quarts
$\quad$ 1 quart = 9.5 deciliters
$\quad$ 1 cup = 2.4 deciliters
$\quad$ 1 ounce (liquid) = 0.3 deciliters
$\quad$ 5 tablespoons = 1 deciliter

Miscellaneous:
$\quad$ 1 deciliter butter = 100 grams
$\quad$ 1 deciliter cooking oil = 90 grams
$\quad$ 1 tablespoon butter = 20 grams
$\quad$ 1 teaspoon butter = 10 grams
$\quad$ 1 tablespoon syrup = 20 to 25 grams
$\quad$ 1 tablespoon extracts = 10 grams
$\quad$ 1 tablespoon salt = 10 grams

Equivalents

5 oz. can almonds	1 cup slivered toasted
2 slices bread	1 cup soft crumbs
5 slices bread	1 cup fine crumbs
¼ lb. cheese	1 cup grated
20 square crackers	1 cup cracker crumbs
½ cup whipping cream	1 cup whipped cream
1 clove garlic	¾ teaspoon garlic salt
1 clove garlic	⅛ teaspoon garlic powder
8 oz. pkg. noodles	3½ cups cooked
13 oz. can evaporated milk	1⅔ cup
4 oz. can mushrooms	½ lb. fresh
2 t. minced onion	1 t. onion salt
1 cup rice	4 cups cooked

Ingredient Substitutions

Ingredients	Substitute
1 tablespoon flour (used as thickener)	½ tablespoon cornstarch or arrowroot starch
1 cup sifted all-purpose flour . . .	1 cup unsifted all-purpose flour minus 2 tablespoons
1 cup sifted cake flour	⅞ cup sifted all-purpose flour or 1 cup minus 2 tablespoons sifted all-purpose flour
1 cup corn syrup	1 cup sugar plus ¼ cup liquid (use whatever liquid the recipe calls for)
1 cup honey	1¼ cups sugar plus ¼ cup liquid (use whatever liquid the recipe calls for)
1 ounce chocolate	3 tablespoons cocoa plus 1 tablespoon fat
1 cup coffee cream	3 tablespoons butter plus about ⅞ cup milk
1 cup heavy cream	One-third cup butter plus about ¾ cup milk
1 cup buttermilk or sour milk . . .	1 tablespoon vinegar or lemon juice plus enough sweet milk to make 1 cup (let stand 5 minutes) or 1¾ teaspoons cream of tartar plus 1 cup sweet milk

INDEX

HOSPITALITY

Harvey Woman's Club
P.O. Box 1058
Palestine, Texas 75801

Please send _____ copies at . . . . $11.95 each $_____

Postage & handling . . . . $2.00 each $_____

State tax for Texas residents . . . . $.60 each $_____

Enclosed is a check payable to **HOSPITALITY** for the total amount of . . . $_____

NAME _____

ADDRESS _____

CITY _____ STATE _____ ZIP _____

- -

HOSPITALITY

Harvey Woman's Club
P.O. Box 1058
Palestine, Texas 75801

Please send _____ copies at . . . . $11.95 each $_____

Postage & handling . . . . $2.00 each $_____

State tax for Texas residents . . . . $.60 each $_____

Enclosed is a check payable to **HOSPITALITY** for the total amount of . . . $_____

NAME _____

ADDRESS _____

CITY _____ STATE _____ ZIP _____

Please send names and addresses of bookstores and gourmet/gift stores in your area where you would like to see **HOSPITALITY** carried.

_____

_____

_____

_____

_____

_____

- -

Please send names and addresses of bookstores and gourmet/gift stores in your area where you would like to see **HOSPITALITY** carried.

_____

_____

_____

_____

_____